Born in Aberdeen in 1968, BARROW started his career as a f Scottish International Relief, a Mary's Meals. He is married to Julie, a nurse, and they live together in Dalmally in Argyll with their seven children.

Praise for *The Shed That Fed A Million Children*:

'MacFarlane-Barrow ... writes simply, modestly and movingly. It is a book full of kindness that stirs you, on every page, to want to be better.' *Independent*

'It is a remarkably straightforward aim, but one that changes lives.' *Telegraph*

'The power of the message lay in its simplicity and the no-frills ethos ... inscribed on Magnus' heart.' *Daily Record*

'This is a heart-warming book, written in an engaging manner, and one which deserves to be read.' *Africa: St Patrick's Missions*

'It's a modern-day miracle of the multiplication of the loaves and fish!' TIMOTHY CARDINAL DOLAN, Archbishop of New York

'Mary's Meals has come of age by holding firm to its governing values, negotiating corrupt regimes, poor infrastructure, natural disasters and even Ebola to keep on feeding some of the world's poorest people.' *Scotsman*

'It's a compelling read about one man's vision and compassion, and how it has had a remarkable effect on children many thousands of miles from its base in Dalmally, Argyll.' *Evening Times* (Glasgow)

'The impact has been breathtaking.' GORDON BROWN

'The unshakeable Christian faith on which Mary's Meals was founded shines through every paragraph in this book.'
Daily Mail

'Clearly a great deal is being done with comparatively little.'
Observer

'The two basic things that matter most are food and education ... MacFarlane-Barrow has got the message, [and] there's no stopping him.'
Tablet

The Shed That Fed Two Million Children

Fully Updated Edition

Magnus MacFarlane-Barrow

WILLIAM COLLINS

The author has donated all royalties from the sale of this book to Mary's Meals, SC022140.

William Collins
An imprint of HarperCollins*Publishers*
1 London Bridge Street
London SE1 9GF

www.WilliamCollinsBooks.com

HarperCollins*Publishers*
Macken House, 39/40 Mayor Street Upper
Dublin 1, D01 C9W8, Ireland

First published as *The Shed That Fed A Million Children* in Great Britain in 2015 by William Collins
This fully updated paperback edition published in Great Britain in 2021 by William Collins

Copyright © Magnus MacFarlane-Barrow 2015, 2021

10

Magnus MacFarlane-Barrow asserts the moral right to be identified as the author of this work

A catalogue record for this book is available from the British Library

ISBN 978-0-00-757831-3
Special Sale ISBN 978-0-00-876931-4

Printed and bound in the UK using 100% renewable electricity at CPI Group (UK) Ltd

All rights reserved. No part of this publication may be reproduced, stored in a retrieval system, or transmitted, in any form or by any means, electronic, mechanical, photocopying, recording or otherwise, without the prior permission of the publishers.

This book is sold subject to the condition that it shall not, by way of trade or otherwise, be lent, re-sold, hired out or otherwise circulated without the publisher's prior consent in any form of binding or cover other than that in which it is published and without a similar condition including this condition being imposed on the subsequent purchaser.

Without limiting the author's and publisher's exclusive rights, any unauthorised use of this publication to train generative artificial intelligence (AI) technologies is expressly prohibited. HarperCollins also exercise their rights under Article 4(3) of the Digital Single Market Directive 2019/790 and expressly reserve this publication from the text and data mining exception.

MIX
Paper | Supporting responsible forestry
FSC www.fsc.org
FSC™ C007454

This book is produced from independently certified FSC™ paper to ensure responsible forest management.

For more information visit: www.harpercollins.co.uk/green

*This book is for Julie, without whom there would have been nothing at all to write about.
Thank you for loving me.*

Contents

	Preface	xi
	Prologue	1
1	Driving Lessons in a War Zone	9
2	A Woman Clothed with the Sun	33
3	Little Acts of Love	51
4	Suffer Little Children	73
5	Into Africa	97
6	A Famine Land	117
7	One Cup of Porridge	143
8	A Bumpy Road to Peace	167
9	In Tinsel Town	191
10	Reaching the Outcastes	215
11	Friends in High Places	237
12	Friends in Low Places	259
13	Generation Hope	283
	Old Epilogue	303
14	Love Reaches Everywhere	309
	New Epilogue	337
	Acknowledgements	341

Preface

When I wrote the first edition of this book, in this same shed in which I am typing now, I could never have imagined the extraordinary things it would inspire in the lives of some who read it.

One reader was prompted to make a £1-million donation to the work of Mary's Meals. Another young couple in the Czech Republic, having saved for many years to build a new family home, were given a copy of the book and after reading it decided instead to use their funds to start a new branch of our mission in their homeland.

Many other readers let me know that reading this book reawakened in them a faith they had lost or had never had. And many, many more joined our movement, offering beautiful, freely given acts of love for the little ones we serve.

I cannot claim the credit for any of these good things. They are not related to my writing skills, or lack of them, or my part in the story. The book has had this impact only because the story itself – one I could never have made up – points us towards some deep truths: like just how wonderful human beings really are.

Of course, not every reader had a profound life-changing experience (and one or two didn't like it at all, like the person who described me in their review as '... Adolf Hitler's Alsatian', and in doing so made my children laugh a lot). But the publication of the book also had a huge impact on my own life – providing all sorts of enriching and sometimes uncomfortable experiences. More importantly, its success has acted as a powerful catalyst for amazing growth in our mission.

The publication of the first edition of this book marked the milestone of reaching one million children with nutritious meals each school day. It had taken us twelve years to reach that happy number. Reaching two million children, which this new edition marks, has taken just six years – and the book has certainly played a key part in that much-needed acceleration.

As well as celebrating the reaching of this wonderful new landmark and recounting some of the astonishing events that have occurred in the years since first publication, I hope this updated version of my book proclaims more loudly than ever that 'this is possible!' Our vision – that every child in this world can at least eat one meal every day in their place of education – can and must be realized. That this is indeed possible is made clear by the continued extraordinary story of Mary's Meals, a story comprising countless demonstrations of the startling goodness of people.

For each of these servants of hope, I thank God, especially because we live in a world where the need to reach the next hungry child feels more urgent than ever. If humanity, through enormous investment and determination, can find a

Preface

way to defeat COVID-19, why can we not do the same with hunger? So many people continue to die of hunger, but we have long known the cure. Food is not waiting to be discovered. And so hunger in this world of plenty is a scandal that cries out to heaven.

But this book is less a discourse on how to defeat hunger than a collection of stories about a disparate bunch of people who are determined to try, and in doing so, make some pretty remarkable discoveries, mainly about themselves.

The Shed That Fed
Two Million Children

Prologue

I am writing this in my father's shed. An east wind is blowing from behind Ben Lui, whose snow-powdered flanks I can see through the window above my desk. Some of the cold air buffeting and moaning around my corrugated-iron shelter has found a way in. There is a draught gnawing my feet. I can hear someone using a power saw in the distance, perhaps my brother-in-law at the firewood, and every so often a tractor chugs down the track towards the farm.

We don't know exactly when the shed was built. It was certainly here a long time before we arrived in 1977. It is clearly marked on a map, dated 1913, hanging in an old wood-panelled corridor of Craig Lodge (my favourite part of the house when it was our family home), meaning it has been standing here for over a hundred years. That the shed is quite clearly leaning to one side today is therefore easily forgiven and it is understandable, perhaps, that I can now hear something clanking in the wind on the roof above me.

Initially, after we arrived, it served as Dad's garage and workshop. It was the perfect size for parking the old Land Rover, in which I would one day learn to drive. Later, he converted it into a playroom, surprising us one Christmas by opening its door to reveal a magnificent pool table. My brothers and I spent many hours enjoying that gift, while at the back of the shed, right outside my window, was our football pitch. Seumas, Fergus and I played for hours there every day, shooting at home-made wooden goals, our pounding feet creating a muddy, grassless strip. In the winter months, when the darkness arrived frustratingly early, we would sometimes turn on the lights of the shed and all the neighbouring outbuildings, in a desperate attempt to create enough illumination for at least a few extra minutes of play. Later, in our rather wild teenage years, friends would join us in the pool shed. Sometimes beer would be smuggled in. Once, when my parents were away, it was the catastrophic scene of the experimental sampling of my home-made cider. I had brewed this secretly, using apples from trees in the little orchard above where my own house stands today. I have never been able to drink cider since.

Later, after we had left home and Craig Lodge had become a Catholic retreat centre, the shed, for a few years, became a little 'rosary factory', where members of a resident youth community made prayer beads of various styles and colours. Then, in 1992, I asked Dad if I could borrow this shed, as well as the one next door, to store donations of aid that were arriving in response to a little appeal we were making for the refugees in Bosnia-Herzegovina. Of course he didn't hesitate in saying yes. Indeed, he and Mum were doing most of the work involved in collecting and preparing the aid. Even if he had known then that he would never get either of his sheds back I believe he still would have agreed, mainly because he is a man more generous than any other I have met, but also because it would have given him an excuse to build some new sheds. Fortunately, this is something Dad loves to do. He is, in fact, a serial shed-builder.

Eventually, after serving for some years as a storage space for parcels of clothes, food, toiletries and medical equipment, the shed became our office, first for me as the sole employee of the charity, before I was joined by my sister Ruth and eventually a team of five. At this stage it was so cramped that some, without desks, worked with laptops on their knees. And so at this point Dad's adjoining shed was demolished and he along with George, a very gifted friend of ours, constructed an amazing purpose-built timber office with their own hands. It is a thing of beauty and extremely practical too. But when the time came to move into the bright new office, I chose to stay here, in the old shed. This was a good decision. To some it may seem odd, perhaps even stupid, to retain the HQ of a global organization in this lopsided and tired-looking shed, in a very remote part of Scotland. But being here helps remind me how and why we began this work. Besides, I know some people, living in poverty, who would be deeply grateful to have a house as large and secure as this for their family to live in.

Indeed, among the collection of photographs and notes stuck to the wall above my desk is one of a family who lived in a house as small and more sparsely furnished than this. My meeting with them in 2002 during a terrible famine in Malawi, ten years after we had driven that first little collection of aid to Bosnia-Herzegovina, changed my life – and thousands of others – forever.

In the picture six young children are sitting beside their dying mother. She is sitting on a straw mat. I remember it being unpleasantly hot inside their mud-brick house. My shirt was drenched and even though I stooped, my head rubbed their low ceiling. I felt awkward; like an oversized intruder in their tiny home at the most intimate of family moments. But they had welcomed me in warmly and so I squatted down beside them to talk. My eyes, with the help of some light that was seeping in through a small glassless window, had adjusted to the deep gloom inside the tiny space and I could see that Emma, wrapped in an old grey blanket, was wringing her hands continuously as she spoke to us.

'There is nothing left now except to pray that someone looks after my children when I am gone,' she had whispered, and, softly, she began to tell me about the reason for her torment.

Her husband had died a year previously, killed by AIDS, the same disease that was now about to steal her from her children. All of the adults she knew in the village were already caring for orphaned children in addition to their own. She did not know who would be willing to look after hers, she explained. Her physical pain was excruciating too. The neighbour who was looking after Emma, and who translated our conversation, was a trained 'home-based carer' and was doing her heroic best to ease Emma's suffering, but she was unable to offer even a simple painkiller, never mind drugs to treat HIV/AIDS. Not that those drugs would have helped much anyway, because for them to be effective a patient needs to be eating a healthy, nutritious diet. Emma and her children had not had enough food to eat for a long time. Their hut was surrounded by parched fields in which their maize had not grown properly that year. The tummy of Chinsinsi, the youngest child on the mat, was noticeably distended from his malnutrition.

I had begun to speak to Edward, the oldest of the children. He sat straight-backed, as if wanting to appear taller than he actually was. His black T-shirt was several sizes too big for him, but unlike the filthy torn rags adorning the waists of his siblings it looked clean. He told me he was fourteen years old and explained that he spent most of his time helping his mother in their fields or in the house. Maybe I was just desperately grasping for a chink through which something brighter might steal into our depressing conversation, when I asked him what his hopes and ambitions were. I was certainly not looking for an answer that would change my life and the lives of hundreds of thousands of others.

'I would like to have enough food to eat and I would like to be able to go to school one day,' he replied solemnly, after a moment's thought.

When our conversation had finished, and the children followed us out into the scorching Malawian sunlight, those simple words, spoken like a teenager's daring dream, had already become inscribed in my heart. A cry, a scandal, a confirmation of an idea that had already begun to form, a call to action that could not be ignored; his words would become many things for me. The horrible family tragedy unfolding in that dark hut had synthesized a multitude of sufferings and intractable problems with which I had become closely acquainted during the previous ten years. And his words authenticated an inspiration recently shared with me; they were the spark that ignited the already smouldering notion that became Mary's Meals.

On the shed wall behind me, a poster, headed boldly, proclaims our vision statement:

> That every child receives one daily meal in their place of education, and that all those who have more than they need share with those who lack even the most basic things.

With every passing week, in the years since my encounter with Edward, that vision has grown ever brighter and the belief it can be realized proclaimed more confidently. We have seen repeatedly that the provision of a daily school meal really can transform the lives of the poorest children by meeting their immediate need for food, while also enabling them to enter the classroom and gain the education that can be their escape from poverty. And the number of those daily meals served by local volunteers to hungry impoverished children in schools around the world has grown in an extraordinary manner. Today, over a million children eat Mary's Meals each school day.

I am very fond of my shed. It provides me the quiet space I often crave, while having just enough room for four or five visitors to sit with me round a table, have a cup of tea and talk. And my confinement to this office also gives my co-workers the space they most certainly need from me, an incurably untidy man. It is also the obvious place in which to write this book. The picture of Edward and his family is just one of many things stuck to my wall that illustrate landmarks on our journey: a Bosnian man playing with a dog outside his destroyed house; children laughing in a dusty African playground; a blind Liberian man with a home-made white stick and the most beautiful smile; another group of children from Dalmally – my own among them – painting the outside of the shed; a young Julie driving our truck just after I first met her; a middle-aged Julie and I meeting Pope Francis; a recent picture of me and Hollywood star Gerard Butler laughing as we carry buckets of water on our heads; a passport-sized picture of Attila, one of the first of our children in Romania to die; a card on which is written *Thank You from Texas*, surrounded by lots of sweet, handwritten notes from school pupils there; a postcard from Medjugorje; a simple, wooden cross made in Liberia; and a photograph of Father Tom pretending to punch someone in Haiti. Above the window, under the rusty casing of a strip light, hangs a little crucifix. Some large maps adorn the other walls – the world, India, Malawi, the New York subway and several others.

A scatter of letters and notebooks lie around my laptop. There is a polite note from the president of Malawi (where we now feed over 25 per cent of the primary-school population), thanking me for our recent meeting and for our work. Another is from someone in Haiti, pleading with us to start Mary's Meals in some schools there with desperate need. And another anonymous one, which made me cry when I first read it:

Dear Mary's Meals
Enclosed is a $55 check to help feed another child. This comes from a man who is in a nursing home, is

wheelchair bound, right-side paralysed and unable to speak. He is financially supported by Medicare and Medicaid. The $55 represents his entire savings account. He pulled it out from two different hiding places when he heard about Mary's Meals. I am certain it will be put to good use.

God Bless you.

I never planned to get involved in this kind of work, and certainly never set out to found an organization. I am a rather unlikely and poorly qualified person to lead such a mission. Mainly, it has unfolded despite me, through a whole series of unexpected happenings and comings-together of people, and gentle invitations responded to by all sorts of people with extraordinary love and faithfulness. The meeting with Edward, while crucial in focusing us on the work we now do, was only one more in a chain of events that had already spanned twenty years by the time he spoke those words to me. And that chain had begun to form when I was only fifteen years old, in an obscure village amid the mountains of Yugoslavia, where I had encountered another loving mother concerned about her children.

1

Driving Lessons in a War Zone

> Be humble for you are made of dung.
> Be noble, for you are made of stars.
> SERBIAN SAYING

We knew that the men who launched death from the top of the mountains overlooking the city normally slept off their hangovers in the mornings. For this reason we set off early, confident that we could get in and out of Mostar before the heavy weapons resumed their relentless task of tearing the homes, churches, mosques, vehicles and people of the city apart. Squeezed into the passenger seats beside me, for this last leg of our four-day drive from Scotland, were Father Eddie, a short, plump, middle-aged priest, and Julie, a tall, beautiful young nurse. Over the last few days the three of us had become good friends. Two nights ago, parked beside a filling station in Slovenia, we had talked long into the night. Father Eddie surprised and disturbed us a little by explaining that before leaving Scotland he'd had a feeling he might never return home and so had given away most of his worldly possessions to his parishioners. Later, Julie told us how, a few months earlier, she had awoken in the middle of the night feeling strongly that God was asking her to give up her job to help the people in Bosnia-Herzegovina. Her story moved me because of her deep faith and because it had some similarities to my own. I felt a little ashamed that when she had first phoned me to ask for a lift to Bosnia-Herzegovina I had not been at all enthusiastic about the idea. By now I was very glad she had managed to change my mind.

As we drove through a harsh Bosnian landscape of jagged rocks and thorn bushes, we prayed a Rosary together and then chatted a bit nervously as I concentrated on the twisting narrow road. Soon we began to pass the remains of people's homes. Some were reduced to piles of rubble, while those still standing had become burnt-out bullet-marked carcasses. We drove on in silence. The road began to snake downhill and Mostar appeared below us, sprawling along the Neretva, the famous river which has often been described as a dividing line between the cultures of East and West and which today was the frontline between Serbian forces and the Croat and Muslim territory through which we were driving. The minarets of mosques were visible down in the old Ottoman quarter, and for a moment I thought of my first visit to this town many years before when we had browsed little street stalls beside the river and watched young men prove their bravery by leaping from the famous Stari Most Bridge into the rushing green torrents below. On the descent into the city we were stopped at a checkpoint manned by HVO (Bosnian Croat Army) soldiers. A thin man with a machine gun on his shoulder and cigarette in his mouth walked to my open window and stared at us sullenly, his brandy breath drifting into our cab. Unsmiling, he held out his hand, and we gave him our passports and the customs papers for the medical equipment in the back of the truck. The delivery of this equipment was the reason for our journey and now, about a kilometre away, on the slopes of the city below us, we could see Mostar's general hospital, our final destination. It was easily recognizable and we stared at the modern, shiny high-rise building, which towered above the surrounding houses. Even at that distance we could see that a shell had ripped a massive ragged hole in its side. The soldier waved us on and we drove carefully through streets of twisted metal, shards of glass, piles of rubble, burnt-out cars, chewed-up tarmac and hate-filled graffiti. We entered the hospital grounds. Outside the hospital several refrigerated trucks were parked with their engines running; makeshift morgues for a city that had long run out of space for its dead. Under the front-door canopy, three hospital staff in white overalls recognized our arrival and waved. My anxiety eased and a feeling of elation took hold of me. I was beginning to congratulate myself silently on a job well done, and found myself wondering if Julie was impressed, when I suddenly realized, a little too late, that the welcoming party's waves were turning to urgent *stop* signals and their smiles to cringes. My heart hammered hard as I jammed on the brakes and heard a crunching noise above my head. In front of us, our welcome committee now doubled up in laughter and it was then I realized what had happened. Their hospital had just taken another direct hit; this time by a small, battered truck from Scotland, whose amateur driver had misjudged the height of the canopy overhanging the entrance and instead of parking under it had driven straight into it! A quick inspection revealed that I had torn a hole out of the top corner of the truck's box, while the damage done to the hospital's canopy was hardly significant compared to the punishment the rest of the building had been taking. The greatest, most lasting damage done was to my own ego.

We unloaded the equipment quickly and drank a hasty cup of coffee with two young male doctors. They suggested we get out of town before the shelling started and that we follow them to a safer venue for a chat. Near Medjugorje, where we were to stay the night, they stopped outside a roadside hotel that had been raked by gunfire and damaged by shells.

Over a coffee the doctors explained to us that, because of the extensive damage caused to their hospital by the shell strike, only the ground floor was now in operation. The building was becoming impossibly overcrowded and they were lacking even the most basic of medical supplies. They were particularly delighted with the external fixators we had brought them as they were treating so many patients with smashed limbs, and they urged us to deliver them more supplies. We explained to them that Julie had travelled with me because she was a nurse and was willing to give up her job in Scotland to work as a volunteer here. They replied that they had enough nurses but not enough medical equipment. They suggested that perhaps Julie join me in my efforts to collect surplus medical equipment in Scotland because by now they had realized that as well as not being able to drive a truck particularly well, I also didn't know the first thing about medical supplies, so someone who did would have to get involved if I was to be of much further help to them. I was surprised by how delighted I felt at the prospect of Julie working with me, but just mumbled that we could mull it over. Julie said something similar and I decided I had better not get my hopes up. From medical matters the conversation drifted inevitably to the war situation. The doctors described how the 'Chetniks' on the mountains were now targeting not only the hospital, but ambulances too. Several had been destroyed while trying to carry patients to the hospital. By now they had swapped their Turkish coffees for Slivovitz (a local plum brandy) and they began to express how they felt about the war. They were filled with hatred towards their enemies the 'Chetniks' and it became a disturbing conversation. The two doctors, who had been talking to us for hours about what they needed to heal badly injured people, began to describe the terrible things they would do to any Chetnik soldier they could get their hands on. Clutching lists of urgently needed medical items, we took our leave, promising we would return with more supplies as soon as possible.

This was the fifth trip I had made to Bosnia-Herzegovina in quick succession, and on each previous one I had been accompanied by a different family member or friend. Each had been a precipitous learning curve for a twenty-five-year-old fish farmer who had not ever aspired to be a long-distance truck driver. I discovered a whole world with its own culture, inhabited by long-distance drivers, one which was not always welcoming or easy to understand. Language itself was a problem. There were new technical terms to learn such as the 'tachograph' (the device which records the driver's hours and speed at the wheel) or 'spedition' (the agents who prepare necessary customs papers at border crossings). This was made all the harder by our lack of European languages and our Scottish accents. On one of my early trips my co-driver was Robert Cassidy, a good friend from Glasgow, whose accent therefore was stronger than my own one from Argyll. We were driving a 7.5 tonne truck full of donated Scottish potatoes to Zagreb. It was midwinter and bitterly cold. We slept in the back of the truck at night between the pallets of potatoes, and we woke one morning near the Austrian–Slovenian border to find that our large bottles of drinking water had frozen solid, while a sign at the petrol station told us it was six degrees below freezing. One of the new technical terms we were about to learn on this trip was 'plomb'. This refers to the small seal made of lead, which the customs officials place on the back of a truck when you enter their country, so that when you exit you can prove you transited their territory without opening the trailer and depositing goods. But we didn't know yet what this term meant and with growing irritation a customs inspector barked a one-word question through his glass window at us. 'Plomb?' He wanted to know if our truck was sealed. After answering this repeated question with a blank stare several times, Robert finally answered in his finest Glaswegian accent. 'Nae plums, just tatties. Loads of tatties.' This time it was the turn of the customs officer to answer with a bemused stare. He didn't even know what language to reply to us in.

At this time some of the bridges on the main Adriatic coastal route that took us towards our routes into central Bosnia-Herzegovina had been destroyed by shells, and so to travel that way involved taking a small ferry to Pag (a long, narrow island running parallel to the coast), driving its length and getting a ferry back on to the mainland further south. On one occasion Ken, my brother-in-law and co-driver on this particular trip, and I joined a queue of hundreds of trucks waiting for a small makeshift ferry, on a road that certainly hadn't been designed for large vehicles, just as an incredibly ferocious storm blew up. The ferries stopped sailing and, like all the other drivers, we found ourselves trapped in our cabs while a freezing wind blasted our truck, rocking it back and forth so violently it felt like we would be blown over. There was no way to turn a truck on that narrow road and so we all had no option but to wait for the storm to blow over. The only food we had in the cab was a large box of Twix chocolate bars, which we carefully eked out over the next forty-eight hours. A couple of times, to meet the call of nature, we fought with the door to climb outside and found ourselves slipping on a frozen stream of truck drivers' urine that ran from the top of the hill to the little jetty at the bottom of the winding road. I made a mental note to carry a more varied, nutritious stock of emergency food supplies in future – or at the very least a greater variety of chocolate bars.

I also began to learn, on these early trips, that the donations of aid in the back of our truck were not always the most important things we brought to those in desperate need. My father and I once delivered aid to a little institution for children with special needs near the port of Zadar. At this time the Serb forces were attacking that part of the Croatian coast and we could hear the rumble of shells in the distance as we arrived outside the shabby little building. We found rows of children confined to cots, dressed in ragged pyjamas, and some terrified staff trying to care for them. Not only were they stressed about no longer having even the most basic supplies for the children, but the war was getting closer and they knew that to flee quickly and suddenly with these children would not be possible. As we unloaded our boxes of aid from the back of our truck, the staff's delight soon evaporated as a shell exploded much closer to the village. And then another. They urged us to unload as quickly as possible and to get back on the road north immediately. As soon as I passed the last box from the back of the truck I said my goodbyes, jumped into the driver's seat and revved the engine ready to go. A few seconds went by and I became annoyed that Dad hadn't climbed into the seat beside me. When I looked in my rear-view mirror, I saw him hugging the most distraught nurse and giving her words of comfort and a promise of prayers. Only then did he climb in and we sped off. Thirty years later, when I heard Pope Francis use the term 'sin of efficiency' for the first time, I thought immediately of this incident. The Pope was reminding those of us who work with people in poverty, that real charity is not just about material goods or 'projects' and their 'effectiveness'. It should also be about looking people in the eye, spending time with them and recognizing them as brothers or sisters. But even today I am not sure whether Dad's hug had to take quite that long!

On each of those drives across Europe, as we came closer to our usual destination, Medjugorje, we would invariably see all sorts of other vehicles heading for that same world-renowned place of pilgrimage. Little convoys of small trucks like ours, solitary vans or family cars pulling trailers piled high with clothes, food and medicine, all converged on that little village in the mountains of Bosnia-Herzegovina. Flags, car stickers or home-made signs proclaimed their mission and their homeland, and gave clues to their destination. While we loved the opportunity to return to Medjugorje, given that our lives had been changed there many years earlier, we started to consider whether we should also begin taking our aid to other overlooked places, where less help was arriving but where even greater numbers of refugees were suffering.

One such place was Zagreb, the capital of Croatia, where thousands of desperate people were arriving from areas that were being 'ethnically cleansed' by the Serbs. At this stage nearly a third of a newly independent Croatia was under Serbian control, and war raged along all of the front lines of a country fighting desperately for its existence. Refugees and displaced people, Croats and Muslims from both Croatia and Bosnia-Herzegovina, were pouring into the city having lost their homes, their possessions, and often their families. Living in Zagreb was a remarkable man called Dr Marijo Živković. A mutual friend from Glasgow had suggested we meet. He had explained to us that Marijo was doing wonderful work for refugees and poor people, and also mentioned that he was a well-known and outspoken Catholic who had been persecuted by the communist regime for that reason. We arranged to meet him at the office of a Muslim organization called Merhamet with whom we were working to distribute medical aid. We had earlier that day arrived with an anaesthetic machine they had urgently requested and had spent the morning with a passionate young doctor and his Merhamet colleagues, learning more about their work and how we might help further. We were a little nervous about the meeting with Dr Marijo because, tragically, the Croats (mainly Catholic) and Muslims, who had until recently been allies in Bosnia-Herzegovina while fighting their common enemy, the Serbs, were now at war with each other, and a burning hatred was now raging between these two peoples. How stupid and thoughtless had we been to have invited a well-known Catholic Croat to come and meet with us while we were with our Muslim friends? We sensed that our hosts were also a little apprehensive and an awkward silence had taken hold of the hot stuffy room by the time Marijo finally arrived. Tall and broad-shouldered, he burst in cradling a huge pile of frozen chocolate bars.

'Please take some!' he laughed, approaching each of us in turn, inviting us to help ourselves to the treats on offer, as if he were an old friend of everyone in the room. Eventually, we were able to shake hands and introduce ourselves, and amid much laughter Marijo explained to us, in very good English, the story of the ice cream.

'You see, a large Italian company wanted to donate all this ice cream – half a million ice creams! They contacted lots of the large aid organizations. Each said it was impossible for them to accept – a crazy, ridiculous idea, to send ice cream in mid-summer to people who had no way of storing it in freezers. Eventually someone told the Italians they should phone me and when they did, of course I said yes! How could you say no to all that ice cream when it could make so many people happy? So before it arrived I phoned lots of people to ask them to be ready to take quantities and give out to all their friends and everyone they meet – to take them to children – to schools. And I am sure they are nutritious too …' He guffawed as he began to eat another one.

'So today all over Zagreb people are eating free ice cream!' He roared with laughter again and slapped the backs of his new Muslim friends, who were by now also in peals of laughter.

This was the first of many lessons I learnt from Dr Marijo over the coming years. He had a wonderful appreciation of the art of giving and receiving gifts. He didn't like to use the word 'aid'. He liked to talk about 'gifts'. And rather than saying no to gifts that were offered, he found ingenious ways to accept. Before the war was over, he had even managed to better the famous ice-cream distribution incident when we asked him if he could accept hundreds of tonnes of potatoes from Scottish farmers. This time he solved the logistics, which seemed impossible to others, simply by unloading them all into a huge pile in a public square in the city centre. He then got on the public radio and invited the people of Zagreb to come and help themselves! The hungry inhabitants of the capital responded quickly and every last potato found a good home within hours.

Dr Marijo, an economist by training, had for many years been involved in promoting Catholic teaching on family issues in the former communist state of Yugoslavia. He began to be invited to give talks in various parts of the world and eventually he and his wife, Darka, were invited by the Pope to become members of the Pontifical Council for the Family. The communist authorities finally lost patience and took away his passport to prevent him from travelling. Undeterred, he instead began to organize international conferences in

Zagreb, inviting people from many countries there, until eventually he was given his passport back. Meanwhile he and his family founded an organization called the Family Centre, to provide pregnant women living in poverty with practical help – baby clothing, food, prams, nappies, and so on. The desperate need for basic essential items – and not just those needed by babies – had become huge among the arriving refugees and the general population, and thus the Family Centre now devoted its attention to receiving and distributing goods to all in desperate need. After we had established that the Family Centre was giving aid to all, regardless of their ethnicity or religion (in fact the majority of the aid was being given to Muslims), we began delivering truckloads of Scottish gifts to Marijo's old railway warehouse. On each visit we got to know Marijo, his wife Darka and their children better, often sleeping one night in their house before beginning our homeward journey. A man with a formidable intellect and a love of speaking publicly, he regaled us constantly with his words of wisdom and philosophy. He was not shy to speak of his various impressive achievements, but often these would be followed by him saying: 'My greatest achievement in life is to have met and married Darka … my second greatest achievement in life are my five children … my only regret is we did not have more …' He spoke about family – its beauty and importance – in a profound and sincere way.

Much of the aid we distributed with Marijo was delivered to various makeshift refugee camps, full mainly of women and children. In rows of overcrowded wooden cabins, built originally as accommodation for migrant workers, lived a group of women and children from the town of Kozarac in northern Bosnia-Herzegovina. Despite their trauma, or perhaps because of it, some of them wanted to speak about the horrors they had endured. Before the war, the overwhelming majority of their town was Muslim. For some time that area had been controlled by Serbs and the inhabitants in Kozarac were among the first to experience the evil of 'ethnic cleansing'. The women told us how they had fled to the forest as the Serbs shelled their town, and when the last few Muslim fighters eventually surrendered, they heard the Serbs announce, through loudspeakers, that those in the trees should surrender and come to the road and that none would be harmed. Crowds of them, waving makeshift white flags, made their way out of the woods and assembled on the road. Shells then began to rain down among them, killing and maiming hundreds. When the shelling stopped, the Serb soldiers lined up the survivors and separated out all the men of fighting age. Many of them, who were identified as being leaders or high-profile members of their community, were shot or had their throats slit by the side of the road. Some of those telling the stories had seen this happen to their husbands, fathers and sons. The rest of the men were taken to newly set-up concentration camps. Huddled in their overcrowded cabins, the women told us their stories in the belief that no one in the outside world knew or understood what was happening. They would insist on sharing some of the food we had brought with us and also asked if it would be OK if they set aside a quarter of the gifts we had brought, to smuggle to refugees they knew of still in hiding in northern Bosnia-Herzegovina, who were even more hungry than them. I came away from those encounters with a mixture of feelings. Each of these horror stories made me feel more outraged and angry at these 'barbaric Chetniks'. I found it difficult to remain impartial in this war that I had no part in, or to remember that I was only hearing one side of this tragic story. So often, too, I was deeply moved by the kindness and strength of spirit shown by those telling me their stories, and troubled by the question of forgiveness in a way I had never previously been in my life. If I was beginning to build up anger and prejudice against the Serbs who were committing these crimes, how could I, as a Christian, expect those who had actually suffered such evil to forgive? How could that be possible? How would a true peace ever be born here again?

Sometimes we would drive on east of Zagreb, navigating unsigned tracks (the old motorway had been shelled) to the city of Slavonski Brod. It lay on the banks of the River Sava, which separates Croatia from Bosnia-Herzegovina, and was being shelled and sniped at from across the slow-moving waters. The road bridges lay snapped in half in the river and all the buildings closest to its banks had planks of timber propped up to cover every window and door. After carefully unloading our food to a long line of people, who had been invited to queue at the back of our truck clutching one empty plastic carrier bag each (a self-imposed, practical way to ration their share), we were offered accommodation in a little house on a hill above the town, currently occupied by an elderly couple who were refugees from northern Bosnia-Herzegovina. Our dinner was eaten in awkward silence as all earlier attempts at communication had ended in failure (their English was even worse than our Serbo-Croat). But, afterwards, our host Mladen and I sat outside drinking Slivovitz, and after a few glasses we somehow found we began to understand each other a little. He explained to me that his house lay on the plain that we could see stretching into the distance on the other side of the river. It would now be occupied by Serbs. He had owned a little land and a few plum trees; in fact the Slivovitz we were drinking was made from their fruit. Before they finally fled, having already packed up all the belongings they could carry (including this Slivovitz), he took his axe and chopped down his precious plum trees. Some Serbs might now be living in his house but they wouldn't be enjoying his plums. He laughed a loud bitter laugh at this point, trying to convince me, and perhaps himself too, that this was a funny story rather than one filled with burning hatred.

I began to dislike the terms 'refugees' or 'displaced people'. Of course these are simply necessary, useful ways accurately to describe people who have fled their homes. But I realized that these terms, until I met the real people categorized that way, and got to know them, had begun to represent inaccurate stereotypes in my mind. In another Zagreb camp, during a conversation with a likeable, sparkly-eyed, articulate middle-aged man, I learnt that he had previously been the CEO of a haulage company with a large fleet of trucks. The fact that at that particular moment in time I was the one who happened to be driving a lorry and giving him aid, even though I had a poorer education, a much smaller experience of life and far less knowledge of how to organize the transportation of goods by truck, most certainly gave me no reason to feel in any way superior to him. Although I found it hard to admit, I had caught myself beginning to feel that way: I the giver; this stranger the receiver. I with power; he with none. I began to realize that this kind of work was a very dangerous one indeed.

Meanwhile, Marijo had found a new way to distribute our gifts of clothing to those in great need. He had come to realize that many found their newfound reliance on aid the greatest suffering of all. In order to respect their dignity, he would take over a hall or large space, and lay out the clothing on long rows of tables. He would then advertise an invitation for people to come and choose whatever they wished 'so they could give to people they might know in great need'. Thus he found a way for people to come and select the clothing they needed and liked without public humiliation.

And so it went on, truckload after truckload, filled with an ever-growing torrent of donations from Scotland. Julie, to my delight, had indeed decided to continue helping and was now my co-driver on most journeys. As the volume of support increased it became clear to us that a very small truck was not the most cost-effective way to be transporting large quantities of goods over long distances. We needed something larger. To be able to drive the largest trucks we had to sit our Heavy Goods Vehicle driving test and so, during November of 1993, we stayed with Julie's family in Inverness (who had been among the greatest supporters of our work before I had even met Julie) and began to take the necessary lessons. To my great discomfort, after a couple of lessons together, it became rather obvious that Julie was much better than I was at driving an articulated truck. In fact, after the first 'lesson' with Julie at the wheel, the instructor said to her in an incredulous tone, 'You are kidding me on, aren't you? You're not a beginner, you've been driving these things before, haven't you?' My heart sank a little and I climbed into the driver's seat for my turn.

'You might need a little bit more work,' he stated tactfully at the end of my drive, 'especially on the roundabouts.'

This was kind of him given the drastic measures at least one car driver had taken to avoid being squashed by my trailer. I had not previously understood all that needs to be considered while driving a 16-metre vehicle that bends when you go round corners. At his kind words, a little knot of fear formed in my stomach and over the next couple of weeks this became something closer to panic. It was not so much thoughts of crushing a fellow roundabout user, or even demolishing a petrol station with one clumsy swish of my enormous tail, which caused me this anxiety. It was, rather, the prospect of having to tell my friends back in Dalmally the news that Julie had passed the test and I hadn't. This would provide them with ammunition for jokes at my expense for years to come.

And indeed it has, for in the end Julie did pass her test with flying colours and I failed (yes, my trailer had strayed into another lane while negotiating a roundabout). My excuse that I was starting with a disadvantage, having passed my original driving test in an old Land Rover, in our neighbouring village of Inveraray – a village entirely bereft of roundabouts – did not wash with any of them. To my enormous relief I passed at the second attempt, and before long we had bought a huge 44-tonne articulated truck. Julie had a habit of naming all our trucks and for some reason, which I never understood, she called this one 'Mary', the most unlikely name I could imagine for this gigantic beast. We were delighted to discover just how much aid we could fit inside this truck, all the more so when we were suddenly immersed in a bigger wave of donations from the public than ever before.

For several months we had been closely following the disturbing events unfolding in Srebrenica. Another Muslim town in a Serbian-controlled area of Bosnia-Herzegovina, it was now surrounded by enemy forces and hugely overcrowded. Like several other towns in similar situations it had been declared a 'safe haven' by the UN, who promised they would ensure the safety of all those who sought refuge there. By July 1995, over 30,000 Muslims were crowded into what had previously been a tiny town in a small steep-sided valley. Each building was full of people and thousands slept outside. As the months wore on many began to die of starvation, while even more were killed by the shells being fired from the mountains above the town. Finally, while we and many in the world watched in disbelief and horror, the Serb soldiers invaded the town. The 400 Dutch UN soldiers surrendered without firing a shot. The Serbs then proceeded to select all the Muslim men of fighting age, took them to an abandoned factory and murdered over 8,000 of them in two days. Most of the women (after many had been raped) and children were left to flee through the forests. The majority of them made their way to Tuzla, the nearest large town, where a makeshift camp of tents was hastily erected at an old airfield. All of this unfolded before the eyes of the world. We were kept up to date by regular bulletins. In addition to the anger I felt at the

Serbs, I now experienced a burning rage at the UN and our own government, who had simply let this pre-planned atrocity happen in a place they had the audacity to call a 'safe haven'. I felt ashamed.

Immediately after this event donations poured in faster than ever, both from an outraged public and food companies who offered us pallets of flour, sugar, canned foods and much more. And so, with an enormous, precious cargo, we set off in our new articulated lorry, determined to get this aid to the women and children recently arrived in Tuzla – not a straightforward task given the only way to reach that town would be to cross central Bosnia-Herzegovina where the war was still raging in a complicated way. We knew our large truck was not designed for the mountain tracks that we would need to navigate and so we agreed to collaborate with another UK charity, which was using small trucks to deliver aid within Bosnia-Herzegovina.

We met them in the Croatian town of Split and, in an industrial complex, we decanted our load into their five trucks, under a searing sun. After a much-needed dip in the Adriatic we headed north, Julie and I now co-driving the smaller trucks with our new colleagues. By the second day of driving we had left behind the tarmac for safer dirt tracks in the forest. These felt familiar to me as they were similar to roads in Scotland on which I had learnt to drive as a teenager. And the surrounding landscape was familiar, too, although the mountains were a bit taller and more dramatic than those in Argyll. But I soon began to realize that these trucks, unlike the Land Rovers and pickups I was used to, were not four-wheel-drive vehicles and were clearly not designed for this terrain. The roads became rougher and steeper. Wheels began to spin and I started to worry. And my growing concern was not just caused by the unsuitable vehicles we had found ourselves in, but by a realization that among the new team we were now part of some appeared more interested in thrill-seeking than the safe delivery of aid. Just north of the city of Mostar we had seen and heard shells exploding in the distance. I was horrified to hear one of our co-drivers suggest we take a route closer to where the smoke was still rising so we 'could see what was going on'. It appeared to me as if some of them wanted to play at being soldiers. When we stopped at UN bases to gain advice on the safest routes to proceed on, some of our co-drivers persuaded the soldiers to lend them their machine guns so they could pose for photographs.

I began to understand for the first time why the larger aid agencies often saw some smaller charities' efforts as amateurish and dangerous. As we all settled down for the night to sleep outside, beside our row of parked trucks, Julie and I quietly discussed our misgivings about working with these people, but we realized that right now, having reached a part of central Bosnia-Herzegovina that neither of us knew, we had no real option but to go on with them towards Tuzla. And besides, we needed to tell all the donors back home that we had seen their donations arrive safely. I climbed into my sleeping bag in a bad mood. Our co-workers had not even brought decent supplies for us to eat, and going to bed hungry never failed to make me self-piteous. During the night, we awoke to find a pack of wild dogs running over us. It was the weirdest sensation. They scampered over our sleeping bags, apparently disinterested in us, and disappeared into the pitch-black. I wondered what had happened to their owners and what they were running from or to.

The next day the roads got worse. The stronger trucks were now towing others up the steepest hills and progress became painfully slow. For our own safety, we really needed to reach Tuzla before nightfall, but that looked less and less likely. As the afternoon wore on, the number of stops to repair punctures increased and I became worried that some of the trucks would simply break down beyond repair. And as the light faded, the endless black forest on each side of the road began to look a little sinister. Just as the situation started feeling very bleak, a convoy of huge 'all-terrain' Norwegian trucks drove up behind us. Their friendly drivers – civilians working alongside UN troops – saw our predicament and stopped to ask if they could help. They were even kind enough not to laugh at us and said they would accompany us to their base in Tuzla, towing us whenever we needed their help. With our unexpected 'guardian angels' pulling us on, we began to make steady progress. Finally, we arrived at the UN base at 3 a.m., where we all collapsed exhausted into a deep sleep – but not before Julie had the chance to tell me excitedly that she had driven one of the huge all-terrain vehicles on the last leg of our journey through the night. She told me this as if her biggest lifelong ambition had just come true. I began to think she might just be a little weird.

The next morning we drove into the town of Tuzla and were met by a grateful but tired-looking mayor. We happily unloaded our precious cargo – thousands of boxes of dried food, soap, nappies – into a makeshift little warehouse from where it was being brought in manageable loads to the refugees at the nearby airfield. Later, we ourselves arrived at the huge camp, now home to 30,000 people. We walked down a path between the tents. A girl was trying to wash her hair in a bucket, while nearby an old lady in a headscarf was struggling to make a fire with a little pile of cardboard. In one tent medics were examining severely malnourished children with gaunt expressionless faces. I realized it was only ten days since the fall of Srebrenica. Ten days since these women and children, sitting outside their tents, emaciated and sunburnt, had watched the murder in cold blood of their husbands, sons and fathers – and many other horrors besides. Ten days during which they had walked through the forests in terror. On the way, at least one of them, a twenty-year-old called Ferida Osmanovic, hanged herself from a tree with a scarf. And while they had endured these things, I had been moaning about my own lack of sleep and good food.

While our recent travelling companions set off on the return journey back to Split along the same the roads we had just travelled, Julie and I decided to take our chances with a military helicopter flight that the Norwegians told us about. We were advised to assemble at a nearby landing pad and wait for its arrival. The first day it never came. The soldiers waiting with us told us it was because they had been unable to find sober pilots. I had thought they were joking but the next day, when the enormous helicopter did finally land, the Ukrainian crew members who emerged to unload the cargo were clearly very drunk indeed. Our Norwegian friends had told us that no one was allowed on these helicopters unless they had a flak jacket. We had no such thing and when we explained our predicament to a friendly UN monitor, also waiting for a lift back to Split, he kindly lent us some blue postbags, saying that they were the same colour and shape as the standard flak jackets.

'Just clutch them as you board and the crew will never notice,' he advised us.

He was correct. As we climbed into the cavernous empty hold of the helicopter, the crew stared at us with inane drunken grins and watery eyes and I realized we probably could have been holding anything at all, or nothing, and they would have been oblivious to it. The beast swallowed us like Jonah's whale and took off. We bounced about in the huge metal barrel, as the pilots employed 'tactical flying' which meant flying horribly low, hugging the hillsides and swinging from one side of the valley to the other. This presumably was necessary to reduce the risk of being shot down, but I did wonder how much of it was just caused by drunk driving. Either way I secretly wished we had decided to return by those forest tracks. But we did eventually land safely in Split and found our large truck, Mary, waiting faithfully to take us home. We would have hugged her if our arms had been long enough.

2

A Woman Clothed with the Sun

> To believe in something and not live it is dishonest.
> MAHATMA GANDHI

Right through our childhood and beyond, the River Orchy was normally our friend, especially on days like this when the incessant rain and gushing feeder streams had it lapping the edge of our only road out. The prospect of a flooding river cutting us off from the rest of Dalmally was usually an exciting one, particularly when it meant a day off school. The Orchy had been a water playground running through every season of our childhood. On warm summer days we would carry our rubber dinghy up to Corryghoil, a slow-moving pool with a sandy beach, and swim in the cool deep water. Sometimes Dad would put the little boat on his old Rover trailer and take it further up the glen so we could ride it over waterfalls and beneath overhanging branches, all the way down to the old stone bridge. Occasionally in the winter the ice froze thick and we would meet our friends who lived on the other side, to 'skate' in our trainers or play 'ice hockey' with our shinty sticks and a stone for a puck. In the autumn we spent long hours trying to catch salmon as they battled upstream to spawn, our rare successes worth the wait, as we returned home victorious with a delicious silver fish and excited tales of how it had been caught.

But on this late autumn day in 1983, we worried as we watched the water's creeping invasion of the fields below our house and noticed that neighbours Alasdair and Donald were moving their sheep to higher ground, for the following morning we were meant to be on our eagerly awaited flight to Yugoslavia. Long before the time arrived to begin our overnight drive to Heathrow Airport, the river was in full flood, the road submerged under an impassable torrent. It was then Dad explained he had thought ahead. He had parked our car earlier in the day, beyond the part of the road now flooded, and then walked back home. He handed us a torch and told us to get moving along the muddy hillside path above the flooded road. And so it was that our life-changing adventure began with a walk through darkness and driving rain, ankle-deep in mud with our luggage on our backs, while laughing at how Dad was always one step ahead.

It had all begun a few weeks earlier as we were sitting round the kitchen table after breakfast. Ruth, my sister, back home on holiday from university, looked up from her newspaper and said, 'Look at this! It says here there are reports that the Virgin Mary is appearing to some teenagers in a place called Medjugorje in Yugoslavia!' An excited conversation ensued. We were a devout Catholic family and knew about famous places like Lourdes where Our Lady had appeared in times gone by. We had even been, the previous year, on a family pilgrimage to the Marian shrine of Fatima in Portugal. But the idea that Our Lady could appear today, in our own time, was something that had never occurred to us before.

'Mum, if this is even possibly true we should go,' we implored. Our parents explained that they could not travel during the forthcoming Christmas holidays because of work to be done on the guest house (our home was a rambling old shooting and fishing lodge). We persevered and were amazed when they suggested that we should go on our own. Ruth and her boyfriend Ken were nineteen years old, while my brother Fergus and I were sixteen and fifteen respectively. Between that breakfast discussion and the day of the flood we discovered that the village of Medjugorje was near the town of Mostar but, beyond that, we hadn't managed to locate it on a map, let alone figure out how we would travel there from the airport in Dubrovnik or where we would stay when we got there. 'All part of the adventure,' we thought, as did several of our cousins and a couple of university friends of Ruth and Ken's who had asked to join us. So it was then, that ten of us, some rather muddy from the waist down, eventually boarded a flight from Heathrow to Dubrovnik.

In the stunningly beautiful walled city of Dubrovnik, perched on the edge of the sparkling blue Adriatic Sea, we managed to find a night's lodging with a man who had only one English phrase, presumably learnt from watching American films. 'Take it easy, sonofabitch!' he would exclaim with a smile in answer to every question we asked of him. As far as we could understand, his boarding house was illegal, a little private enterprise that had no right to exist in this communist country. The next morning we discovered that during this holiday period there was no public transport available and eventually we resorted to hiring a couple of cars to reach our destination. Before long we were winding our way along the pretty coast and then up into steep mountains towards Mostar, all the while still laughing about the 'sonofabitch' man from the night before. We had been well warned that the police and communist authorities were not at all enthusiastic about the reported apparitions taking place in Medjugorje or the idea of foreigners travelling there. In fact, before our departure from Scotland, our parents had received calls from the Yugoslavian Embassy suggesting it would be irresponsible of them to allow us to go there. And so we were not terribly surprised when, a few miles from Medjugorje, we were stopped by policemen who questioned us about our reasons for being here. They let us go after a few minutes but did not look impressed when Ken had the audacity to ask them directions to the village from their roadblock.

Finally, we arrived in the little scattering of stone houses amid vineyards and fields of tobacco, and parked outside a white church with two spires that looked far too big for the tiny village around it. The other thing of immediate note was an enormous cross on top of the hill overlooking the village. On that weekday evening, we entered the church and to our amazement found it packed full. The people were saying the Rosary and we could see that Mass was about to begin. It seemed nearly everyone else there was local. Tall, weatherbeaten men, with huge farmers' hands, old ladies dressed in black and families with young children sang and prayed with all their hearts. It was a Mass unlike anything we had ever experienced before and we were profoundly moved by this incredible spectacle of faith. After Mass the priest approached us, introduced himself as Father Slavko and asked us where we were from. He was amazed to hear we had travelled from Scotland and asked us where we planned to stay. We told him we didn't know yet and he explained that there were no hotels or guest houses in the village. He introduced us to his sister and her family, who immediately insisted that we come and stay at their house. There were three sons in the family of similar ages to us, as well as their cousin Gordana, who was visiting from Australia on holiday. She patiently began translating for us, and for the next few days she never stopped! Aside from some conversations about Italian football – a shared passion of ours and the sons of the family – we talked about the extraordinary events that had been happening in this village.

They explained to us that on 24 June 1981, two teenagers from the village, while walking along the road one evening, saw a lady on the hillside who they recognized as the 'Gospa', the Croatian term for the Virgin Mary. The following days they were joined by four other children, who also saw her and heard her speak to them. She told them she was the Virgin Mary, the Queen of Peace. One of the first things she said to them was, 'I have come to tell the world that God exists. He is fullness of life, and to enjoy the fullness and obtain peace you must return to God.' From then on these six children began seeing and talking to the Virgin Mary daily and, within a few days, thousands of local people were gathering on the hillside to be with the children as they dropped to their knees and conversed with someone that all others present could not see. But as the word spread, and people from greater distances began to arrive, the communist authorities became unhappy about these public displays of religious fervour and began to clamp down. The youngsters were taken to a psychiatric hospital where they were questioned and threatened with detainment, but none retracted any part of their claims – not even the youngest of them, nine-year-old Jakov Colo. The gatherings on the hillside were forbidden but the crowds started to fill the church each evening instead, where the children now began to have their apparitions. Meanwhile, the parish priest, Father Jozo Zovko, who had initially been sceptical about the claims of the children but came to believe them, was jailed for three years because of the stand he took on their behalf. Our hosts, through the ever-patient Gordana, explained to us how this incredible chain of events had unfolded in their village and they also told us of the numerous extraordinary miracles that they, along with many other local people, had witnessed. For example, often they had seen the sun spin in the sky (reminiscent of the famous miracle witnessed by tens of thousands at Fatima nearly seventy years earlier). There had also been various healings of people with all sorts of ailments.

We were spellbound by these stories that were told to us in a calm matter-of-fact way, by a clearly sane and well-balanced family. They told us there were many other stories of miracles, and some wild rumours too, but they were only telling us things that they knew for certain to be true. We were overwhelmed by the kindness of this family. It was only after the first night we realized with huge embarrassment that they had all given us their own beds to sleep in while they slept on the floor. On the following nights of our short stay, no matter how hard we tried, we could not persuade them to let us sleep on the floor instead. The family knew the visionaries well. Marko, one of the brothers, explained to us that he was actually going out with Mirjana, the oldest of the six. They insisted on organizing for us to be there with the visionaries, in the small side room of the church, when they would have their apparition. And, sure enough, for the next two evenings we found ourselves in a little crowded room just off to the side of the altar. Along with the bigger crowd in the body of the church we prayed the Rosary together with the young visionaries, who again were of similar ages to ourselves. At a certain point all the visionaries suddenly stopped praying and simultaneously looked up towards the wall. Silence descended. We watched them smiling broadly and talking, but we could not hear their words. They appeared to be in deep conversation with someone we could not see. I was sitting so close to them I could have reached out and touched Marija, as she mouthed words to someone and seemed totally captivated and delighted. This lasted for a few minutes and then the children stopped looking up and became aware again of the rest of us around them. Together we resumed and finished the Rosary.

During those few days in Medjugorje, I experienced a feeling of deep joy unlike anything I had felt before. I felt exhilarated. Our Lady had come to tell us that God existed. I believed her with every fibre of my being. I decided to respond to Our Lady's invitation in my life as best I could.

The rest of our little party seemed to be having very similar experiences. We laughed so much together that week, and cried too. It was as if we were finding out who we really were.

Later in the week, we saw for ourselves the sun spinning and vivid colours radiating outwards from it across the sky. An incredible sight, but by then, given the events taking place in our own hearts, it certainly did not seem like the most amazing experience of that week.

We returned home to Scotland very tired and very happy. Mum and Dad and our grandparents, who lived with us, along with two trusted priests, awaited us armed with a tape recorder and a number of crucial questions, which they insisted we answer before we went to bed. They were determined to ensure we were not being fooled by some mischievous prank, or something worse, and they wanted to thoroughly check our information against the teaching of the Church. Mum and Dad were anything but cynical about this, though. In fact, in hindsight I think that perhaps all of us from the moment Ruth first read the little article in the newspaper at our breakfast table somehow knew in our hearts that this was true. I cannot think of any other reason for Mum and Dad encouraging us to go and see. But now they wanted to be sure, and they wanted to be well prepared to answer the questions that would undoubtedly be posed by others.

They were impressed by the information and answers we gave but, even more, in the days following, the changes they could see that had taken place in us. Their teenagers were now the ones encouraging them to spend time in prayer together – it had previously always been the other way round. They could see something profound had happened to us.

Ruth, meanwhile, wrote an article about our experience, which was published by the *Catholic Herald*. They put our address at the end of the article and we started to receive many letters asking for more information. In fact, over a thousand arrived at our home over the coming weeks and while we headed back to university and school, Mum and Dad wrote handwritten replies to each. One letter arrived from a lady called Gay Russell in Malawi. She explained she was a pilot who flew a small plane across Southern Africa and she asked for more information. Mum sent her a letter. Of all the letters that arrived this was the one we remembered, even though we never heard from her again. The image of a lady flying around Southern Africa telling everyone about Medjugorje became a family joke. We could not know then that twenty years later, in very different circumstances, we would eventually meet Gay, in her African home, and that through that coming together something very extraordinary would happen.

Two months later, having written all their replies, Mum and Dad visited Medjugorje themselves. They had similar experiences to us there and when they returned, also convinced that Mary, the mother of Jesus, was indeed appearing on earth in our own day, with a message for humankind, they felt God was asking them to turn our family home and guest house into a 'house of prayer', a place where people could come on retreat and spend time with God. They began to block out some time from the normal paying guests (most of whom until then had come to fish for salmon and hunt deer) and to organize retreats. Our largest room soon became a chapel, the snooker table replaced by an altar, and, after some months, Craig Lodge the guest house, became Craig Lodge Family House of Prayer. As well as a multitude of visitors who came for a day or two, others would stay longer and soon a little community was born (the Krizevac Community, named after the hill of the cross in Medjugorje), comprising young people who came to live with us, who wished to devote time to deepen their spirituality and discern their calling in life, or who perhaps just needed a place of refuge to recover from what life had thrown at them thus far.

So our idyllic, quiet country house became a hive of activity. Having lived in a guest house or hotel since my earliest memory, I was used to others often being in our home. It was also not the first time Mum and Dad had made a dramatic decision that would alter the life of their family. Two years previously we had fostered Mark, a seven-year-old boy with a dreadful skin disease, who had been abandoned in a hospital in Glasgow. At twelve years old I was surprised and discomforted to find myself no longer the 'baby of the family'. Suddenly we had in our midst a small boy with some serious behavioural problems, prone to spectacular outbursts of rage. We very quickly learnt from this little city kid a whole new range of swearing and ways to insult people. But Mark very soon became our much-beloved little brother and before long we adopted him. Not only did he become a permanent member of our family, but also for all of us an incredible blessing.

But Mum and Dad's latest decision to open their doors was a new kind of invasion of our family space; a nice friendly invasion, but not one that I always found easy. The stream of house visitors was incessant and the boundaries around private family space were sometimes nebulous. Most of my social life was with friends who I had grown up with in the village of Dalmally, and as I grew into my late teens most of my time was spent away from Craig Lodge, playing sport or in the local pub. In that company I would almost never speak of my faith, the retreat centre or my experiences at Medjugorje. It was almost as if I began to lead two separate lives. I never lost my faith, and still prayed every day, but outside of my family there was no one I would speak to about this. My closest companion was my brother Fergus and together we were part of a very tight-knit group of friends who had grown up together in the village. From an early age we were all fanatical shinty players (the Highland sport with a slightly unfair reputation for violence) and most Saturdays we would turn out for our village team, Glenorchy. A close relation to the Irish game of hurling, shinty is often described by those who see it for the first time as field hockey without rules. But shinty was my passion. I loved both the game itself and the fact that nearly all my teammates were boys I had grown up with. We had won the Scottish Cup at primary school and stuck closely together ever since. Our early glory inspired us to believe that we would one day be national champions at senior level, something our village had never managed, but as the years progressed our success diminished. This was probably largely due to the amount of time we spent in our village pub rather than training on the shinty pitch.

Following the match, most Saturday evenings were spent in our local pub, or heading to one of the nearby towns and villages for a ceilidh or party. Often on Sunday mornings Fergus and I failed to get up in time for our local Mass, and so frequently Sunday afternoons were spent driving to attend an evening Mass as there was none near us. We never missed one ever, but most were attended with sore heads and parched throats. We would talk together about our faith and pray together – actually we had always done that from my earliest memory when we shared a bedroom – but we would never speak to our other friends about this part of ourselves, close though they were to us. So our double lives became more disconnected and as they did so I became less happy. But I never lost my faith or my very deep respect for my parents and their choices. I could see that what they were doing was something very beautiful, something that was changing the lives of many people. Their decisions made no worldly or economic sense; those who came to stay were invited to make a donation to cover costs, but those who could not afford to give anything were never turned away. In time, to make ends meet, they sold the salmon fishing they had owned on the Orchy and happily continued to welcome all with smiles. Mum's home-made soup became famous far and wide; Dad's 'bear hugs' even more so.

Meanwhile, I headed to Stirling University to study history, although in my heart I never wanted to leave Argyll. Much of my childhood had been spent deer-stalking and working outside and I had never held a desire to move to a city, nor had any particular career in mind. And my best friends were all staying and finding jobs around Dalmally. But I had done well in my exams at school, and because it seemed expected of me I headed off for the university. History had been my favourite subject and so I chose to study that. I did not last long in Stirling, though. I found my shyness, which I had coped with so far by staying in the company of close friends when socializing, became crippling in this new environment. I could not talk to the other students never mind make friends with them, and every weekend I would hitch-hike home to see my friends and play shinty. With my beloved Glenorchy stripes on and shinty stick in my hands, I would become happy and confident again for ninety minutes. 'Well played, the Big Man!' the older men watching on the sideline would shout when I won a tackle or hit the ball up the field (fortunately, teammates such as Foxy, the Heekor and Pele had earned more imaginative nicknames). Then I would travel back to the university campus and hide in my room. After six months I nearly broke my mother's heart by giving up and dropping out. I returned to Argyll to work outside again – planting trees for the Forestry Commission, stacking timber at a sawmill and then eventually becoming a salmon farmer. For six years I was part of a small team looking after the salmon that swam in the huge net cages that floated on Loch Craignish, a secluded deep-sea loch 4 miles from the nearest tar road. It was a place of great peace and I enjoyed the quiet but strenuous daily routine. It was good place to think and pray, and the boys I worked with became good friends too. I thought I would probably spend the rest of my days living and working in this part of Scotland and most of the time I was quite happy at that prospect, although the long, dark, cold winters often prompted thoughts of exotic warmer lands and new experiences.

But then one rainy evening, in November 1992, Fergus and I walked down to our local pub for a pint. It was unusually quiet. There had been no shinty match that day because of a waterlogged pitch and very few of our mates had shown up. We began to chat about what we had seen on the television earlier that night. A news report had shown the suffering of the people in Bosnia-Herzegovina who had fled ethnic cleansing and who were now in refugee camps. The Yugoslavia we had visited as teenagers was tearing itself apart. In 1991, Slovenia and Croatia had declared themselves independent; a move which ignited a war between the Serbs, who had dominated the Yugoslav state, and those wishing to break away. A year later Bosnia-Herzegovina, home to Croats, Muslims and Serbs, exploded into civil war – a gruesome conflict played out in front of the world's cameras. In Medjugorje, Our Lady Queen of Peace was still appearing to the same six young people, and the title she had given herself had taken on a new significance. Over the years her messages were invariably about the way to peace, about how wars would be avoided if we lived the Gospel message. Exactly ten years to the day after she appeared to those six children in Medjugorje, the first shots of the war had been fired. As the horror unfolded and a stream of reports of bloody massacres, ethnic cleansing and mass rape stunned modern-day Europe, the reason for some of Our Lady's messages and the urgency with which she had spoken them became much more clear. Perhaps too few of those of us who had been privileged to hear and believe her messages had really ever put them into practice in our lives.

This particular bulletin had focused on a camp near Medjugorje and probably for this reason we began talking about how much we would like to help the people there. We knew of a group in London that was organizing the transport of aid to Medjugorje, and we began discussing the idea of making an appeal locally for aid and driving it out with one of these convoys. After closing time, walking back home alongside the black river which had, all those years earlier, nearly stopped us from visiting Medjugorje, we talked ever more enthusiastically about a return visit.

The next day we shared the idea with the rest of our family and almost immediately, before we could ponder it further, our little appeal was launched. Mum and Dad phoned various friends and regular visitors to the retreat centre to ask if they would help, and before long parcels of food, clothing and medicines were being delivered to our house. Donations of money also started to arrive in the post, much to our surprise. Hurriedly, Fergus and I organized a week's holiday from the fish farms we worked on, and we used the donations of money to buy a second-hand Land Rover. We had learnt from those organizing the convoys out of London that four-wheel-drive vehicles were urgently needed for the distribution of aid in the mountains of Bosnia-Herzegovina. The plan, therefore, was to drive out with the convoy from London and to leave both the aid and the Land Rover in Medjugorje before flying home.

Barely three weeks after that conversation in the pub, we found ourselves driving out of London, in a dangerously overladen Land Rover, heading for Dover and then on to Bosnia-Herzegovina. Our employers hadn't been able to give us more than a week off work at such short notice and so, to ensure we could get there and back in the time available, we had roped in some friends to drive the first leg of the journey from Dalmally to London while we flew down to cut one day off the journey.

And so it was that we arrived in Medjugorje once again, with a Land Rover bulging full of gifts for people we had never met, many of them living in abandoned railway carriages in a nearby refugee camp. This was the first time either of us had returned here since our visits in the early 1980s – our first visit here as grown men – and initially it jarred to see all the guest houses and hotels in places where there had once been only vineyards. But by the time we climbed Mount Krizevac, praying the Stations of the Cross as we went, and sat together at the foot of the enormous white cross at the summit, we knew that all of the blessings and graces we had experienced here as teenagers were being poured out for us again. We returned home with grateful hearts. And what I discovered at home surprised me. The donations of aid and money that had poured into Craig Lodge in response to our first little appeal had not stopped – in fact the trickle had become a deluge. The sheds that I had borrowed from my dad, beside Craig Lodge, were now full of medical aid, dry food, blankets and clothing. Mum and her friends were busy categorizing and packing the aid. I realized I had a decision to make and after praying and thinking about it for a few days, I handed in my resignation letter at the fish farm and put my house up for sale. It was not a difficult decision. I had for some time been searching for something else in my life and here, unexpectedly, was an opportunity. Mum had recently inherited a fairly valuable painting from a distant relative, which she sold to raise the money we needed to buy a small truck. Whenever I wasn't sleeping in it I could sleep back home at Craig Lodge, she told me. And so with no particular time frame or 'grand plan' in my mind, and without any previous relevant experience, I found myself organizing the collection and delivery of aid to Bosnia-Herzegovina.

3

Little Acts of Love

> Give something, however small, to the one in need. For it is not small to the one who has nothing. Neither is it small to God, if we have given what we could.
>
> ST GREGORY NAZIANZEN

All the while, back at home, Mum and Dad continued to phone everyone they knew. Over the years, thousands of people had stayed with them at the retreat centre and many had become dear friends. The calls, telling them about our new effort for the people of Bosnia-Herzegovina, quickly mobilized an army of co-workers. Not satisfied with that, Mum then wrote to every Catholic parish in Scotland seeking support. The response was incredible. All day long the phone rang with offers of help. Each morning the postman arrived with piles of letters containing cheques, representing personal donations, church collections or the proceeds of fund-raising events. Julie would spend hours on her typewriter writing thank-you letters, while I spent most of my time driving all over the country to pick up donations of goods and bring them back to the sheds at Craig Lodge, where we would sort through and pack them ready for shipment. It was hard work and we would not have managed without the numerous friends who helped on a regular basis. One of my favourite tasks was loading the trucks bound for Bosnia-Herzegovina. I felt a huge sense of responsibility to ensure that every last square centimetre was fully used so that each expensive, time-consuming journey delivered as much as possible to those in need. Fitting in the goods of different sizes, weights and fragility became like some kind of huge 3D jigsaw game. It was also hard physical work, something I was missing since leaving the fish farm where I had spent all day every day for six years doing physically demanding manual work. My least favourite job meanwhile was that of giving talks and presentations to people who were, understandably, asking for reports and feedback. Or more accurately, I *imagined* this would be my least favourite job, because for some time I managed to avoid each invitation by persuading Mum or Julie to do these talks to churches, schools or various other groups of supporters, while I conveniently prearranged to make a collection in some different corner of the country.

In Glasgow, Scotland's largest city, a wonderful retired couple, John and Anne Boyle, came to our rescue. They set up a volunteer support group in the city, and obtained a free warehouse from the city council as well as a van to carry out local collections. Before long this became the biggest part of our operation. The free warehouse was a very welcome gift but hardly ideal in design. Our space was on the fourth floor, meaning all goods were transported in and out using a very old lift. On the days we loaded the truck for transport overseas, one team would repeatedly fill the lift on the fourth floor, before sending it down to the team below, who carried it out to the truck. More than once the lift broke down. We came to understand that the city authorities would only send out a technician immediately to repair it if there was someone stuck in the lift, otherwise we could be left for hours, or even days, without a way to complete the loading. We eventually discovered we could climb inside the stuck lift, through its roof, and sometimes resorted to doing this prior to phoning the council.

'Yes, there is someone inside,' we would answer honestly and accurately. I think probably they had a very good idea what we were up to, when they arrived to find one of us inside, red-faced and squeezed in beside a stack of boxes, but it seemed like they, along with everyone else in the city, just wanted to be part of the effort and keep the aid moving. While, initially, much of our support in Glasgow came through the churches, when the large Muslim community there heard of our work, they became very involved too. They organized collections of food at the mosques on a regular basis and would deliver huge quantities to our stores. Many in this Asian community, mainly of Pakistani descent, were involved in wholesale food retailing and they often donated us their surplus stocks. But we could never get enough dried and tinned food. It was always top of the lists of urgent requests we were being sent from Bosnia-Herzegovina. We began to approach supermarkets and seek their permission to carry out food collections. They would allow us to park an empty shopping trolley at their entrance and hand leaflets to customers entering the store, inviting them to buy an item on our list and deposit it in the trolley on the way out. A small team of us would target a different store every weekend with this approach and the willingness of people to donate this way amazed us. It was efficient, too, as a team in the back of our van would categorize and pack each product separately as it came in. We usually returned to the warehouse late in the evening with full boxes ready to deliver, marked *Tinned veg*, *Pasta*, *Sugar* and so on. Nearly all the boxes we used as packaging were donated by whisky distillers. They were strong boxes, ideal, but could cause huge excitement and consternation at border posts. Customs officials and police would stand open-mouthed when we responded to their requests to open the back of our truck for inspection, their immediate assumption being that these 'humanitarians' were actually whisky smugglers. They usually seemed a little disappointed when we opened the boxes to reveal their more mundane contents. As time went on we became aware of another interesting pattern at the supermarket collections. At those in the deprived areas of Glasgow – often housing schemes with some of the worst rates of unemployment and poverty in the UK – we noticed that we would be donated significantly more than at those in the more affluent suburbs. Not something I can pretend to explain the reasons for, but something real and quite marked none the less.

I found 'giving patterns' a little harder to predict while doing street collections for money. This was an activity I enjoyed much less than the supermarket collections. Somehow it always seemed harder to ask a stranger for money than for food. Even though it should have been obvious that this was not a personal plea, there was something about rattling a can while saying 'please help the people of Bosnia-Herzegovina' I found very difficult. There was a little humiliation involved; perhaps the tiniest taste of what it must feel like to have to beg for your own needs. To pass the long hours on the pavement I would sometimes enter into a private game of guessing the response of each pedestrian as they walked towards my solicitation. The guy with the muscles and tattoos; the woman pushing the pram; the schoolkids on their lunch break; the busker who had looked annoyed by my presence on 'his patch'. Each one would, more often than not, surprise me. I could not form any conclusions on categories of people and the likelihood of them dropping some coins in my can. And I could not compare and distinguish giving patterns between men and women, young and old, meek-looking and fierce, or the singers of old depressing Scottish songs and upbeat-but-off-key bagpipe players. I am sure others have carried out more scientific experiments in this matter, and could therefore prove me wrong, but I certainly concluded that people of all sorts could be extremely generous and extremely mean. Our experience of this even included the potential of a much more controversial comparison when we were given permission to do a street collection outside the national football stadium before a Scottish Cup Final, which was to be contested by the two giants of Scottish Football, Glasgow Rangers and Glasgow Celtic. Rivalry between these two teams has a reputation for being perhaps the fiercest in world football, representing as they do the Protestant and Catholic communities of the West of Scotland and the rather unsavoury, historical baggage that goes with that. So it was with some trepidation we ventured out with our collecting cans among the swarming fans, approaching the stadium in their tens of thousands. I wondered if they would even notice our presence or hear our invitation. They certainly did and their giving was incredible – the most generous we had seen. I suspect there may have been a competitive element involved. Perhaps they thought we would keep separate totals for amounts donated by fans wearing blue and those wearing green and publish it for the world to see. Or maybe it is just that pre-match beer helps open hearts and wallets. Whatever the reasons (and I am sure in reality they were much more laudable than those I mention), we collected a record total in a very short space of time as the fans entered the stadium. The link with those Glasgow football clubs actually has continued in various ways ever since.

A couple of years after that event I was introduced to two famous former footballers, Frank McGarvey and Gordon Smith, who used to play for Celtic and Rangers respectively. They decided to organize a match between former players of both clubs to raise funds for us. As a Celtic fan myself and a lover of football, I could not have been more excited. They booked a small stadium in the East End of Glasgow and phoned their old friends from both clubs. Many famous players agreed to play. The day before the event I chatted briefly to Frank about some last-minute arrangements. I asked him how his team was shaping up.

'Not too great, actually,' he replied. 'A few have called off at the last minute. You better take your boots along yourself.'

I laughed.

'No, I'm not joking. Take your boots. You're a big lad and you told me you could play a bit.'

He hung up. I stopped laughing. Then I phoned around my friends to tell them the news. Then I looked for my old boots, which had not been usefully employed for some time. The next day I found myself sitting in a dressing room with a group of players who had all been boyhood heroes of mine, talking about tactics and how to beat Rangers. I remembered having lots of dreams just exactly like this when I was young. This was very strange indeed.

'Where do you like to play?' asked Frank as he began to organize his team, and I realized he was talking to me.

'Umm, up front – striker.'

'Great. You and I will play up front together.' He smiled. 'Don't worry. I'll keep you right.'

And so it was that I ended up playing in a Celtic–Rangers match. Actually, I was playing directly against one of their most famous former players and recent captain of the national English team, Terry Butcher. He was a big man. I think he went easy on me during the game, although his kindness didn't extend to letting me have many touches of the ball. In truth I didn't play very well, missing a couple of chances that I should have scored. And we lost the match. A few of my friends from Dalmally had travelled down to watch me, something that meant a lot to me, although afterwards in the bar they had some fun analysing my performance.

This whole experience felt like God was giving me a little treat. A wonderful, surprise gift. Something completely unexpected but connected to some heartfelt desire (even a childish one that I might not dare to articulate as an adult) or longing of mine that only He understood. And a sense that He wanted me to know that He understood me. And this has happened to me many times since. Undeserved, unexpected, gratuitous gifts that can only be unwrapped when feeling like a small child.

Meanwhile there were lots of things to do which were a little less exciting. Now that this work seemed to have developed into an ongoing mission we realized we needed to register a charity. Originally the name we had written on the side of our old truck was *Scottish Bosnia Relief*. When the word 'Bosnia' became politically sensitive during the war, it began to create a risk when we drove through certain areas or border crossings and so we scrapped off those particular letters. After some time we decided to paste the word *International* in the untidy space between *Scottish* and *Relief*. After all, we reasoned, we were delivering goods to Croatia as well as Bosnia-Herzegovina, and who knew where else in the future? So we had named the organization: Scottish International Relief. My brother, Fergus, then spent some time doodling various ideas for a logo. We choose a blue Celtic cross he had drawn, with the letters SIR – the acronym we became known by for many years – written on it. This ancient symbol, a cross on top of a smaller circle, is a very familiar sight across Scotland and Ireland, representing the transition by our ancestors from Paganism to Christianity, from worship of the sun (the circle) to worship of Jesus (the cross). Next we needed a slogan, and once again round the family table we bandied about different ideas, finally agreeing on 'Delivering Hope'. 'Hope' has always been my favourite word. We also briefly discussed whether this work should be an extension of Craig Lodge Family House of Prayer – which had existed as a registered charitable organization for several years – and therefore a Catholic organization, or whether we should be non-denominational. While we all felt this was a work of God and a fruit of Medjugorje, we also felt unanimously and strongly that this should be an organization open to people of all faiths and none. And so we set up a new non-denominational charity and, in addition to members of our family, we invited on to the first board two non-Catholic friends who had already done a huge amount of work. We worked with a lawyer in our nearest town, Oban, to write up a constitution and at our first, rather informal meeting we elected my brother-in-law Ken, Ruth's husband, as Chairperson. This board would meet three or four times a year, while Julie and I, with huge support from Mum and Dad (despite the fact they were also running the retreat centre) did the daily work, with the help of a multitude of volunteers.

Julie, who among her other gifts fortunately had a talent for administration, took responsibility for thanking donors and recording their names and addresses. I did most of the driving within Scotland to collect the aid donations, as well as the planning and preparation for deliveries. This included communicating with our partners on changing areas of need, request lists, customs paperwork, route planning and trying to repair holes in the roof of our truck. I also wrote the appeals and newsletters we began to send to our growing band of supporters, and to my surprise found I enjoyed this very much. In fact, to make ends meet (I was still an unpaid volunteer living off my savings and Mum and Dad's free lodging), I began writing a few articles on other unrelated topics and sold them to various publications. And, of course, a huge amount of our time was spent driving the truck back and forth across Europe. In the year since our first trip with the Land Rover I had driven to Bosnia-Herzegovina over twenty times.

While I learnt things every time I made one of those deliveries, I was learning at least as much from people who, in all sorts of incredible ways, were supporting our work at home. I was very deeply moved and challenged by some of the generosity that I experienced.

Mrs Duncan Jones lived in a little cottage – the sort you read about in fairy tales – at the end of a very rough track near the village of Kilmartin. We always enjoyed visiting her with our van to collect various goods – both her own donations and things she had collected from friends in the area. Each time we visited her she would give us wonderful bowls of home-made soup, and, 'in order to provide sustenance on the journey to Bosnia' she baked us the most delicious fruitcakes I have ever tasted. These cakes contained a truly amazing quantity of brandy. She would sometimes leave them for us to collect at a particular filling station on our road to Glasgow, neatly wrapped, along with a note of encouragement. Her husband, an Episcopalian minister, died shortly after we met her but her hard work and support of our efforts never wavered. Once, I remember visiting her to collect yet another pile of donations. When she served me my soup I noticed that, rather than a ladle, she used an old mug to fill my bowl. I began to look around her kitchen at her empty cupboards and shelves, and noticed nearly everything was gone. Worried, I asked her if she was OK.

'Yes, fine,' she smiled.

'Are you moving house?' I enquired.

'No, no. I love it here. No, I just thought about those families in Bosnia returning to their homes with nothing at all. They need these sorts of things more than I do now. I mean, does an old lady like me, living on her own, really need a ladle? Or extra plates and pots?'

I trundled down the hill from her home, my van full of her household belongings and carefully wrapped cake on the seat beside me. In my rear-view mirror I could see Mrs Duncan Jones waving. She wore a wonderful huge smile.

I was being challenged in lots of other ways too. A few weeks prior to this, Julie and I (by now engaged to be married) were chatting on the last leg home from another trip to Bosnia-Herzegovina and she gently began to question me about my shyness – and my clothes. I had, to her dismay, just told her, quite smugly, that I could fit all of the clothes I owned (apart from my kilt) into one washing-machine load. For her, it was a horrible realization that I didn't look this bad just because I was currently driving and loading trucks all day.

'Well, I suppose that is why all of your clothes are that same sort of horrible grey colour,' she said dryly after a short silence.

'What do you think you will do after this finishes? Will you go back to being a fish farmer?' she asked me.

'I really just don't know,' I replied after a little thought. 'What I am sure of, though, is that it won't be something that has anything to do with people!'

As the months went on, however, and I had to spend more time speaking to people I didn't previously know, I very slowly grew in confidence. With Julie's encouragement I would sometimes even relent and give talks to some of the support groups. And I found myself even beginning to enjoy some of these encounters and the sense that I had a particular thing that I could do – and do well. I found our supporters were hungry for information about our latest aid deliveries. We started taking pictures and bought an old slide projector so we could illustrate our presentations. And we developed our newsletters to include pictures. I began to derive an enormous sense of purpose from being able to communicate the needs and words of those who were suffering to those who wanted to help them. For a little while I thought that perhaps I could try to become a journalist. One day I noticed a fish-farming magazine advertising for a reporter and I applied. To my surprise they asked me over to Edinburgh for an interview. The two men across the table were complimentary about some samples of my writing that I had sent them and it seemed to be going well. Then they posed me a hypothetical question.

'What would you do,' they asked, 'if you came across evidence that a product sold by a company, who had a very substantial advertising account with this magazine – say a chemical used for getting rid of parasites on salmon – was having a hugely detrimental effect on wild shellfish in the area?'

'Of course I would write a factually correct, well-researched article, exposing this. It would be an important story to tell,' I said with some relish, not for one second thinking that, to them, my answer was hopelessly naive. But then I noticed them looking at each other, one with raised eyebrow, the other smirking. Too late, I realized that my fantasies of writing award-winning journalism as a weapon of truth and justice were not necessarily compatible with writing for a Scottish fish-farming magazine. Julie was waiting for me outside and when I told her what had happened we laughed so much, realizing that our hearts had never really been in it. In fact our hearts were not really in anything outside of the work we were already doing. And in Julie I had a fiancée who not once, ever, expressed any concern about our future financial security or well-being.

However, we *were* running out of money. It was a year since I had given up my job. We needed to make some choices. The board of trustees proposed that I start to take a small salary so that this work, which was growing steadily, could continue. Eventually, after much discussion, thought and prayer, I accepted. It was a very difficult decision. This had not been part of the original plan, and to take even a small portion of the money given us in order to support myself made me feel very uncomfortable. We wanted our organization, and still do to this day, to be as low-cost and as reliant on volunteers as possible. But the alternative was for me to go back to another job and for us to wind down the organization, just at a time when more and more people were supporting us and encouraging us to go on. And one small salary represented a very small percentage of the value of donations. So I accepted the offer and I am very glad I did.

We continued, relentlessly, to look for the most effective ways to deliver the aid that people kept entrusting us with. I was happy that our new bigger lorry had reduced the costs of transport significantly, but now I became bothered that we were driving back across Europe on each return trip with a huge empty trailer. I began asking people if there was anything someone would pay us to carry back from Eastern Europe to help offset costs. Around this time I came to know Sir Tom Farmer, perhaps Scotland's best-known entrepreneur and founder of Kwik Fit, the enormous car tyre and exhaust-fitting company. He had, years previously, visited Mum and Dad at our retreat centre in Dalmally and been very kind in supporting them. It turned out that at this time he was importing lots of tyres to Scotland from Slovenia and northern Italy. He was happy for us to carry some of these as 'return loads' back to his Kwik Fit depots and to pay us the going rate. Sir Tom became a great friend and mentor over the next few years, giving me his time whenever I asked, and some hugely important words of wisdom.

'Target your values, don't value your targets,' he told me when I mentioned growth figures or ambitious plans. On other occasions, when I talked of new ideas, he would refocus me by saying, 'Magnus, just stick to the knitting!'

The return loads worked wonderfully well and, in time, through agents, we also began to arrange other cargo (refrigerators, flat-pack furniture, etc.) that we could carry back. To do this we had to obtain an Operator's Licence to run a haulage company, which necessitated me doing some study on international haulage and passing an exam. The return loads worked really well in offsetting much of the cost of transport, but before long I realized that I was now spending most of my time running a trucking company. I felt that was not what I should be doing with my time. So I began to think about it the other way round. I observed on our journeys that there were lots of Eastern European trucks delivering goods to the UK. They must also have empty trailers to fill on their return journeys? And so that is what we began to do. Now that we had established, trusted partners, like the Family Centre in Zagreb, we could load a Croatian truck in Scotland and pay them a very reasonable cost to transport it for us. This became our preferred way of working, allowing us to concentrate on raising awareness of our work, collecting aid and thanking our donors. It also enabled us to cope with the ever-increasing scale. By the peak of our aid deliveries, during the Kosovo crisis in 1999, we were loading a 40-tonne truck almost every day for two consecutive months, from four Glasgow warehouses. We asked a radio station in Glasgow to make an appeal for more volunteers, and over just one weekend 500 people registered at our warehouses to help pack and sort the goods. These trucks took the aid by road to Split where, with the help of the redoubtable Dr Marijo, our trusted friend in Croatia, it was transferred to ships for the final leg of the journey into Albania, where huge numbers of refugees from Kosovo were arriving.

Also, the kind of aid we sent evolved as we went on. As stability returned to certain areas of Bosnia-Herzegovina and Croatia, some refugees began returning to homes that had been damaged and looted. An urgent need grew for the things they required to start life again. Now our trucks began to carry cutlery, kitchen utensils and tools.

One group of people who were grappling with the possibility of a return home were good friends of ours. They were Bosnian Muslim refugees living in Glasgow. They had fled their hometown, Bosanski Petrovac, which lay in a Serb-controlled part of Bosnia-Herzegovina, in 1992, and eventually arrived by chance in Glasgow, having been evacuated by the UN. It was there, when they began coming to our warehouse to volunteer their time to help prepare the aid donations for shipment to their homeland, that we got to know them. They became part of the 'team' of warehouse volunteers and told us that being able to do this gave their broken lives a purpose. Not only were they struggling to learn English and adapt to a foreign culture; they were also finding life on the seventeenth floor of a block of flats in the city very different from their former rural existence. There were twelve of them, all closely related, and sometimes we invited them up to visit us in Dalmally where they would enjoy barbecues with us. Suad, and his wife Zlata, who had a young son, were about our age and we became friends. As their English improved, they wanted to tell us more about what had happened to them. They explained that before the war their village had been home to Serbs and Muslims who had lived peacefully together. Many of their neighbours were Serbian whom they had known all their lives.

'We were just working in the fields like normal,' Suad explained. 'Shooting just started. There was tension in the village. We all knew what was happening in other parts of Bosnia-Herzegovina. But even one week before we had been invited to a party at the house of our Serb neighbours. The shots were coming from near that neighbour's house, beside our field. My father and my brother Mersad fell. They were bleeding. I was hit too.' He pointed to the scars on his withered arm.

'My brother Mersad took a long time to die. He kept shouting "Suad, help me," but I couldn't. I was all bloody too.'

'We were watching it all happen from our house,' Zlata said quietly. 'We wanted to run out to them in the field but the Serb was shooting from some bushes nearby. He would have killed us. Edin, Mersad's son, was ten. He kept on trying to run out to his dad and we had to hold him back. Eventually when it became dark Suad managed to crawl home.'

The next day they squeezed on to overcrowded buses provided by the UN to evacuate them to Zagreb. They were shot at by Serbs and endured an appalling journey in the heat, without food or water.

'I had to use my shirt as a nappy for Zlatan – he was still a baby then,' Zlata told us through tears.

By 1995, the fortunes of war began to change and the Serbs had largely lost control of that part of Bosnia-Herzegovina. We were able to begin sending trucks of aid into the city of Bihac, which had endured a horrific three-year siege, and then to our friends' hometown of Bosanski Petrovac. Suad began to receive messages from people who had already returned home to their town, urging them to come back too. And so, despite having no savings, no paid employment opportunities there, no assurance of safety, only a badly damaged home and some fields that might now have mines in them, they decided to go home. And we decided to go with them. We filled a large truck with all the belongings they had accumulated in Glasgow, as well as various other goods and tools to help them begin their lives again from scratch. Meanwhile, we had also been donated a minibus for a psychiatric hospital in Croatia to which we regularly delivered aid, and so we formed a plan for me to drive the group home in that minibus and then leave it at the hospital before flying home. The BBC heard of our plan and decided to make a documentary about our journey. And so, for the benefit of the cameramen, we waved goodbye to the bulging truck as it departed ahead of us from our Glasgow warehouse, and climbed into our bus. The group ranged from a two-year-old to an elderly granny. We headed south towards the ferry and Europe.

On arrival in Belgium we stopped at the customs post to show our passports. The police studied the Bosnians' papers and were clearly unhappy. They asked questions and made phone calls. They told us the papers were valid for entry into Croatia and Bosnia-Herzegovina only, but not for transiting the European countries in between. They decided to deport us back to the UK. We also asked questions and made phone calls, but to no avail, and later we found ourselves travelling back on the boat to England. I realized the Bosnians had no homes to return to in Glasgow and that their belongings were already well on their way to Bosnia-Herzegovina, along with the BBC film crew. I phoned Julie to check what money we had left in our bank account and what flights from Heathrow would cost. We calculated that we had just enough to fly the whole group to Zagreb. So I drove them to Heathrow Airport from the ferry terminal and put them on their plane. I then headed south again, catching my third cross-Channel ferry in two days, and pointed my bus towards Zagreb. By now I could drive to our various destinations in the former Yugoslavia without needing a map, and this time it was pleasing to see just how quickly I was transiting countries compared to the slower pace of progress I had become used to in the lorry. Meanwhile Julie arranged for the Bosnian families to be met by Marijo on their arrival in Zagreb, who took them home to stay with them while waiting for me to catch up. When I finally did arrive the next day, they all climbed back in the bus for the final leg of their emotional journey over the border into Bosnia-Herzegovina. It amazed me, when I finally watched the documentary broadcast by the BBC about this journey, to see how skilfully they pieced together the footage so there was no hint of the deportations and flights that had occurred in between the Glasgow departure and the arrival into Bosnia-Herzegovina!

After the usual checking of papers at the Bosnian border we were finally waved through. As we entered Bosnia-Herzegovina, Zlata broke the silence with a cry.

'We are no longer refugees!'

Everyone in the bus was crying. And the sobs grew louder when we finally reached Bosanski Petrovac, which was in ruins. Every building was covered in bullet holes and many houses had been reduced to pitiful piles of rubble.

The welcome they received from dear friends they had not seen for over three years was full of raw emotion. There was so much news to exchange. So many terrible things experienced that they had never had a chance to discuss and to try and understand. So many changes, too, in their old town. The Serbs were now gone. The town was now Muslim in a way it never had been before. A new mosque was being built even while many of the houses still lay in ruins. For Muslims like those I had just arrived with, their religion had not been something they previously practised. In fact I had met some young Muslims during the war who told me they never even knew they were Muslim before the war. Only their surname denoted their religion and sometimes sealed their fate. Bosnanski Petrovac might be home, and their hearts rejoiced at being back, but in some ways it was an alien land. I felt a little awkward. These encounters and exchanges that I found myself in the midst of were so personal and intimate that I wanted to leave them to work through it without me, however they could.

I left Bosanski Petrovac very early the next morning, leaving Suad and his family sleeping in their own home. I should have felt elated, but my drive was not a comfortable one. I travelled for many miles through a countryside and villages utterly devoid of people. Wild dogs, the only other sign of life, roamed amid the rubble and rubbish. This was part of the *krajina*, an area occupied by the Serbs for most of the war. They had only recently been defeated here and I became increasingly scared as I drove through this wasteland on my own. I began to doubt whether those in Bosnanski Petrovac, only recently returned themselves, had been well-informed when they advised me it would be safe to drive this route to Croatia and the Adriatic coast, where the hospital was awaiting the minibus. And given the lack of road signs, and any other way of checking I was on the right road, I began to fear I would drive into an area where I should not be welcome. The hours went past without seeing a human. As well as fear, a new overwhelming loathing for war and its futility rose in me. I wondered what would become of all the Serbs who had now been forced to flee the empty houses by the side of road and the villages to which they had belonged for generations.

It was clear there were no winners in this war, only people taking their turn to lose in very horrible ways.

Eventually, I did find my way out of the mountains of Bosnia-Herzegovina and that same evening I found myself in a different world, eating delicious fish by the sparkling Adriatic with some friends from the hospital, who rejoiced over their new bus.

It was only on the flight home that I remembered our bank account. The £4,200 we had spent on plane tickets to Zagreb had left us with almost nothing. The aid donations would be piling up. I began to wonder how we would pay some outstanding bills and find a way to finance the next delivery. When I arrived back, a smiling Julie could not wait to tell me her news.

'A cheque arrived this morning from a priest in Ireland. We don't know him. He doesn't want a thank-you letter. He wants this to remain anonymous,' she said, her voicing cracking with emotion. 'It is for £4,200.'

4

Suffer Little Children

> First they ignore you, then they laugh at you,
> then they fight you, then you win.
> MAHATMA GANDHI

It took me a long time to decipher how the jumble of numbers on my train ticket related to the carriages, compartments and bunk beds of a night train pulling out of Bucharest railway station, bound for Transylvania, just before midnight, on a very cold and dark April night in 1998. When I eventually found the right compartment I was dismayed to discover it full of young Romanian soldiers drinking beer. They did not look particularly happy when I entered and I felt a little intimidated. It took lengthy persuasion and much pointing at my ticket (they didn't have English and I had no Romanian) before a young, well-built man with a shaven head gave up my bed upon which he had been sitting. As the train chugged through an area of bleak-looking high-rise flats in the suburbs of the capital city, one of the soldiers surprised me by offering me a swig of his beer. I accepted and just as I was handing the bottle back the window of our carriage smashed inwards. A small rock landed on the floor between the bunks and shattered glass sprinkled the cabin. The reaction of my travel companions suggested this was just an act of random vandalism, but as the cold night air rushed into our compartment, and we did our best to snuggle under our meagre blankets, I questioned the wisdom of travelling to this country I knew so little about. But then I remembered the email that had led me here. I had received it, out of the blue, a few weeks earlier from an American lady called Kristl Killian. She introduced herself as a volunteer who was working with children in Romania who had been abandoned in hospitals in the city of Targu Mures, and she was making a desperate plea for us to send basic supplies.

'At the AIDS hospital where I work, we lost nine children over Christmas,' she had written. 'The rest are dying from AIDS-related illnesses or starvation. The situation is serious. The stronger children steal from and prey on the weaker ones and with two nurses for forty children, the smaller weaker ones are eventually starving. PLEASE help us.'

By now we were beginning to receive many requests for help, but there was something about the tone of this one, a sense of sincere desperation, that moved us to act. Already our first truckload of food, clothing, toys and medicine was on its way to Targu Mures, and now I was here to learn more about the situation and what we might do to help.

When I walked, shivering, from Targu Mures railway station, early the next morning, I was relieved to be met by Kristl, a small pretty lady, with bobbed dark hair and a big smile that never left her face for long. We made our way to a nearby cafe and over a badly needed hot drink she told me her story. She had first visited Romania as a tourist, been injured in a car crash and ended up spending a short time in a local hospital, before being flown back to the USA. While she was recovering fully back home, she could not stop thinking about the abandoned children she had met in the hospital wards in Romania and she decided that when she was well she would return to do whatever she could to help. After coming back to live in Targu Mures, she began visiting the hospitals and slowly a small group of Romanian friends joined her.

Kristl explained to me that during the 1980s and early 1990s, thousands of Romanian children had been infected with the HIV virus during basic hospital procedures. Contaminated syringes, vaccines and blood had passed on the disease and resulted in Romania having the highest incidence of paediatric HIV cases in Europe. The fact that the majority of the children infected this way seemed to be Roma (Gypsy) – a marginalized and often discriminated against ethnic group – led to various conspiracy theories. Whatever the reasons for the contamination, all over Romania thousands of HIV-positive children who had contracted the disease during that era were living in hospitals – often abandoned by parents who had been encouraged by the authorities to do so. There were currently over 100,000 children living in institutions in Romania. The last communist leader there, the infamous Nicolae Ceausescu, who had ruled Romania for twenty-five years, had been overthrown only nine years previously. Along with his wife Elena, he had been captured, condemned to death and shot by firing squad. But the odious legacies of his rule were still horribly evident, perhaps most especially in the thousands of orphanages, hospitals and city streets where children who had never known the love of their families endured broken lives.

Kristl, and her dedicated band of helpers, now visited some hospital wards in Targu Mures on a regular basis to spend time with the children, trying to speak and play with them. The situation for the children in the Hospital for Infectious Diseases – the ones she had described in her email – was the most terrible they had witnessed. The abandoned children there were neglected in every sense of the word. All of them faced the rest of their lives there and every week children were dying all alone in their cots. There was growing tension, even animosity, between the paid staff and these volunteers who were seen as being critical simply because their attitude to these rejected children was in such contrast to that of the nurses and doctors. The words poured out of Kristl as if she had been eager to tell the whole story to someone. Even amid this grim report a sparkling humour was evident. She was amused by her own everyday mistakes in this foreign land where she was working hard to learn the language and culture.

'This morning when I got to my car I realized I had parked it very badly last night, trapping one of my neighbours' cars. There was note on my windscreen,' she laughed. 'It just said *Cretina*. I can't stop laughing about it. I'll need to find the neighbour tonight and apologize.'

I was struck by her bravery and strength of spirit, but especially by her very evident faith in Jesus. She had been raised a Baptist and even during those first conversations, we began to discuss our different Christian traditions and discovered that we held in common a love for the writings of C. S. Lewis.

By the time I had drained my second coffee and swallowed the last bite of my chunky salami sandwich, I had learnt a lot about Romania and the particular situation Kristl and her friends were working in. Her comprehensive briefing complete, Kristl suggested that we head immediately to the Hospital for Infectious Diseases. We climbed in her old, battered car, where the sight of the crumpled 'CRETINA' note she had left on her dashboard prompted peals of laughter again, and we drove through some pleasant tree-lined streets, before she parked outside an inconspicuous brick building, not immediately recognizable as a hospital. We walked through the front door and made our way along dim corridors, without seeing a single member of staff. Kristl, by now, had stopped laughing.

I will never forget the overwhelming stench of faeces and infection, or the silence when we entered the 'ward'. In a cold, gloomy, bare room were long rows of cots, each one containing a child. Emaciated and dressed in torn, stained pyjamas, most were rocking rhythmically back and forth. From time to time the silence was broken by a moan or shriek. One girl began to bang her already bleeding head repeatedly against the bars of her cot, shrieking as she did so. Many of them had grotesquely swollen heads. Their faces looked wizened, almost like old people's heads on children's bodies. Some had limbs that seemed to stick out at impossible angles from their bodies. Their hair had been cropped short and I could not tell girls from boys. Most had scabs and sores and what looked like scabies. At first they seemed oblivious to us, but as we approached them some began to push their stick-thin arms out to us between the metal bars. Accepting the invitation, we lifted them and held them. They hugged like limpets, even when we tried to prise arms and legs off so as to pick up the next child now reaching out for a hug. Some gave me unexpected, beautiful little smiles. As the shock wore off (even Kristl's briefing had not prepared me for this), I began to think I should take some photographs. Already I knew I desperately wanted to do something to help these children and realized that in order to persuade others to help us, we would need evidence that this was really happening. I fumbled in my bag for my camera and Kristl continued talking to the children as I began taking some pictures. She knew many of their names. She explained to me that some of them were unable to walk, at nine or ten years old, simply because no one had ever lifted them from their cots for long enough for them to learn. There were forty chronically sick children here and only two nurses on duty at any one point to care for them. It seemed that most had long ago given up trying to do so.

Then a nurse entered the room for the first time. She looked unhappy to see us and her frown deepened when she saw my camera. She told Kristl (who already spoke pretty good Romanian) that she wanted us to speak to the director of the hospital and led us through some corridors to a small office. The director, a bespectacled, middle-aged woman with badly dyed orange hair, gave us a short lecture. She asked us to leave and left us with the impression that Kristl and her friends might not be allowed back.

I felt distraught that I might have made things even worse, but back at her apartment Kristl and her friends, who had gathered to discuss a way forward, tried to reassure me. Over coffee and cake, they explained this was not the first time they had been asked to leave and that their relationship with the staff had already broken down. They explained how even the toys, pyjamas and soap they had recently taken to the hospital for the children were going missing, presumably stolen by the staff.

'Thank you for the gifts you send them from Scotland, but as long as those kids are in that hospital we cannot really change their lives,' they told me.

Later that evening I walked back to the hospital on my own. For a very long time I stood outside the grubby brick walls and I prayed. I asked God to have mercy on those children. 'Please, Lord, give them a new life. Let them experience love. Show us what to do. Please, Lord.'

The next day I talked to Kristl about the idea of us creating a decent loving home for at least some of these children – perhaps a kind of children's hospice where they might receive care and love during their short lives. She told me that she had been thinking and praying about the same thing, but explained there were many huge obstacles that would have to be overcome. The hospital authorities didn't necessarily want the children to leave as they received funding from the government to keep them. Most Romanians knew little about HIV/AIDS but had a great fear and prejudice about this disease and so there would probably be strong local opposition to opening such a home. Qualified, caring staff might be hard to find too – although the amazing local volunteers and friends from Kristl's church were perhaps good places to start looking. Then, of course, there was the small matter of finding the funds to open and run such a home, and the fact that neither of us had done anything like this before. Despite the realization that the odds were firmly stacked against us, a dream was born that day and, in retrospect, I am grateful that we were so naive about the scale of the problems and obstacles we would face.

I began to travel to Targu Mures frequently. It was a town I grew to like very much with its Austrian-Hungarian architecture and beautiful town square that was closed to traffic on Sundays. In the evenings, if all my meetings were finished, I would visit some of the many churches there. Much of the large Hungarian population in the town was Catholic and so, most days, I could attend Mass in one of several of their churches, but often I would also visit the beautiful and huge Orthodox church, where I was struck by the beauty of their singing and their wonderful icons. Some Sunday mornings, after Mass I would also go to the 'church' Kristl attended, which took place in a meeting room in a hotel, and which featured a lot of guitar and piano-led praise music. Members of the small congregation were demonstrative and passionate in their prayer and songs of praise. I started getting to know a number of Kristl's close friends here. Among them were Gusti and his wife Ibi, whose two gifted teenage boys led much of the singing in the church. One day, over dinner at their home, Ibi told me how she had been brought up by communist parents and knew nothing of Christianity. When she was a young child she became sick and eventually was diagnosed with cancer. She ended up in the same hospital where the abandoned children now lived. When she was there she had a mystical experience during which she met Jesus. She left hospital completely healed of cancer and with a burning Christian faith that never left her. I was happy to find myself among these people who believed in miracles and who unfailingly exhibited an attitude of great faith and hope. Together we began looking at different properties that might be suitable for our children's home. Meanwhile, back in Scotland, I began telling others about the suffering of the children in the hospital and our need to raise funds to open a home for them. Just as our fund-raising for this project was beginning, a great-uncle of mine, Nigel Bruce, died. I hardly knew him, having only met him three or four times in my life, and so I was shocked to discover that he had left me a sum of money in his will. The lawyers sent me a note in which Nigel had written, 'I know Magnus will know what to do with the money.' The amount he left was very similar to the amount that we had estimated as a minimum requirement to buy and set up a home. Great-Uncle Nigel was right, I certainly did know what to do with his extraordinary gift. Once again, it seemed as if everything we ever needed was being given to us. Meanwhile, many generous supporters responded to our specific appeal to meet the running costs of the home. For the first time we had invited people to set up monthly donations so we could be confident about budgeting and we were amazed by how many began pledging regular amounts to us. However, fund-raising for this project turned out to be the easiest bit.

After some weeks searching, during which we visited all kinds of properties in and around Targu Mures, we found what appeared to be the perfect place. It was a large, two-storey house, set amid cornfields on the edge of a small market town, thirty minutes' drive from Targu Mures. The second time I visited it I was accompanied by my sister, Ruth, who was by now working with me and helping with a multitude of growing tasks. Being a gifted writer, she was beginning to take the lead on developing our style of communications with donors, including the production of our first newsletters. We would laugh about this, remembering how as children we played at producing our own little newspaper. We called it *Craig Lodge News*. It was properly laid out in columns with news stories, drawn pictures, adverts and even a letters' page. It was nice now, as adults, to be producing 'newspapers' that we hoped people might actually read! At this stage we had no exact division of roles, or job descriptions, and Ruth was supporting me with whatever needed doing. So we stayed a couple of nights in the house, among the rolling fields, trying to learn more about the local community. At breakfast time a fierce housekeeper would slam on the table a jar of pickled vegetables, a chunk of white bread and a bottle of vodka, while Ruth and I tried not to laugh. I never did manage to acquire a liking for pickles at breakfast.

Along with Kristl and our Romanian collaborators, we had discussions with various local authorities. We met the mayor of the town and explained what we wanted to do with the house. We asked for his approval and were delighted when he agreed to give it. He signed various necessary documents, stating his support for the opening of a home for abandoned children who were HIV-positive. We went ahead and bought the house. Two weeks later the mayor contacted us and told us there was huge anger in the town about our project and that he had even received death threats from people because he was supporting us. The people were terrified at the idea of children with AIDS coming into their town. He told us he was now withdrawing his support. After some fruitless attempts at entering into dialogue with him, and those in this community who were opposed to the plan, we realized it was pointless to persevere. Time for the children in the hospital was too short. We set about reselling the house while beginning to look for an alternative. Gusti, who himself ran a children's home for an American church group, told me that they now had a property in Targu Mures for sale. I went to see it and found a well-built spacious house, in a quiet part of the city with large grounds. By now we realized that our best chance, given the strength of local feelings, was to open the home in the city rather than in a smaller community. This house was perfect for our needs but the asking price was far too much for us.

'Are you interested in buying it?' asked John, the American owner, immediately my tour of the house was completed. He was in his sixties, very spritely with bright eyes and a disarming direct style of communication.

'I certainly am,' I replied, 'but we don't have enough money. Even if we sell the other house soon, it is not worth as much as this one and so we will need to find more funding from somewhere else. I am sure we can do that but I don't know how long it will take.'

He asked me to tell him more about the project we had planned. When I had finished speaking there was a long silence.

'I believe this is a work of God,' he said firmly. 'I would be happy for you to pay what you have now and then just pay off the rest when you have it.'

He asked for no written contract, no specific timetable of payments and no interest payments. I was dumbfounded. We went ahead and bought the house based on this incredible offer. Suddenly things began to accelerate. The next major hurdle was the massive amount of paperwork required to obtain various permissions by local government and to officially take these children into our care. In some cases, and quite rightly, despite the fact most had not been in contact with their children for many years, we had to obtain the signatures of parents, giving permission for the children to be moved from the hospital to the new home. Armed with a list of names and addresses, Kristl and her new English fiancé, Matt, set off to find these people. After hundreds of miles driven on pot-holed roads, dirt tracks and endless searches in country villages, derelict farms and city slums, all of the necessary signatures were captured. The opportunity was taken also to invite the parents to visit their children whenever they could.

Meanwhile, perhaps the most important part of all was developing nicely; an amazing team of loving Romanian staff were being recruited. Many of them were those who had initially been helping Kristl visit children in hospitals, initially as volunteers. They were people who wanted to do this because they had it in their hearts to help these children, rather than an interest in personal gain. But we still needed someone who could lead the whole project and I had talked with Ibi about this. She was someone I admired hugely, but she was also an accountant with a good, relatively well-paid job in local government. While she felt very drawn to helping these children, she decided she could not give up her career at this time. I did not have long to feel disappointed before her quietly spoken, earnest husband Gusti, who already had experience running a children's home, said he would love to come and work with us in that role. Having agreed details with Gusti on the final evening of one particular visit, I flew back to Scotland happy that at last everything seemed to be falling into place. Almost as soon as I arrived home, Ibi called me to say that just after I left them Gusti had become seriously ill. Over the next few weeks it transpired that he had had a stroke and would be unlikely to ever recover enough to work again. A short time later, despite the fact her own world had been turned upside down and she was now having to support her two teenage boys, as well as her sick husband, Ibi called me again to say she felt God wanted her to give up her government job in order to run the home. She wanted to make sure those children would be loved. And to that task she has been devoted ever since.

We had chosen the ten healthiest children to take out of the hospital first – believing they would be likely to benefit most from their new home, which we had now decided to call Iona House after the famous Hebridean island of that name in our part of Scotland. Over the course of two days, the wide-eyed frightened children were driven carefully by Ibi and her staff from the hospital to their new home. The first few days were full of surprises and challenges for the new carers in the home. Most of the children did not know how to use knives and forks; nor were they used to sitting at a table to eat. Some were terrified and wanted to run away. Many of the children ate until they were sick as they had never had more than enough food put in front of them before. All of our advisors with expertise in HIV/AIDS made clear the importance of correct diet, and so from the outset we wanted to make sure we were able to serve these children very good and appropriate food. Most began to put on weight very quickly. The carers immediately began helping some of the children to learn to walk properly. Part of the garden had become a little play park and, for most, exploring outside was a huge new thrill. After the initial trauma of the move was past and we felt the children were ready, we decided it was time for an 'opening day celebration'.

On the morning of the party – their first ever – I spent time with the children picking apples and hazelnuts from the trees behind the house. Laci, a tough ten-year-old, giggled as he played with the puppies. It was a time of wonder and awe and I will never forget it. Mandra, for the first time in her life, wore a dress. Carla laughed at her and said she looked funny, while everyone else said she looked beautiful, which she did. Vasile spent that afternoon painting a picture of birds, rivers, mountains and trees, with paints recently arrived from Scotland. 'I have a very good imagination,' he explained to me when I complimented him on it. At sixteen years of age, he was a bit older than the rest of the children and had come to us via the local authorities rather than the hospital. He told me his story. His alcoholic father had abandoned him in a railway station when he was three years old. Since then he had lived in various orphanages until becoming ill and spending a long time in hospital. One day, a doctor who had been examining him left the room, saying he would be back a few minutes later. When after an hour no one had returned, Vasile decided to look at the doctor's notes which were spread on the desk. That is when he learnt he was HIV-positive.

'I hugged myself for a long time,' he said quietly, looking at the ground.

He explained that some time after that, when he was feeling suicidal, he was invited by some kind people to a Christian summer camp. 'I loved it. After that I began praying every day that God would give me a family,' he said, smiling. 'But until now I could not imagine how God could ever answer that.'

In the evening we had a barbecue in front of the house. The children crowded round, eyes wide with delight at this strange drama of outdoor cooking and laughing as the smoke chased us in the breeze. As the setting sun began to glow orange through the fruit trees, we sat down together to chew on succulent pork steaks, bowls of salad and chips, and we made a toast with our wine and juice. We had waited a long time for this. When we had finished the meal some of us began kicking a ball about in the fading light. Upstairs in the house one of the children opened a window and music began to float across the yard. Kristl, whose faith had led us to this day, got up and, taking Laci in her arms, began to show him how to waltz. I watched in awe as they, with big smiles on their faces, danced.

By the time we had opened Iona House only twenty-four children were still alive in the hospital. As the ten children in Iona House began to settle in, our thoughts soon turned back to the fourteen still left in the hospital. We decided to build a second large house in the grounds of our existing one if we could find the money to do so. Around this time someone introduced me to Duncan Bannatyne, a well-known Scottish entrepreneur, whose public image was one of a gruff, hard, self-made man. I met with him for lunch in a restaurant near his home and, over our fish and chips, told him about our work in Romania and our desire to open a second home. He had been to Romania before and was extremely interested in what we are doing. Only an hour after having first met me he said he would give us all the money we needed to build the home and that he would like to come out with me for its opening the following year. He told me the date by when he expected it to be finished and left me with no doubt that I should ensure it was indeed complete by then. Luckily, we managed to stick to the timetable and in early 2001 Duncan and I travelled to Targu Mures. We were accompanied by Sister Martha, a young nun in white habit, who I had recently come to know. I had invited her to visit with us as she had huge expertise in the care of children with special needs and we were looking for help and advice. We made an unlikely group. Duncan, who I had already discovered had a huge and tender heart beneath his gruff, 'hard-man' exterior, was fascinated by the peace that this beautiful young lady, who had taken vows of chastity, poverty and obedience, exuded. Duncan quizzed her to try and discover why she had chosen this path and why she, who had nothing in the eyes of the world, was so obviously full of joy. We had some lively discussions about the meaning of life and in response to Duncan's questioning she promised she would pray for him every day. The highlight of this visit was the official opening of

Bannatyne House, which had allowed us to take a further ten children from the hospital. This brand-new house was to become the girls' home, while Iona House would now be for the boys. Some of this group were much more seriously ill and disabled than the first group. Another celebration with all of the kids – there were now twenty of them – took place in our garden. Duncan, whom the kids loved, told us it was one of the happiest days of his life. After our lunch we sat outside and talked while the kids played around us. I noticed at one point that Duncan had disappeared for some time behind the house and when he returned he looked as if he had been crying. He seemed to be struggling for words. He told us he had just had an experience of God.

'God wanted me to become like you lot,' he said, trying to smile. 'God gave me a choice. I decided no, and then He left me. But I can't do it – I can't give it all up.'

'But God doesn't want to take things away from you, Duncan,' Ibi said to him gently. 'He wants to give you something.'

Duncan remains a good friend of mine and has given me and our work huge support over the years. In his autobiography *Anyone Can Do It*, he describes this encounter with God and I find his frank account of this experience disarmingly honest and humble, and I pray that one day he will find a way to accept that gift.

Duncan's generosity and the opening of Bannatyne House meant that now only four very sick children were left in that ward. So we set about raising money to buy a small house adjacent to our property that we could convert into a suitable home. During the course of completing this third home I visited the hospital again. One of the girls, Juliana, was continually banging her head, which was matted with blood, against the bars of her cot, while her skinny arms were twisted into the metal springs beneath her mattress. Her face was expressionless and she seemed oblivious to everything around her. I felt a surge of anger. How could the staff see her like that and not even do something to pad the cot or protect her head from the iron bars? The doctor in the ward, who seemed unable to see any worth in these children at all, and who was mystified why we were going to such great lengths to provide homes for them, pointed at Juliana.

'You know,' he said, 'I have no idea why you are creating another home. She will certainly be dead before you even open it.'

When I came back a few months later and for the first time visited our third home, Rosie's House (named after one of the little girls who died in the hospital), I was met at the front door by Juliana, who was being supported by Ana Maria, a member of staff who had devoted hour upon hour to her care and was teaching her to walk. Juliana looked so different. Her hair was growing in and her head wounds had healed. She had already gained 5lbs in weight. She took my hand and began to show me around her home. She was particularly eager to show me her beautiful, colourful bedroom. On her bed was a cluster of cuddly toys; her toys. That room in the hospital now lay empty.

The running of these three homes was a daunting task for Ibi and her team. The children had a multitude of pressing medical and emotional needs. We had to build a network of experts around the core team of carers; doctors, physiotherapists, counsellors, psychiatrists, pastors and nuns were all involved. For the first time the children were able to benefit from anti-retroviral drugs and appropriate nutrition. As if this enormously demanding project was not enough, Kristl and Ibi felt compelled to do more for other suffering children in Targu Mures – especially those at risk of being abandoned. Working with the local authorities, they also began to support families caring at home for children who were HIV-positive. They also continued to develop their work in a notorious Roma community on the edge of the town called Hill Street. Twice a week we would trundle up a steep dirt track, lined by hovels, some constructed only of various pieces of plastic thrown over rough branches (a hopeless defence for the snows of winter), with containers of thick soup and bread. At the sight of our van, a swarm of children, each clutching a bowl or pan, came hurtling towards the queue, already forming as we parked. The race was not strictly necessary. There was always enough for the slowest of the seventy grubby, long-haired, barefoot children who lived on the street. These children lived in a chaotic and despised community, who to a large part survived by working on the 'Rampa', the huge city dump on the hill behind. Here they worked long hours to salvage goods for recycling. None of the children attended school. They were put off from doing so by the hostility towards their community from other parents, teachers and children, a lack of presentable clothing to wear and the fact that their parents often felt that their help on the rubbish dump was a more pressing priority than going to school. As we spent time with the people of Hill Street, we began to realize that nothing would really change there unless the children had an opportunity to gain an education. Eventually, we built a small kindergarten for the younger children and made a rule that only the children who attended for the day, and thus began to get used to a daily routine of learning, would receive a meal. And because of the promise of that meal their parents sent them, for the first time, to a place of formal education.

Meanwhile, over the next few years, the lives of many of the children in our homes began to change more dramatically, and certainly much more beautifully, than we could ever have expected. A combination of medicine, nutrition, hugs, love and prayers produced miraculous results. As many of the children grew marvellously into teenagers and then young adulthood, we slowly realized it was not, after all, a hospice we had opened. But during those years since we took them from the hospital seven of the children have died.

After two years in Iona House, Claudiu was the first child we lost, quite suddenly. He was a boy with learning difficulties and a happy disposition. The other children, who had been used to seeing their friends die when they lived in the hospital had, by then, almost managed to forget about death. They were devastated by Claudiu's death. Next, it was Ioana, a beautiful, smiley girl, who never stopped moving and laughing. One week before she died she told us she had decided to give her life to Jesus.

Then it was Attila, a hyperactive little boy with limited speech, who passed away very peacefully, the following spring. A week before he died, even though there was no medical reason to be particularly alarmed, Ibi had been overcome with a sense of foreboding and decided to celebrate his birthday early. When the other children had left the room, taking their balloons and laughter with them, he surprised Ibi by asking her to sing to him, which of course she did.

Sany had grown from an unusually sweet little boy to a typically awkward teenager by the time he died. Big Codruta, who was blind but never stopped talking, then brave Olimpia, who had survived an operation on a tumour below her eye and who loved to play with her dolls, and finally Small Codruta, who lived in her own little world and who would only occasionally give us a glimpse of what she was thinking, all died over the next few years.

Ibi and the other carers cherished each one almost like they were their own children and every death pierced their hearts. On each occasion they battled with their overwhelming grief and sadness while also trying to provide the other shattered children with the love and reassurance they needed. A certainty that each of those children died having experienced joy, knowing that they were precious and that they were loved, helped keep Ibi and the others going. And of course the marvels unfolding in the lives of the other children helped too.

Most of the children we took from the hospital are now young adults. Some will always require intensive care, while others are living independent or semi-independent lives. Juliana, the girl who used to bang her head on the cot, the one that the doctor said would die before we built our home, is now a young woman. She needs lots of care but she is happy and she is certainly alive. Some of the young men are now in paid employment. Some have managed to build a relationship with their families for the first time. On one more recent visit, Laci, now a strong, stocky young man, who had recently found and visited his own family, asked if he could speak to me on my own. We found a quiet room and Ibi joined us to translate. I had always been particularly fond of Laci. He had an air of quiet reliability and faithfulness. When he was still a very small boy, I remember an occasion when Ibi had given him the task of looking after some vegetables in the garden. A few weeks later the staff found him watering the plants in the pouring rain and asked him what he was doing.

'But Ibi asked me to water them every day!' he answered.

I noticed now, as he sat in front of me and began to speak, that the long twisted scar across his neck, chin and cheek had become more conspicuous, probably because of the refusal of his facial stubble to grow on the old wound. I am ashamed to say I expected him to ask me for help, perhaps even a request for money.

'I want to thank you for taking me out of the hospital,' Ibi translated his first words. 'For giving me food and clothes. For giving my family food and clothes.' He hesitated for a moment, looked at Ibi, and then went on. 'Now I want to tell you that I have decided to go home.' He cleared his throat as if to indicate the next statement would be the most important – the crux of the matter. 'You see, I love my mum,' he said, in perfect well-rehearsed English.

This work with Ibi and the children in Romania taught me many things. It changed me. It showed me that faithful, unconditional love – the sort that I witnessed being lavished on those children unfailingly for years – can transform even the most hopeless situations. These experiences also led me to a view of what real charity looks like. The extraordinary giving of people like Mrs Duncan Jones – as well as my own parents – had planted some seeds, but these things I saw and experienced in Romania created in me a deeply rooted sense that charity, without suffering or sacrifice or even failure, is actually something else. Philanthropy perhaps? Or aid work? Maybe international development? Good things, all of them, if done well, but they are not charity. It was charity itself that attracted me and beguiled me with its beauty. It became something I wanted to learn how to practise.

In the summer of 2010, nine years after we opened Iona House, I returned there for yet another party in the garden. This one would be the most special celebration yet; I even wore my kilt. That day three of the girls – Adela, Carla and Ilidi – wed their sweethearts. In their white dresses, they danced on the lawn with their new husbands. And long into the evening, we danced too. And each of them has since become the mother of a healthy child.

5

Into Africa

> Peace demands the most heroic labour and the most
> difficult sacrifices. It demands greater heroism than war.
>
> THOMAS MERTON

Father Pat Maguire used to arrive with a roar on his very large motorbike in full leather biker's gear. Among the regular visitors to Craig Lodge House of Prayer were many dear friends, but my children were always particularly excited about his appearances. Father Pat had become one of our biggest allies in the collection of donations for Bosnia-Herzegovina. His house in Dunblane had become a collection point for aid from that part of Scotland, and I would visit him frequently to load the accumulated goods from his garage into my van. After the hard work was over he would, over a cup of tea, tell me of his time as a missionary in Africa and his love of that continent. He talked a lot about the civil war in Liberia where several priests in his Order (the Society of African Missions or SMAs) were working. He explained to me that over half the population there were living in huge displaced camps around the capital Monrovia and amid them was an English priest called Father Garry Jenkins. He described the suffering and the needs of the people there, which sounded even more acute than those in Bosnia-Herzegovina, and began to ask if we might think about sending aid there too. We started looking at shipping costs and talked to Father Garry more specifically about the needs and the practicalities of moving the goods from the port to those in the camps. He was desperate for us to try it and reassured us he would oversee all of the logistics and distribution if we could just get the containers to Monrovia. And so, during 1996, we wrote up a new 'list of needs', this time for the displaced people of Liberia, and began to ask for help on their behalf. In addition to the food, clothes and medicine we had been sending to the former Yugoslavia, towels and soap were identified as urgently needed items for people living in extremely hot and humid conditions.

Not far from Father Pat's home is the world-famous hotel and golf course at Gleneagles. One of the housekeepers there, another friend of Father Pat's, heard of this urgent need for soap. She and her colleagues then began to collect the bars of soap, until then discarded after one use by the hotel guests, and tie them in plastic bags for our collection. Over the next few years I became a regular visitor to one of the world's most exclusive hotels, and for a while the back of my van began to smell very nice indeed. As well as soap, candles (also desperately needed in Liberia, but not required for more than one use in Gleneagles Hotel) became part of these consignments made ready for my collection. I always drove out of the beautiful grounds of that hotel smiling. There was something about transporting these sumptuous things, discarded by people of great wealth, to those living in abject poverty, that gave me great satisfaction. And although it was all done with the consent of the hotel's manager, I managed to feel a little like Robin Hood and the Perthshire moor I drove across for a moment would become Sherwood Forest. When, some time later, we eventually wrote down our vision, part of it read, 'that all those who have more than they need share with those who lack even the basic things'. Those kindly housekeepers in Gleneagles Hotel certainly made possible a spectacularly direct way to do that. It seemed appropriate that nearly ten years later the UK government, whose turn it was to host the G8 summit in 2005, chose Gleneagles Hotel as their venue and decided that this summit should concentrate on Climate Change and African Economic Development. Sadly, when they made those choices, they were entirely unaware of the soap and candle recycling initiatives that had been pioneered here. However, on several occasions since then, when I have attended meetings involving politicians talking about international aid and development, in order to combat feelings of dislocation and despair, I endeavour to conjure up the perfume of that soap and the mood it engendered.

Soon, alongside the lorries bound for Bosnia-Herzegovina, we were filling and dispatching shipping containers from our warehouses in Glasgow and receiving reports and warm thanks from Father Garry and the recipients of this aid. He amused us by explaining how they were removing the huge, heavy shipping containers from the trucks that transported them from the port (some of these, rather than being returned empty, were kept for use as secure stores). In the absence of a crane, they tied the container securely to a tree and the lorry would then accelerate away leaving the container to crash on to the ground. It didn't always work first time and a number of palm trees had simply snapped in two.

By early 1997, the fighting in Liberia had lulled and Father Pat and I decided it was a good time to visit. Sadly, my first experience of Africa was one of a war-ravaged, dark city. There was no electricity in Monrovia, home to more than a million people, and as we drove through the late evening from the airport, I could see groups of people huddled round flickering fires within the eerie carcasses of roofless buildings. The SMA Fathers had a little flat in the centre of town, which like virtually every other building here had been looted of every single thing it once contained. Even the light-bulb fittings and electrical sockets had been ripped out – not that they would have been much help to us anyway. We unpacked our bags in the dark with the aid of torches and lay down in the hot, sticky blackness for a few hours' sleep.

Liberia was founded in 1847 by American freed slaves to become the first independent African republic. The descendants of those Americans became the rulers of the country and during the 1970s Liberia was considered a relatively prosperous country with huge potential given its enormous natural resources. But a coup in 1980 ushered in an era of gradual decline and eventual descent into civil war by the end of that decade. Various armed factions, divided along tribal lines and motivated by a desire to control the lucrative gold, diamond, iron, rubber and timber industries, had become engaged in a brutal conflict that had already claimed the lives of over 150,000 Liberians. Over 60,000 people had taken up arms, many of them children who were forced to become slaves or 'child soldiers' by armed groups who had ransacked their villages and killed their parents. The notorious warlord, Charles Taylor, leader of the NPFL faction which had controlled much of Liberia's territory for several years, had recently emerged victorious and a fragile peace had now held for a few months. ECOMOG, a West African peacekeeping force, was helping to provide stability and elections were planned for May. As we drove out of the city at first light, we were stopped at checkpoints and asked by Guinean soldiers for our passports. Nearby, a huge rusting tank was parked in a petrol station, as if waiting for an attendant to appear and ask if he should fill her up. Every single building in the city appeared to have been raked by gunfire and many had been shelled. Among the rubble people had rigged up pitiful shelters for their families with pieces of plastic. As he drove, Father Garry gave us updates on the war, explaining its complexities and answering our questions with colourful and disturbing anecdotes. His love for the people here was clearly deep. I had the impression that because they were suffering profoundly then so was he. He spoke fiercely about justice and how there could be no lasting peace without it. He quoted Old Testament prophets on this subject. He also told us a little of his own early life story; how he had been raised Methodist and left home at sixteen to join the British army. He was enormously impressive; a warrior priest, the like of whom I had rarely met before. We crossed the main bridge over the St Paul River (which I recognized as the scene of recent fierce battles shown on news reports) and passed the port where our containers from Scotland had been arriving. Finally, we reached the enormous sprawling camps on the edge of the city, home to hundreds of thousands of people who had been forced out of their villages. These never-ending rows of hastily erected mud-wattle huts were the home of the Gola people, among whom Father Garry had lived and worked for over twenty years. It was to these people that he had been distributing the contents of the containers. And those gifts were immediately and delightfully evident as we walked between the homes and talked to Father Garry's friends, who emerged to greet us. Many were wearing Scottish football stripes, or other shirts whose slogans made their origin clear. *Glasgow's 10k Sponsored by Irn-Bru*, read a T-shirt worn by one of a group of young people who gathered round us eager to say hello to Father Garry and his guests. Some of them, such as Abraham who was sitting in a wheelchair sent from Scotland, wanted to thank us for the gift. We sat and talked for a long time with them. The conversation was an excited one. Some of them believed it might be time to risk a return to their village of Jawajeh, which they had fled in terror three years earlier when one of the factions, Ulimo J, had taken control of that part of Liberia. The men had just heard encouraging news passed back by those who had already left the camp for the villages – they believed the fighters had now left those areas. They sought Father Garry's advice. Eventually he suggested we all go back together later in the week. That way he could give them a lift and carry some supplies. I noticed that as well as the smiles and laughter that this offer elicited, looks of fear, even dread, flitted across some faces too.

Later we visited lots of families in their makeshift homes. Most of them had obviously known Father Garry for many years and the welcomes were warm and sincere. As we crowded into little rooms to talk, it was nice to smell that wonderful Gleneagles soap, now in a very different setting, and to recognize the candles which provided their only light in the hours of darkness. Many of the children were obviously severely malnourished, some with swollen bellies and depigmented hair caused by kwashiorkor. They held my hands and stroked my forearms, fascinated by this enormous, very hairy white person. Some of the babies cried when they saw me and cowered into their laughing apologetic mothers. Later we crowded into a little makeshift chapel where Father Garry and Father Pat celebrated Mass, and the people sang with all their hearts and prayed that God would deliver them from these camps and bring them safely home to their villages. They prayed, too, for all the people in Scotland who had helped them in their time of need.

Afterwards, Father Garry received news that our latest container had been released unexpectedly early from the port and was on its way to us now. Father Garry implored those around us who had heard the message not to spread this information. 'Please be quiet about this,' he pleaded, 'we don't want to distribute the contents of this container immediately as we want to be able to give it to those returning to villages in the coming weeks. We want to encourage and support people to go home to their farms, not stay here forever in these camps. For now we want to unload it into our store. So we do not want large crowds here.'

I looked at the 'store' to which he pointed. It was a previously emptied shipping container sent from Scotland, on the doors of which were roughly spray-painted 'WITH LOVE FROM SCOTLAND'. I smiled at a memory of one of our volunteers, Debbie, who had surprised us all just before the truck bearing that container pulled away from our Glasgow warehouse doors. As the truck driver had climbed into the cab to start his long journey towards the port, she had suddenly clambered on to a stack of pallets beside the lorry and produced a can of white spray paint from her jacket. While we laughed uproariously she, like the experienced graffiti artist that she obviously was, handwrote her message with a flourish. When I last looked, that container with those words as clear as ever, still sits at our HQ in Liberia today, more than eighteen years later!

But Father Garry's plea was in vain. By the time the truck rumbled up, hundreds of people in rags had gathered offering to help. Their desperation was obvious. I had always enjoyed loading and unloading trucks – especially being able to distribute ones that I had helped pack in Glasgow. In fact I had personally collected most of the goods in this load from homes and schools and churches in Scotland. I knew many of the people who had made the gifts. It was usually a thrill to be able to return home and reassure those good people that I had indeed seen their gifts being given to those in need with my own eyes. But this unloading was certainly not one I enjoyed. Father Garry and Father Pat had driven on to say Mass in the other camp and left a group of us to take charge. These people around us were hungry. And they had hungry, naked children at home. They were in urgent need and it was very difficult for them to understand why we could not give this particular container of aid to them. In the absence of a secure, walled compound we decided to make a human chain to move the aid as swiftly as possible to the store, while others tried to keep the pressing, ever-growing, mass of people back. Some began to shout angrily and by now several thousand people had congregated in the fading light. Zinnah, who had worked with Father Garry for many years, and who was calmly organizing the team, told me not to worry and explained that he had sent a message asking for ECOMOG troops to come and help us. To my great relief, a few minutes later, several Nigerian soldiers climbed out of a pickup truck and restored order. Wheelchairs, bundles of clothing, farming tools, boxes of spectacles and bags of familiar soap were carried speedily into the other container which was then firmly padlocked, as the disgruntled and frustrated throng dispersed into the evening.

While the unloading of that container had been difficult, especially for those in need who had had to watch, I absolutely understood how important it was to encourage and support the return of the people to their villages and farms where they could resume their previous self-supporting way of life. There was a risk of aid dependency developing in the camps and it was certainly easy to understand why some would be less than enthusiastic about a return. Apart from the traumatic circumstances in which many had left the villages, the option of returning to overgrown farms in areas that currently had no health care or schooling was not an easy choice to make for families.

But, certainly, the strong men clasping machetes, who squeezed into Father Garry's truck a couple of mornings later, were clearly determined to rebuild their old lives. With fourteen of us squashed into the pickup, we drove out of the city, through ECOMOG checkpoints into what had been rebel-controlled territory for many years. From time to time, as we drove through the war-scarred landscape, with remains of various buildings visible at the sides of the road, the men would start to sing. I could see how emotional these returning exiles were, Father Garry included. We eventually reached Tubmanburg, the county capital and former mining town, where Father Garry used to live. He showed us what was left of his house – not much more than a pile of rubble – and pointed out his looted church. He had chosen to stay here, behind enemy lines, for much of the war to help the most vulnerable – the blind, those with leprosy, amputees, elderly and other sick people – who had congregated around his church. He had been cut off from all his colleagues in Monrovia for fifteen months. During this time, he had experienced hunger, armed robbery, and escaped on foot from ambush and artillery attacks. In 1996, over 300 children died of hunger and related diseases here. He showed us the little mounds of earth near his church where he had buried them.

'While those children starved, the people who caused their deaths continued to dig for diamonds,' he said sadly. 'They say here now that even the trees are crying for the lack of children. Those mangos that weigh down each branch because the kids haven't been here to pick them, they are their tears.'

We squeezed back into the pickup and continued on our way, leaving the tar roads and making our way slowly through overgrown forest tracks. Sometimes we had to wait while the men used their machetes to clear fallen trees or overhanging branches that blocked our way. Eventually we stopped in a clearing, over which towered some enormous cotton trees. As the men scrambled out of the car, I realized that this was Jawajeh and began to notice tumbled-down houses among the undergrowth. The men eagerly slashed some of the overhanging branches as they began to explore. Then they stopped and waited for Father Garry and Father Pat. They spoke quietly with them and then sat down in a circle under the trees. They had asked the two priests to say Mass there in the remains of their village. I noticed, through the trees, a man and woman sitting outside a derelict mud-brick house that had been daubed in the graffiti of Ulimo J. They were watching us.

'A fighter,' said one of the men quietly and then ignored them as the priests, in their white cassocks, began to say the words of the Mass. After we had received Communion the men stood and began singing, quietly at first, 'Jesus Come, Devil Go'. As we walked through the village around their various broken homes covered in vegetation and graffiti, they sang all the louder while their priests liberally sprayed holy water with a palm leaf all around them. In a space where a house had once been lay two human skulls.

Paul, who was about the same age as me, and in fact the village chief, showed me his own roofless home. 'I think I must knock it down and start again,' he said sadly, after a brief survey.

Before we left them in the village, they had already begun a ferocious attack on the encroaching forest with their machetes. They were determined to clear a farm for planting. This, for them, was the first priority. Only when they had planted new crops, made their homes habitable and satisfied themselves that their village was once again safe would they take their wives and children back from the camps.

Later that week, we returned to Jawajeh. In our pickup was a pile of fruit, bags of rice, cassava seeds, new machetes, hoes, wire for trapping animals and a cockerel and hen who would be tasked with beginning a new chicken population here. We could not believe how much of the forest the men had already cleared with their bare hands. They were delighted with the supplies we brought and said they believed they would be harvesting cassava by August. Meanwhile they would live on whatever they could catch or find in the forest. They told me about bush yams, palm cabbage and other wild food to be found in the forest, but asked if we might be able to send them supplies of rice from time to time.

And so it was that our work in Liberia happily entered a new phase. For a time, at least, our focus moved from emergency response to supporting people as they returned to their old homes and worked to rebuild their lives. Much of my time during the remainder of that first visit was spent organizing the purchase of supplies for returnees to seventeen other villages in Bomi County. We used donations to buy thousands of machetes, large quantities of seeds and various other essential supplies. We also funded the rebuilding of village schools and the setting up of a mobile health clinic that would serve this area. This work was incredibly direct and effective. '£1.75 will buy a machete,' we wrote in our newsletter, '£10,000 will rebuild a village school.' People gave the money, and we bought the machetes and rebuilt the schools. Our donors had huge confidence in our very direct approach and they understood that all we were doing was based on a genuine partnership with our friends here. We were supplying some of the basic things they desperately needed in order to become independent again. The mobile clinic we funded grew and began visiting villages across Bomi County, providing the only primary health care available. The local nurses and midwives we employed, and the medicines we shipped, were saving lives every day. As the farms began to produce food there was great hope that the Gola people were entering a new era of peace and self-sufficiency. But the peace was short-lived.

Charles Taylor, the victor turned president, continued to terrorize the population and bleed the country of its natural wealth for his own personal gain. By 1999 a new rebel group called LURD had emerged and Liberia's 'Second Civil War' began. This war, like all wars, was barbaric, but perhaps particularly so. Probably no conflict in the last hundred years has made use of child soldiers in such an extensive way. Both Taylor and LURD were guilty of this hideous crime, and eventually perhaps as many as 20,000 children were forced to become 'ammunition porters' or child soldiers. Other human rights abuses and cruelty became prevalent. The military leadership of many warlords was based on a confused dark mysticism and their young soldiers were often introduced to cocaine, khat and other drugs as a way of control. There were numerous reports of torture, cannibalism and ritualistic killings. The abuse and rape of women was widespread. LURD soon gained control of much of the rural areas, including most of Bomi County, and once again the people of those villages, who desired only to raise their crops and their families in peace, were forced to run for their lives. History had repeated itself. Our friends found themselves back in the camps outside Monrovia, and our focus once again became sending them emergency help.

But Father Garry chose not to flee to the capital. As the LURD forces advanced towards Tubmanburg, all other expats and aid organizations left. The archbishop in Monrovia encouraged Father Garry to do the same. But by now those most in need had once again gathered around the church looking for help. And so, remembering the children who had starved here in 1996, he decided to stay. I talked to him on a regular basis. He used to phone me standing on top of a table under a certain mango tree, telling me with a laugh that it was the only place he could always get a good reception. We were able to send him funding on a regular basis via some Lebanese friends who owned a supermarket in Monrovia and had a way to get the funds, or desperately needed food supplies, to him. Meanwhile, the rebel forces were getting closer. Finally, in May 2002, we heard the news that LURD soldiers had attacked and captured Tubmanburg. None of us had any further contact from Father Garry for three weeks. We were devastated and assumed the worst. Then to our delight and surprise we heard news he was in Guinea. A couple of days later he phoned us and told us his story. The young soldiers who took the town after fierce fighting were surprised to find there among the destitute, an eccentric

English priest. They got on the radio to their commander for advice and were told not to kill him. So instead they took him captive. When Father Garry's two close co-workers, Zinnah and Matthew, understood what was happening, they asked the LURD boys to take them too. They wanted to be with him and try to protect him. A three-week trek through the forest ensued before they released them in neighbouring Guinea.

'I have learnt a lot,' Father Garry told me next time I saw him. 'For years I have been leading communities and assisting others. And then I became completely destitute with sixteen boy soldiers in authority over me. I depended on them for sustenance and survival. One day one of them saved my life when I slipped as we waded a deep river. Another time I watched them fire a rocket-propelled grenade into a pool and collect the floating dead fish for food. I experienced powerlessness, vulnerability and physical weakness in a new way. I also felt empathy with my captors. I joined the army myself when I was only sixteen, so I was a child soldier once, I suppose. I thank God for that experience, that journey.'

Finally, in late 2003, following fierce fighting in Monrovia, Charles Taylor resigned, was extradited and later tried for war crimes. The war was over and the largest UN peacekeeping mission in the world was deployed. A short time later I visited Tubmanburg once again. Huge efforts were now under way to disarm the population, including the child soldiers. On the streets some of the boys still had their AK47s and grenade launchers. They still retained their 'war names': Kill the Woman, Quick to Fire, Dissident Baby and a dishevelled eleven-year-old called Down to my Level were among the children we met and played football with. But eventually all of them handed over their weapons and referred to those 'war names' as if they had been a different person. Twice during that visit, once in a petrol station on the edge of Monrovia and once on a lonely forest track, we ran into Father Garry's former captors. They greeted him warmly and embraced him. Their mutual affection and respect was obvious. Now they only wanted to regain their childhood and their chance for education. They asked Father Garry when he would reopen St Dominic's School.

This became one of our next priorities, the repair and refurbishment of this, the only high school in the area. It had been ransacked and looted of everything. A carpet of spent bullet cases covered the playground in which there was also at least one unmarked grave. We shipped containers full of books and teaching aids to re-stock the school library and re-equip the school, while he set about recruiting new teachers. Of the 600 pupils who eventually enrolled, over half were former child soldiers.

An incredible hunger for education, and a desperate recognition that without it there would be no escape from grinding poverty, was evident among all the young people I met at the start of that new school term. It was sometimes in jarring contrast to the very different angst that had been gripping my own family at the start of our school year in Scotland – and uncomfortably different to my own childhood memories of dreading the end of each school holiday too.

I had recently watched with relief as the tears dried and Martha's limpet grip on Julie at our school gate weakened until at last she forgot to say goodbye before skipping off to see her friends. Now, in Liberia, I watched as a lady in a wheelchair approached Father Garry as he walked back from early morning Mass to eat his breakfast at home. She was pushed by a boy in his mid-teens and had strategically positioned herself on the well-worn path between the church and Father Garry's house. She explained that she was a mother of nine and had travelled two hours from her home near Monrovia to beg that Father Garry take one of her children into the high school. He tried to explain that he had no places left and that anyway the school only took children from the surrounding three counties. She wailed and shouted in protest. He apologized again and gave her the fare for a taxi ride back to Monrovia. She sat quietly crying while the boy who had pushed her to the door tried to comfort her.

We also realized that the war had already robbed many older teenagers and young adults of their chance of ever going to school. For them we built a small trade school, hoping vocational skills such as carpentry, bricklaying, sewing and computing might give them the means to find work and support themselves. We also attached to this project a working farm to teach agriculture, as many who had lived in the camps or fought in the war had also lost their traditional farming skills. Situated just beside the spot (now marked by a wooden cross) where the children who had starved during the war were buried, we call this farm 'The New World'. We bred sheep and goats with a view to repopulating the animal stock in the village – for they had been completely wiped out. Slowly the people began to readjust to peace. But without justice, peace is a hard thing to keep. One of the younger pupils confided in Father Garry that every morning, as he walked from home, he passed the man who he had seen murder his own mother.

Most of the guns had now gone, piled up rusting in UN compounds, but in some ways that was the easy bit. Truth and reconciliation in a land where tens of thousands of children were drugged and trained to kill is a difficult business. I was talking about this one day to Moses Flomo, an old friend in Tubmanburg, who was a physician assistant and senior member of the mobile clinic team, and he said to me, 'You have to understand this is not just about the guns. We Liberians need to disarm our hearts.'

The growth of our work in Liberia was only made possible by the growth of our support back home. By now, a formidable group of fifty volunteers from the Glasgow area had begun to visit a different parish every Sunday where the parishioners had been previously invited to bring their unwanted clothing and bric-a-brac to place in the back of our van on their way into church. These goods were taken back to our warehouses and categorized. Some ended up on containers and trucks headed for Liberia, while others were sent to be sold in our charity shops, which were also being set up and run by groups of amazing, dedicated volunteers. The team collecting goods at the parishes then also began to give talks to the congregations at the invitation of the priests and ministers, and then to sell raffle tickets outside the churches as the congregations left. In time they recruited an incredibly committed team – among whom were teenagers, elderly people, a lady in a wheelchair and a blind gentleman – big enough to be present in at least three parishes each weekend and raising hundreds of thousands of pounds. They created massive awareness and respect of our work. To this day they continue this initiative, sacrificing their weekends, wind, rain or shine, and they humble me and teach me much with their good cheer and self-giving love. I like to describe our work as just a series of lots and lots of little acts of love, and when I do so, I usually think of them standing laughing outside a church in the face of the horizontal Scottish rain.

6

A Famine Land

> It is love that asks, that seeks, that knocks, that finds,
> and that is faithful to what it finds.
> ST AUGUSTINE

During the first half of 2002 our newspapers and TV stations began to report extensively on a famine unfolding in Southern Africa. Millions of people across several nations faced starvation. The country worst affected, and the one which we heard most about on our news bulletins, was Malawi where at least three million lives were said to be at risk. Despite the many strong historical links between Scotland and Malawi that I would learn of later, I knew very little about this slither of a country, landlocked between Mozambique, Zambia and Tanzania, other than it had once been part of the British Empire and was today among the poorest ten nations on earth. When we began talking about Malawi and discussing if there was anything we might do to help there, the question we all began to ask was, 'I wonder what ever happened to Gay Russell?'

Gay was the lady who, nearly twenty years earlier, had written us a letter asking for more information about Medjugorje, having read Ruth's article about our experience there as teenagers. She had described herself as a pilot in Malawi who flew a small plane. This conjured up romantic images, perhaps partially inspired by a family favourite book, *Out of Africa*. Although we had received over a thousand letters at that time, Gay was the correspondent that had stuck in our minds. Mum had written her a letter, received a lovely reply and sent another. That was the last we had heard of her.

While we were having those discussions, and wondering aloud about Gay, the only person we had ever had contact with in Malawi, there was, as always, a group of interesting people staying at Craig Lodge on retreat. Among them was a businessman from the English Midlands called Tony Smith. We had never met him before. When Tony told us that he not only knew Gay Russell, but was currently working with her in Malawi, we were incredulous. Tony described how, following his own conversion experience in Medjugorje some years before, he had had an inspiration to build a replica of the huge cross there on a mountain somewhere in Africa, for those who would never be able to afford to make a pilgrimage from that continent to Medjugorje. In time he had been introduced to Gay and together they were currently building the concrete cross on top of the mountain overlooking the city of Blantyre, in which Gay lived. Tony put us in touch with Gay by email and, following an eighteen-year break, we resumed a warm correspondence with her. Among other things, we learnt that she and her husband David were also involved in supporting famine relief projects in her country. They invited us enthusiastically to come and visit them when we could.

Meanwhile, we also began to make connections with other people carrying out emergency work in Malawi. Among them was an anthropologist from St Andrews University, who had previously lived in and studied the matrilineal society of the Chewa people in certain villages in the central region. Working with her friends in those villages, she had designed a project to provide food aid in particular villages. The project had two purposes: first to save the people from starvation, and second to allow them to stay in their villages rather than moving to towns and cities in their search for food. In this way they could plant and care for their next crop and prevent their way of life breaking down (as so often happened in famine situations). We launched another appeal to our ever-growing band of generous supporters on behalf of the famished people of Malawi. Hundreds of cheques written by kind people began to arrive at Dalmally and, very soon, Ruth and I began to make plans for our first visit to Malawi. We wanted to visit Gay and the groups she was working with in the southern region, but before that we would take part in the first delivery of food to the two villages in the central region.

As we drove south from the airport in Lilongwe, towards those villages, we passed the huge government grain silos. We recognized them from recent newspaper articles reporting that the food reserve that should have been stored here, just for a catastrophe like this, had in fact been sold by the government. The silos that could store 167,000 tonnes of maize were found to be completely empty. The government claimed they had been advised by the International Monetary Fund (IMF) to sell the reserve in order to help pay off their debt – a claim denied by the IMF who said they had received no payment. Meanwhile an investigation by the Anti-Corruption Bureau had revealed that senior politicians and individuals in the private sector had profited hugely from the sale. Among those accused was the minister responsible for poverty alleviation.

As we left the city and continued our journey we began to drink in our first impressions of Malawi. It was overwhelmingly beautiful. Each side of the road teemed with people: women with firewood on their heads, men pushing bicycles piled impossibly high with stacks of charcoal and children carrying brightly coloured buckets of water. In the fields beside the road, people were tilling the fields, exposing the soil with hoes, ready for planting. Homes made of mud brick or mud and wattle, with generous thatched roofs, were clustered into little villages by the roadside. Funny-looking baobab trees delighted us, their enormous trunks that tapered towards relatively small crowns giving them the look of a tree turned upside down. Curiously formed hills began to take shape in the haze. On the southern horizon Bunda with its rounded top and Nkhoma, steeper and dramatically pointed, rose brazenly from the surrounding plain, disdaining the support of any foothills. The truck we were following was stacked high with bags of beans and maize flour, the first food consignment for 'our' villages, bought from merchants in the city. While helping to organize the procurement of these rations from merchants in the city, I began, for the first time, to consider the fact that hunger and malnutrition are very rarely caused by there being no food available. People starve because they do not have enough money to buy food. Children become malnourished because their parents cannot afford to purchase their most basic daily needs. The fact that hunger is caused by poverty is something I thought about as we left the tar road and made our way along bumpy tracks where thin people were trudging, with a cloud of dust billowing behind us.

The first thing I noticed when we entered Ngwanda, a village nestled among huge rocks, was a group of men huddled closely on the steps of a house. They surrounded a little transistor radio. I learnt from them later that they were listening to the crackling commentary of Malawi's biggest football match for years – a cup clash with neighbouring Zambia. But as soon as they saw the truck with food bouncing down the steep track towards their village they rose to greet us with huge smiles. Women hurried from their huts, some with babies strapped to their backs, and children came running from every direction. By the time we climbed out of our car, the women were singing and dancing their welcome to us. The commentator's voice from the crackling radio was drowned out by their song and shrieks of joy.

The maize and beans in the truck were an answer to the prayers of this village. Of course they had been informed it was coming. Our friends had worked with the leaders of the community to establish the population of the village and their needs, and to ensure they were ready to organize an orderly distribution. The amount we were delivering here was calculated to be enough food to meet their needs for the next two months. But despite that the people of the village seemed astounded that there, before their very eyes, was the food that would save their lives and the lives of their children. Perhaps more than once they had been made promises that had not been kept.

Nearly 85 per cent of the people of Malawi are subsistence farmers, living in villages like Ngwanda and surviving on the food they grow on their smallholdings of between one and two acres. Hunger for those that live off the land here is never far away. Their staple is a corn – a white maize – that they grind into flour, dry in the sun and then cook into a paste with boiling water. The result is a dish called Nsima, which my over-stimulated Western palate finds almost tasteless and hard to eat in any quantity. Maize is indigenous to the Americas and was introduced to Malawi by Europeans during the sixteenth century. With its high yields, it soon largely replaced millet and sorghum, which had been the mainstays of the African diet for thousands of years. Today those indigenous crops account for less than 10 per cent of the total planted area, while maize, as a subsistence crop, has become for Malawi what rice is for Asia. But maize is a thirsty, hungry plant, sucking up large quantities of water and nutrients from the earth, and a series of droughts during the 1990s combined with a lack of fertilizer for the increasingly depleted soil had triggered a spiral of worsening famines. A good harvest might yield just enough for a farmer to feed his family for the year. But now most years were not so good. December, January and February were known as the 'hungry months' when the home-grown fare ran out and food prices soared. This year the little roundel stores in the villages had been found empty many months earlier and, by now, starving people across Malawi had in desperation begun to eat roots of trees, maize cobs, sawdust, water lily bulbs and various other things they would not normally have considered as food.

After the welcome party of Ngwanda eventually stopped singing, one of the older ladies called the people to order. They sat in long rows in the dust and waited for their name to be called from the list. A member of each household, usually a mother or grandmother, took their turn to walk forward to collect their allotment of maize and beans. Each ration – based on the family's size – was weighed carefully on scales and poured into sacks. I was struck by the patience of those sitting quietly and, while this very lengthy process continued, I noticed an old lady and her grandchild kneeling in the red dust, carefully picking up the few tiny beans that had been spilt. They placed their precious find into a small pot to carry home. Eventually, as the light began to fade quickly and I remembered how short dusk was here, and that we had planned not to be driving after dark, the chief called out the last name on the list. Everyone in the village now had enough food to see them through the next two months. We promised we would be back with more supplies before they ran out, and seeds too so they could plant next year's crop – the crop that would, hopefully, set them free from reliance on our aid.

We left the people of Ngwanda much later than planned. The sun had already set as we followed the truck, now half full, further on round Nkhoma Mountain to a more remote village at the very end of the road. We felt guilty as we knew the people of Mgonzo had been waiting for us all day. When we finally arrived, the light of a full moon was casting shadows between the little cluster of homes set on the side of a steep hill. Here we were met with whispered greetings. These people were even more hungry and certainly much weaker. They explained to us that they had been eating leaves, roots and unripe bananas during the previous few weeks. In some ways the quiet, almost speechless, thanks of these people was more moving than the demonstrative lively welcome that we had received earlier that day. For several minutes after unloading we sat beside the dark pile of food in complete silence – a profound and grateful silence that I will never forget – and it was with reluctance that we eventually got up to take our leave. The peaceful villagers whispered their farewells and, after whispering our promises to return, we left them sitting again in silence beside glowing fires.

The next day Ruth and I boarded a crowded bus from Lilongwe to Blantyre. The views on the four-hour journey were exhilarating, and at one high point on the road we thought we could see Lake Malawi sparkling in the far distance and what we presumed were the faint blue hills of Mozambique beyond. When the bus finally pulled over in the city centre of Blantyre we saw a white couple standing on the pavement waving at the bus. The husband, perhaps sixty years old and a little overweight, wearing unusually thick glasses, was sporting a sweatshirt with *Russell Athletic* emblazoned on it.

'That must be David and Gay!' said Ruth, pointing and laughing, as we grabbed our bags and climbed off the hot bus. We really had not known what to expect and that first impression of a man with a self-deprecating sense of humour was not, we soon discovered, misplaced. After warm hugs and a thirty-minute drive, we found ourselves in the living room of their house, perched on a hilltop with a breathtaking view across the city to the hazy plain and hills beyond. Over dinner their stories came tumbling out. We learnt that both of them had spent almost their entire lives in Africa, having grown up in Zimbabwe (then Rhodesia) before moving to spend their married life in Malawi, where David worked with Knight Frank and as an economic adviser to government, while Gay flew as a pilot for a large sugar corporation. We were entertained by them telling one hilarious anecdote after another. Gay also explained that after receiving Mum's letter she had visited Medjugorje herself for the first time in 1986. After that she began helping to set up prayer groups and Medjugorje centres across Southern Africa, as well as organizing several large groups to travel from Malawi to Medjugorje on pilgrimage. In 2000, Tony Smith had contacted her and together they began to build a Way of the Cross on the edge of Blantyre, a replica of the Medjugorje one, for all those who could never travel to Europe.

'Oh, and by the way,' Gay said, 'I still have that letter.' She went out of the room and a few minutes later returned with Mum's handwritten note. With it was a faded photograph of Ruth and me as teenagers, with the visionaries in Medjugorje, which Mum must have sent her with the letter. We laughed and cried. So did Gay. We were moved by a very deep sense of God's plan unfolding in our lives. 'You God botherers!' exclaimed David. 'A lot of stuff and nonsense!'

For the rest of that evening, and on many others, David poked fun at Gay and us, but somehow he never managed to sound truly cynical, and certainly when it came to acts of kindness and good works it soon became very apparent that he had a lot to teach the 'God botherers' in the room. Later, Gay told us that David had actually bought her those flights to Medjugorje as a present and insisted she went. It also seemed that half the priests and nuns in Malawi used their house as a regular place of retreat, with constant comings and goings through David's open door. And he and Gay were also heavily involved in the famine relief effort, supporting various groups and providing a wealth of local knowledge and experience to people like us who were hoping to do something useful.

'I hope you don't mind, but we have a busy few days organized for you two!' Gay told us as at last we headed, dog-tired, to our beds. 'And we'll make sure we take you to the top of the mountain where we are building that silly cross,' said David.

The next few days certainly were busy. We visited various friends of Gay's who were involved in famine relief and other good works. Among these were some young volunteers from Israel who were running a small primary health-care clinic on the shores of Lake Malawi. To get to Chembe, where they worked, we drove down an uncomfortably bumpy track and laughed at the baboons that were hanging from trees beside the road. We gasped when we finally saw the famous lake, sparkling azure blue, and a little thatched-hut village strung along the edge of a sweeping, white sandy beach. It was just like a picture from a glossy tourist magazine, complete with fishermen beside dugout canoes, mending their nets. At first glance it looked idyllic, but it wasn't. Irit and Yogi, the two young Israeli girls, welcomed us at their clinic and gave us a hugely informative and depressing overview of life here in the lakeside community they had made their home. As we walked through the village, they explained that of 11,000 people living here already 800 were orphans – and that figure was growing rapidly. The AIDS epidemic was wiping out a huge swathe of people of childbearing age, leaving children to be cared for by their grandparents or other wider members of the family. This was a horror story unfolding across every village in Malawi, a country in which 16.4 per cent of those between fifteen and forty-nine years of age were infected – the second highest HIV/AIDS rate in the world. The numbers dying of the disease were already staggering, but now the chronic hunger that was stalking the land was making an already catastrophic situation even more terrible. The average life expectancy had plummeted to thirty-nine years and, while approximately 140 people were dying every day, it was predicted that Malawi was still some years away from its AIDS peak. As we had already learnt in Romania, a healthy diet with plenty of protein is the first most essential need for someone who is HIV-positive. And yet here, in this village, people were going three days at a time without food. A group of children gathered round us as we continued our tour, jostling for position beside us. Irit pointed out a graveyard at the back of the village, where sandy mounds stretched back to the hillside.

'There are four or five funerals every day now,' she told us, as an elderly man greeted her and beckoned us urgently into his courtyard. Inside his wife was lying on a mat, trying to comfort her grandchild. The thin child moaned continuously and they explained to us that his parents had died and they were now 'mother and father' to the child, rather than grandparents. Irit, having examined the boy, surprised us by asking if we could pay the fare for a car to take him to a proper health clinic. 'He needs to get medicine immediately,' she said as we handed over the pitifully small amount of money required.

Having arranged things for the couple, Irit led us on through the village. A lady carrying a very large metal bucket of water on her head stopped to chat to Irit. The bucket had a leak and the water was trickling out. As she smiled and joked with Irit, she held a small tin mug to catch the precious water trying in vain to escape from her.

Nearby we stopped at a little market where Irit bought some fish for our lunch. 'The hunger is terrible here not just because the crops have failed, but because the lake is over fished.' She pointed out the drying tables nearby. Some had a few small silver fish on them while many were bare. 'These tables used to be covered with fish. They would dry them and sell them. So not only did they have fish to eat but a source of income too.'

We took the fish to Mrs Kaswaya, a friend of Irit's who was to cook lunch for us at her home. She greeted us shyly and placed a mat on the ground for us to sit on. We sat quietly with her and ate the fish and Nsima with our hands, struggling with the heat of the food. Mrs Kaswaya and her four children giggled at us. On the way back Irit said she would like us to meet a friend of hers, Teresa, an eighteen-year-old girl who, in the face of hunger, had turned to prostitution to survive. Now she had AIDS and was dying. Irit called outside her door and eventually we heard some movement. Teresa crawled slowly out. Her stick-thin legs were no longer able to support her; Irit was as shocked as us. We sat down on the sand beside Teresa and Irit chatted to her quietly for some time. She held her hand tenderly and eventually said goodbye. She did not have anything else to give her.

We eventually left Chembe and bumped back up the rough road, past the baboons, in silence, realizing that what we had witnessed that day was a microcosm of Malawi. The battle against hunger, AIDS and degrading poverty was one being played out in every village across this land. It seemed to me that these malnourished, weakened people, deprived of the weapons of education and good health, were engaged in a horribly one-sided fight.

The itinerary put together by the Russells over the remainder of our stay gave plenty of other opportunities to learn about Malawi and to meet some of the warriors who were refusing to give up. Among such characters was a tiny, but formidably strong, nun from the Philippines, who was running day centres for children below school age in Blantyre. Most of these children were orphans and in desperate need of food and care. Her approach was to support and train local volunteers to run this project and to ensure they saw it as 'their project and responsibility' rather than that of some foreign organization.

'These are your children, not mine. This is your responsibility more than it is mine,' Sister Lilia said quite fiercely to the group of local volunteers at one of her training days, to which she had invited us. At first I was a little taken aback by her apparent lack of compassion towards these volunteers, who were, after all, giving up their time to do a very noble task in difficult circumstances. However, I soon began to understand that her philosophy was not born out of a lack of love but rather from real, genuine charity that wanted to help set these people free from reliance on aid.

Each of the twenty-one nurseries in her project was run by a management committee with members of the local community taking up the roles of office bearers. Their newfound responsibilities and the training provided often helped them find a new confidence. A recent innovation had also seen them begin to accept children from parents who could pay a fee for 'child care' and in this way some of the funding required to provide meals to the impoverished children was met, rather than the project relying entirely on the support of donations and grants.

I was hugely impressed by the way this project worked. I was growing increasingly uneasy about aid flown in and sometimes imposed on local communities in a way that seemed to strip people of their dignity and sense of responsibility, and that gave little thought to a future beyond such immediate intervention. Of course there was a place for emergency responses, which were at that very moment saving millions of lives in Malawi and among which our own project was playing a small part. But I had come to believe that the war against poverty and hunger here could only truly be won by the people of Malawi themselves, not by aid givers from outside, no matter how important and faithful our support for them might be.

And those U6 centres were a joy to visit! In each one we were greeted by around sixty or seventy toddlers, sitting in rows, being introduced by their volunteer teachers to numbers and letters. Whenever we arrived we would be greeted by a child who would stand and extend to us a well-rehearsed formal greeting.

'Introduction. My name is Paul. I am four years old. I am a boy.' And the next one would stand to repeat the formula. 'Introduction. My name is Veronica. I am five years old. I am a girl.' And after a number of 'introductions' they would sing and clap and melt our hearts.

Some of these little children were by now living in 'child-headed families'. Orphaned, and without adult support, they were being cared for by older siblings who were sometimes primary-school age themselves. The food being provided at these centres was saving the lives of these children and the introduction to education was a gift that might just open up an escape from poverty. The centres were also a place of safety and care for these children while the elder sibling attended school or worked to survive.

On the last morning of this first visit, before heading to the airport, we rose early to climb through the woods to the top of Michuru Mountain, where they had started work on the foundations for their huge concrete cross. The view from there was breathtaking. The whole of the city of Blantyre was spread beneath us, with the vast plains and hills beyond. We prayed a Rosary with Gay as we drank in the vista. When we had finished we took from our pockets some pebbles carried from our own hill in Scotland – the one behind Craig Lodge on which Dad had built 'Stations of the Cross' – and some from the hill in Medjugorje where the apparitions of Our Lady first took place. These we placed into the open foundations, already full of Malawian stones, and we prayed for blessing upon this project and upon Malawi. And I promised the Russells I would be back very soon.

On our return home we began fund-raising furiously. A number of those we had met in Malawi, who were carrying out such great work, were desperately in need of funding to feed more mouths and we had promised them we would do whatever we could. With Gay co-ordinating things at the Malawi end we were able immediately to begin sending funds to our new friends. We wrote about our experiences in Malawi in our own newsletters and managed to generate some media coverage.

Whenever I returned from a trip overseas I would give a little talk and show pictures to the volunteers and members of the youth community living at Craig Lodge, who had given up a year there to pray and serve those coming to stay on retreat. It was very often through the people who came to stay on retreat at Craig Lodge that our work grew, so it was important to keep the community up to date and passionate about our efforts, ensuring they could speak to those guests who were interested and wanted to learn more. Three days after this particular talk Maureen Callaghan, one of the community members, approached me to say that when I had spoken to them about Malawi, she felt a fire burning within her heart and she could not stop thinking about what she had heard and her desire to go and help. She had not slept the two nights since. She had never been anywhere in the developing world and had not previously had any particular desire to do so. Two other girls in the community – Lisa and Nicola – also felt moved in the same way. So they decided to make a 'mission trip' there, funded by Craig Lodge Trust (the charity set up to administer the House of Prayer). Gay was delighted to hear this news and immediately set about finding them a small house to rent at the foot of their 'cross mountain' in Blantyre. Here they lived for five weeks among the poorest of the poor, supporting Sister Lilia, and began to work with the local parish priest to identify children most in need of help.

Three months after my first visit, in November 2002, I returned to Malawi, this time to visit those we were by now funding and other groups that Gay knew needed help. I was accompanied this time by two journalists from the *Herald*, Scotland's largest-selling quality newspaper, who had agreed to write a magazine article about the situation in Malawi and our efforts to help. By now, as predicted, the effects of the famine had worsened. Even without a famine, November often marked the start of the hungry months, but this year people had already long exhausted any reserves they might have had.

I had realized by now that most effective emergency food-distribution projects were very often being delivered by the churches, which had the advantage of a permanent structure which could be mobilized to create networks of community volunteers. On this visit I spent time with several groups of nuns and priests who were carrying out incredible work on a large scale. None seemed particularly shocked by this famine, and all had tried-and-tested systems they had been relying on and developing over many years. In Namitembo, a very remote and particularly famine-ravished area, lived two missionary priests, Father Owen O'Donnell from Glasgow and Father Frank from Liverpool. I stayed with them for a couple of nights. While each of them spoke with the strong distinctive accent of their home cities, I noticed that on their own in the evenings they spoke Chichewa, the local language, and I had the impression that by now they were more at home here than they ever would be back on the banks of the Clyde or Mersey. Their parish was enormous. Within its boundaries lived 80,000 people. A huge network of volunteers of home-based carers had been trained and developed to care for the sick people of the parish (most with AIDS here would die at home) and orphans. On the first evening of my stay Father Owen showed me their newly built secondary school, the only one in the whole area, complete with science laboratories. The creation of this place of education had obviously been a labour of love. At close inspection I noticed that the small sunken sinks in the laboratories were actually made out of cake tins. Beside the school were huge warehouses, piled high with enough food to meet the emergency needs of 880 families for another month, but Father Owen was already worried about how he would buy enough for the month of February. He needed to have it transported here soon before the rains might make the roads impassable.

The planting season here had already begun. Some recent rains encouraged many to plant maize, but without a single shower since, the people were terrified that this crop would be lost. They had no more seeds to replant. Life here was terrifyingly precarious.

I rose early to attend Mass in their simple church as the first beams of sunlight drifted through the windows. The small congregation, dressed in ragged clothes with calloused hands, looked as if they were on their way to the fields. At the end of the Mass, as most made their way out in silence, I noticed a lady walking up the aisle with a bundle on her head. This she rested on the bottom altar step and Father Owen came to it, prayed over it and blessed it. The lady then placed the bundle back on her head and serenely walked out towards the sun rising over the fields. I realized that within that cloth were the precious seeds that she was going to plant that day. I pondered for a while during the 'after Mass silence' on the act of faith I had just witnessed. Those seeds represented her own and her family's future. Within them lay all her hopes and all her fears. Everything. Even life and death. She had been able to lay down all of that and in one simple heartfelt gesture had given it all to God and asked for His blessing. How much more difficult would it be for me to make the equivalent offering? With our Western layers of security and complexity this would not be an easy thing to do. How might it feel to be so utterly dependent on when the next rain will fall and on the God who created it? Or at least to be so acutely aware of it?

Later that day I drove with Father Owen to visit one of his many dying parishioners. Fostino, a thirty-five-year-old man who had been a tailor, lived with his sister, who was caring for him in a house that sat alone among the dry fields. Fostino had no shirt on and was shockingly thin. Each of his ribs was protruding and his arms were horribly wasted. He groaned and his sister helped him to sit upright. It appeared he was only hours from death. They told us that apart from some mangos, growing on a nearby tree, they had not eaten for nearly a week. He had AIDS and was convinced that he was given the disease as a punishment because he had once stolen a man's bicycle. He was desperate for that man's forgiveness as he believed only in that way would he be cured. Father Owen counselled him and prayed with him, before giving him Communion. Fostino and his sister, whose name I never learnt, seemed more peaceful as we left them. As we walked down the path away from the house, the sister caught up with us and with a shy smile handed us a bundle of mangos from their precious tree – a gift for our journey home.

There were many encounters during those days that moved me deeply and left me questioning things and looking at them in different ways. Everywhere was life and death and very little of the stuff that most often obscures them. I had a strange sense of preparing for something and that this was some kind of intense training course. Before leaving home on this trip, Julie, who was expecting our fourth child, had reminded me it was now nearly ten years since our first trips to Bosnia-Herzegovina. I surprised her by saying that for some reason I felt as if these ten years, while amazing, were a preparation for something else. But I didn't expect that my next meeting with a suffering family would change my life in the way it did, and lead to the birth of Mary's Meals.

A couple of hours' drive from Namitembo, along dirt-track roads through dry fields, is the parish of Balaka. On arrival here the Italian priests led me to a church which we entered through a side door. I was taken completely by surprise to find myself on the altar, staring down on 550 young children sitting silently in rows. Every one of them was an orphan. Ten years previously the priests here had decided to find sponsors in Italy to support the ten orphans they knew of in their parish. They didn't intend to do any more than that as they saw no further need. Now there were 8,000 orphans in their parish with the number growing every day. And incredibly, here, and all over Malawi, nearly all of those children orphaned by AIDS were cared for by members of their extended families. Street children and orphanages were not yet known in Malawi. I wondered how different our response in the West might be if we were faced with a disaster that resulted in hundreds of thousands of orphans.

Father Gamba, a young friendly priest, then asked me if I would like to accompany him to the home of one of his parishioners, who was near death. Thus it was I came to meet that family whose picture remains on the wall above my desk: Emma surrounded by her six children, including fourteen-year-old Edward, who, when I asked him about his hopes in life, gave me an answer I will never forget. 'I would like to have enough food to eat and I would like to be able to go to school one day' had been his stark, shocking reply to my question.

The extent of the ambitions of that fourteen-year-old boy, spoken as if they were a daring dream, shook me for a few reasons. The greatest of these was a conversation I had been having with Tony Smith, the man from England who had reintroduced us to Gay. He continued to support the work to build the cross, which was now evolving into a more ambitious project which would eventually see the building of an exact replica of the church in Medjugorje and the placing of identical Stations of the Cross up Michiru Mountain. His stays at Gay's house overlapped with my own and he had been talking to me about something that happened to him about two years previously.

He had been staying at Gay's house and feeling depressed at the suffering he saw in Malawi, especially that endured by hungry children. One evening, back at Gay's, he turned on the TV and found himself watching a speech made by the American Senator George McGovern in which he stated, with some passion, that if America decided to fund the provision of one daily meal in a place of education for every child in the world's poorest countries it would act like a 'Marshall Plan' that would lift the developing world out of poverty. Tony said when he heard this speech he was inspired with the thought that if someone took that concept, gave it to Mary, the mother of Jesus, and called it Mary's Meals, then it would actually happen. He had talked to Gay about this at the time and discussed the idea of beginning such a programme in Malawi. However, the famine situation then began to unfold in Malawi and the funds he sent to Gay under the name of 'Mary's Meals' were instead used for desperately needed emergency food distribution in an area called Chipini, through some nuns we had now met and were also supporting.

So much of our experience over the last twenty years came together within this one simple concept. Our devotion to Mary, the mother of Jesus, and our surprising encounter with her in Bosnia-Herzegovina as teenagers, the numerous meetings with impoverished children in the years since who were unable to go to school because of poverty and hunger, the words I had just heard Edward speak, and a growing recognition that the problems faced by the world's poorest communities would only ever be overcome by people who were healthy and who had, at least, a basic education. The promise of a meal could enable those children who worked for their daily bread now to attend class instead, and would encourage parents to send their children to school rather than keeping them at home to help. We had already seen this happen in a very small way in our project begun a couple of years earlier in Targu Mures for the Roma children.

Edward was certainly not alone in missing class. Around 30 per cent of the children in Malawi of primary-school age were not enrolled in school, despite the fact there were free school places for all. The need to find food, grow food, do paid casual work, care for dying parents and younger siblings was keeping children out of the classroom. Even if they did enrol, all too often they were unable to concentrate and learn because of their hunger, or their attendance rates were dismal because of their own illnesses. Hungry, malnourished children cannot be good students and many, like Edward, had never even had the chance to try.

Over a third of children who die in the world each year do so because of hunger-related causes. Hunger and malnutrition remain, in the twenty-first century, the biggest global health threat, causing more deaths than AIDS, malaria and tuberculosis put together.

Hunger is caused by poverty and poverty is caused by hunger. People suffer chronic hunger not because there is no food, but because they cannot afford to buy it. The world produces considerably more than enough food for everyone. Even in that dire famine situation, Edward, if he'd had money, could have travelled into town and bought his family food. But he had no money and so they starved.

Chronically hungry children cannot develop physically and mentally, nor can they learn at school, and for both these reasons they are deprived of the ability to work productively and support their families as adults. They cannot live the independent dignified life that every person craves. In the developing world, 43 per cent of children are stunted. They will, for the rest of their lives, be smaller in stature than they should have been (and those lives might be very short given that it is estimated that around 18,000 children die of hunger-related causes every day), while 775 million illiterate adults face an almost impossible struggle to earn enough to survive.

The first thing to do for the hungry child is to give them food. Every parent, every person, knows that. But it is clear that the gift of even a basic education is essential too, if chronic hunger is to be truly vanquished. How can people learn how to irrigate their fields, make fertilizer or diversify their crops if they cannot read or write? How can they pursue other ways to make a living and create wealth beyond growing what they eat? How can illiterate people hold their governments to account? How can they defend themselves against corruption? Or combat the spread of HIV/AIDS? How can other pressing health needs be addressed without first ensuring the growing child has enough to eat?

Thus, the mission of Mary's Meals, to provide one good meal every day in a place of education, for hungry impoverished children, was launched by Edward's words.

Of course the idea of serving meals in school is hardly original. Most schoolchildren take it for granted they will eat each day. I certainly did. Each morning in our little primary school in the Scottish Highlands, a sense of anticipation built as a van carrying steel containers of food, cooked at the bigger school at the other end of the loch, arrived at our gates. At least I think that is where it came from – it was always a bit of a mystery to me. We would carry them inside, guessing what might be in them. To find that the bigger containers held steaming meatballs and mashed potatoes made it a good day, although that was a short-lived feeling if the smaller lids were then opened to reveal rhubarb crumble. But I cannot ever remember going through a school day without eating, or even contemplating such a thing. School meals are accepted as essential across the developed world, whether they are funded by governments or by parents handing over 'dinner money'. In fact, globally, around 368 million children are fed daily at school, but while nearly every child benefits in this way in the world's richest countries, only around 20 per cent of children in the developing world are provided school meals, with the UN's World Food Programme feeding nearly 15 million of them. Meanwhile 57 million impoverished children remain out of school, while 66 million more attend the classroom hungry and unable to learn properly.

The more we talked and thought about Mary's Meals, the more the beauty of this idea captured Ruth and me. The board and all those involved in Scottish International Relief back home were immediately supportive of the proposal to start this new campaign. We decided to set up a branch of Scottish International Relief in Malawi to begin this work there (as well as the various other projects we were by now committed to in that country). Gay Russell did a huge amount of work to get the organization set up in the right way, roping in a friend in Blantyre who was a lawyer, and before long she joined Tony Smith and me as the first Trustees of the new Malawi organization. Meanwhile we began fund-raising for our new Mary's Meals campaign.

We all agreed that the vision of Mary's Meals should be for every child to receive a daily meal in their place of education. Clearly there was a lot of work ahead of us. We just had to decide where to begin.

7

One Cup of Porridge

> Yesterday is gone. Tomorrow has not yet come.
> We have only today. Let us begin.
> MOTHER TERESA

At the foot of Michuru Mountain (on which the cross was being built) lay an impoverished township called Chilomoni, clustered along a road that curled out of Blantyre flanked by fruit sellers, barbers, mechanics and a myriad of other small businesses that plied their trade out of little stalls. Rows of tiny houses marched up the hillside behind them, homes to a growing population. In the middle of this settlement sat a large parish church and school.

Two hours north, on a plain beside the Shire River, in the rain shadow of a ridge of hills, lay the remote area of Chipini, reached only by long, rough, dusty tracks. A scatter of tiny villages of mud brick and thatch were surrounded by little fields of maize that often did not grow well. Amid these villages was a clinic run by some nuns, the Medical Missionaries of Mary, with whom we had worked to provide emergency food supplies during the famine.

These two spots presented themselves as good places to begin Mary's Meals. Gay knew people in Chilomoni through the work she was doing to organize the construction of the cross and because the girls from Craig Lodge had spent some weeks there, living in a rented small house which she had arranged for them. Their time there had given us further insight into the plight of orphans in that community and they had drawn up lists of those in greatest need. Gay began talking to the people there to understand their situation and to introduce them to the concept. They expressed a huge desire for Mary's Meals, and together with the community leaders she began planning for these to be introduced to the small primary school beside the parish church. Before long they had built a simple little kitchen and store in readiness for the project to begin.

From the outset we were convinced that Mary's Meals could only be effective and long-lasting, if the local community 'owned it'. We felt strongly that each school community needed to believe in this project and have a desire to support it at least as much as us. We wanted to avoid, at all costs, the mistake of imposing an idea on people; rather, we wanted it to be theirs more than ours. This would require a genuine respectful partnership in which the local community would give what they could to enable the provision of daily meals to their children, while we would support by providing the food and other required assistance that they were unable to afford. Specifically, this concept would depend on local volunteers making a commitment to organize and carry out the daily work of cooking and serving the food. We were determined to ensure this was not seen as another emergency feeding project, but a very specific, community-owned intervention aimed at schoolchildren and linked always to education. At Chilomoni, it became clear that the Parent Teachers' Association (PTA) was the appropriate local body through which to organize. Following some community meetings at which a huge desire and enthusiasm for the Mary's Meals project was amply demonstrated, the PTA agreed to take responsibility for organizing a rota of parents and grandparents who would take their turn in giving up a morning to prepare the meals.

Another thing we felt very strongly about was that, whenever possible, the food we provided should be locally grown rather than imported. We wanted to support the economy of the country and the local farmers at every opportunity. In Malawi there was an extremely popular porridge for children called Likuni Phala ('Likuni' being the name of the place where the dish had been carefully formulated for growing children by some pioneering nuns several years earlier, while 'Phala' simply means porridge). It consists of maize, soya and sugar, and is fortified with vitamins and minerals. It has become the dish of choice for Malawian children and their families. Gay knew a company who manufactured Likuni Phala, by buying the raw ingredients from smallholder farmers all over Malawi and processing them into a ready-mix that simply required cooking in boiling water before serving. The choice of this, as the food we could buy and serve, was a very straightforward one. The ingredients – aside from some of the added vitamins, which came from South Africa – were all grown within Malawi and the product was readily available, easy to transport and simple to cook. It was also wonderfully inexpensive!

During January 2003, the first Mary's Meals were cooked and served at Chilomoni. That same week exactly the same thing was happening for the first time in those remote and hungry villages in Chipini. There, the impressive Medical Missionaries of Mary sisters had organized the school feeding programme, based on exactly the same model of local volunteers cooking Likuni Phala, for seven small primary schools. The rates of child malnutrition were particularly high there, and many children did not attend school because of hunger and poverty. And so it was that Mary's Meals began in an urban and rural setting simultaneously.

My first visit to Chipini after the start of Mary's Meals was, sadly, during another famine, for in 2003 food shortages here were more acute than ever. At Chinyazi primary school, skinny children queued quietly for their Mary's Meals. Far too quietly. Many of the children walked past me, the white man with the camera, as if I wasn't there: none of the usual laughing and jostling to get in the picture. It was already noon and they were more interested in eating for the first time that day. Little groups of children sat down in the dust and silently ate their porridge. For most of them this would be their only meal of the day. Near the school, outside a mud hut, I saw a 'gogo' (grandmother) sitting with her youngest grandchildren and I paid her a visit. She explained that her daughter, the children's mother, had died and that she was the children's sole carer. She told me in despairing tones that there was now no maize she could afford to buy in this whole area. Later on, her two older grandchildren, Allieta and Kondwande, arrived back from school carrying their grubby jotters and empty mugs (in which they had been served their Mary's Meals). They had more energy now. They laughed when they saw me at their home and proudly showed Granny their schoolwork. They explained that the daily porridge was enabling them to attend school for the first time.

Within a few months of serving Mary's Meals a few things became obvious. First of all it was plain to see that this was not just a nice idea. It was something that would actually work. The schools began to report that, after the introduction of the daily meals, children whose attendance rates had previously been very poor, because of illness and hunger, were now attending every day. They also began to see significant increases in enrolment. Children who had never been to school were coming for the first time, sent by parents who were assured their children would now eat every day and were therefore happy to give up the help they might have been providing in the fields and at home.

It also became apparent that there was an enormous and pressing demand for Mary's Meals. As soon as other villages and communities learnt of Mary's Meals they requested we consider them as part of the programme. However we also learnt very quickly that the magnetism of these meals was so powerful it could also cause a problem. While, from the outset, we had wanted the daily meals to draw children into school, we had not realized that they would be so attractive as to prompt children to leave neighbouring schools and enrol in those where the daily meals were being served, even if this meant a daily walk of several miles. This migration of pupils was not what we had intended and the requests of those villages from where children were now walking became all the more difficult to refuse.

Our efforts to fund-raise and increase awareness became even more determined and certainly more focused. It seemed we were developing a replicable model that could save and change lives and transform the future of the world's poorest communities. We wanted to tell the whole world! Given our low-cost fund-raising model based on the activities of volunteers, and communication mainly by 'word of mouth', we knew that this would not happen overnight, but we did start to see that presenting Mary's Meals to people was igniting unprecedented support. I enjoyed greatly the opportunity to explain to people the concept and how it worked. Faces would light up at the understanding that something as simple as a daily meal in school could meet the immediate need of the hungry child and at the same time tackle the underlying cause of poverty. People warmed to this simple solution. And their enthusiasm grew greater still when they learnt that to feed a child for a whole school year cost only £5! A few, understandably, needed some convincing that this could possibly be a true cost and we were happy to explain this. It was indeed a real number made possible mainly because nearly all the work was done by unpaid volunteers, and because the food we bought in bulk was locally grown and remarkably cheap. By now I no longer felt daunted at speaking in public – at least not if I was talking about Mary's Meals. In fact no audience ever seemed too large or too small, I just felt grateful for every chance to tell people the good news. I noticed that the story of Mary's Meals tended to put smiles on faces and not only prompted immediate donations, but often left others feeling equally evangelical about this mission. Before long their friends became supporters too, and so it went on. Our database began to grow faster than ever and so did our income.

While we were not able to say yes immediately to all those many requests for Mary's Meals, we were delighted we could now plan for expansions. To combat migration of children from other schools, we decided to cover entire districts by working outwards from existing schools to the neighbouring ones. If we had realized the need for this approach we might not have begun serving meals in two different areas from the outset, although in many ways it was a good thing to have begun in schools both on the edge of Malawi's largest city and in remote villages. It gave us an opportunity to start learning about those very different urban and rural environments. As we began to move into new schools we gradually refined the procedures and model. The first part of the process, at each new school, was to meet with the community and school leaders and to ensure their desire and commitment to take responsibility for the daily work. Then we would commit to building a kitchen and storeroom on land near the school that we then donated to the community for their own use. So at times when they were not cooking in the kitchen, that part of the building became a little community centre or, sometimes, in the afternoons of the rainy season, an additional classroom. As time went by we spotted an opportunity for further community contributions towards the building of these. In most villages, people made their own clay bricks and so we stopped buying these from suppliers and asked the community to donate them. We also began to ask the men of the village if they would labour beside the qualified builders to keep costs down and speed up completion. Given that most of the volunteer cooks were mothers and grandmothers, this was also a good way to encourage more men to become involved.

During this first set-up stage, we were reliant on advice from a remarkable Malawian called Peter Nkata. He was a local businessman who knew the Russells; David through the Rotary Club and Gay through the church. When I was introduced to him, Peter, in his spare time, was working very closely with Sister Lilia, the Filipina nun we had learnt so much from, who ran the U6 centres for orphans in Blantyre. David introduced me to Peter just as Mary's Meals began, as he knew Peter was desperately looking for funding to keep these centres running. Over dinner at Gay's house, Peter explained that the number of children below school age in desperate need was growing rapidly. The numbers of orphans were increasing and many were now living in 'child-headed' families without adult support. For these children the day centres were the difference between life and death, a place where they were guaranteed a daily meal. We knew this was the most crucial time of development for the growing child and that stunting caused by malnutrition at this stage could not be reversed later. I remembered very well visiting these centres the previous year with Sister Lilia and being incredibly moved by the sweet way the little children introduced themselves. It didn't take very long for Peter to convince us to take on the funding of the nineteen centres. So from almost the beginning of Mary's Meals we were providing daily meals in nurseries as well as schools. After all, the basic principle was the same – a daily meal in a place of education – only the children were younger.

Peter with his local knowledge and entrepreneurial approach began to help us enormously with his advice and very quickly we asked him to become our first Country Director. We were delighted when he accepted and immediately began to build the organization that we now required by recruiting a team of staff, securing office space, establishing processes and procedures and agreements with various suppliers. The monitors became crucial members of the growing team. They were responsible for visiting the schools on a regular basis, at least twice a week. They would check the food stock, ensuring it was hygienically and securely stored and that the correct quantity was being held between the monthly deliveries. In a country where so many were hungry and corruption was endemic, protection of food stocks was a high priority for us. We soon learnt that in addition to our monitoring, the self-policing nature of this locally owned model was just as important. Most of the volunteers were mothers who would not take it lightly if someone attempted to misappropriate food that belonged to their own children. While visiting the schools the monitors also collected data on enrolment, attendance and academic performance, to begin building up a body of evidence around the impact of daily school meals.

Their other job was to check with the head teachers and PTA that sufficient volunteers were giving their support to ensure the meals were cooked in a timely manner. But we were determined not to get closely involved in management of these volunteers. On the two or three occasions when it was found that insufficient volunteers were turning up we suspended the programme. In each case, within two weeks the community leaders, who had agreed at the outset that this was their responsibility not ours, turned up at our office to explain they had solved the problem – normally a local feud – and promised the programme could resume normally, which it invariably did. And these problems were extremely rare. The spirit of these volunteers, often hungry themselves and facing a daily struggle to survive, humbled me. They would rise before dawn to light the fires on which to cook the porridge and while they stirred those enormous pots they would often sing. Teresa was one of them. I spoke to her one day as she was stirring a huge pot of porridge.

'The situation is critical in this area. The food these children receive changes their lives,' she said to me earnestly.

'It must be a big sacrifice, though, for you to do this every day. How can you do it?' I asked her.

'Well, every morning before I come here, I make doughnuts, and send them to be sold at market. That is how I support myself and my daughter – and my sister's kids too. So it is OK for me to come here. I enjoy it!' she said, beaming, as if it were the simplest and easiest thing in the world, to give up every day to do this unpaid work while struggling to support her own extended family.

A few years later, we carried out a survey among the tens of thousands of volunteers who by then were volunteering to cook and serve Mary's Meals in Malawi, in order to understand better what motivated them.

'Why do you volunteer your time?' was the direct question we posed.

'Because we have it in our hearts!' one lady responded, and with that perfect answer she rendered the rest of that survey obsolete and became a spokesperson for all of us involved in this mission.

By 2005, visits to schools that were benefiting from Mary's Meals became exciting occasions. At Goleka primary school Mr Sapuwa, the headmaster, met us with a huge smile and ushered us into his little office. His school had been receiving Mary's Meals for a year now and he was eager to tell us about the results. He pointed to the charts on his wall.

'Our school roll has increased from 1,790 pupils to 1,926,' he said, 'and the government has now provided three extra teachers! Attendance rates are now at very high levels, far better than before. In all the schools nearby where children don't get Mary's Meals the absentee levels are still terrible.'

But it was the next statistic that seemed to give him most joy.

'Based on exam results this year forty-three of our pupils have been offered government-funded places in secondary schools,' he beamed. 'Prior to the introduction of Mary's Meals not one of my pupils had been offered one of these places.'

While primary schooling in Malawi is free and theoretically universal, only a tiny amount of secondary-school places are available. Apart from the small number of fee-paying pupils at private schools, the others who have this opportunity are those who are provided free places based on outstanding results at their final primary-school exam. It was hard to believe such a dramatic change in academic performance could have been brought about at Goleka primary school by Mary's Meals alone, in just one year, and we suspected there may have been some other factors at play. However, it was very clear, both here and in other schools, that children who had begun attending every day rather than just coming now and again, and who were able to concentrate rather than struggling through a whole day of class without having eaten, were going to do significantly better academically. In fact our early collections of exam results from the primary schools which benefited, before and after Mary's Meals, showed an average increase in pass rates of 9 per cent.

Outside Mr Sapuwa's office, there was an eruption of happy sound and we emerged to see hundreds of laughing children queuing for their morning meal. Each was holding a colourful mug. By now, we had decided to issue one of these to each pupil to ensure fair helpings for all. A row of volunteer cooks served the children from enormous pots. One of them, Esther, told me she had four children of her own at the school and so was happy to give up a morning every couple of weeks to take her turn to cook.

'Now they are only ever hungry at weekends,' she said as she ladled out a serving into the next child's mug. 'Please don't ever stop these Mary's Meals!'

Two older boys in the queue proudly produced a little notice they had written for my benefit. They held it up with serious faces. It read *Thank you for giving us polidge*. They smiled broadly when I took their photograph. Then the local chief arrived to add his thanks. He told us Mary's Meals was helping the whole of his community.

By now this scene was being repeated in many schools across Blantyre with the same results. In some cases the increased enrolment was proving too much for already stretched school resources. At Namame primary school, within a few months of Mary's Meals beginning, the school roll doubled from 2,000 to 4,000, a number far too great for the school to cope with. Again, it seemed a large number of the children had migrated from schools not yet receiving Mary's Meals, and plans were already under way to provide Mary's Meals in those so that the school roll at Namame could be reduced to a sustainable level. We also saw in time that at some schools where Mary's Meals prompted a huge increase in enrolment that the government prioritized these for the building of new classrooms and additional teachers.

Mary's Meals rapidly became well known in Malawi. There was a huge sense of momentum and infectious excitement. Every week we received more requests to bring Mary's Meals to new schools. We were ready to expand rapidly if new funding could be found. Ruth and I talked incessantly about finding new ways to spread the word to all those who would want to support this work if they only knew about it.

But already more and more people were learning about and supporting our work, and doors were opening in extraordinary ways. Often these new connections and opportunities originated at Craig Lodge House of Prayer or through Medjugorje. Millions of people from all over the world had by now visited that little village in the mountains of Bosnia-Herzegovina and had life-changing experiences there. They comprised an enormous global network of people who, if they learnt of it, very often felt deeply moved to support this work that they perceived as a fruit of Medjugorje and another way they could express charity in their lives.

For some years, a regular visitor to the Craig Lodge House of Prayer was Milona von Habsburg. She was an Archduchess of the famous Habsburg royal family who had sat on the thrones of Europe for centuries, most notably those of the Austrian Hungarian Empire. But Milona most certainly did not live 'like royalty'. She was another whose life had been profoundly changed at Medjugorje. She had visited there in the early 1980s and had become friends with the visionaries. Her fluency in seven European languages was a wonderful gift to the visionaries and priests just as they were becoming overwhelmed with pilgrims from every corner of the globe. Milona started working as secretary to a priest there called Father Slavko (who became well known as a speaker and author of books about the phenomena in Medjugorje), as well as a translator and close friend of the visionaries. She stayed with them in Medjugorje during the darkest days of the Bosnian war and also began travelling to many parts of the world with them as they were invited to speak and lead retreats. To our delight, on several occasions invitations for them to visit the Craig Lodge House of Prayer were accepted, and a crowd would gather in a marquee erected for the occasion in the garden.

Milona became a much-loved and recognized person in Medjugorje. She was someone who not only spoke about the messages given by Our Lady, but a person who had actually put them into daily practice in her life. She became a dear friend of our family and, after Father Slavko died in 2000, we continued inviting her to the House of Prayer to lead retreats on her own rather than translating the words of the parish priest, because we felt she had a wonderful way of talking about Our Lady's presence in Medjugorje and explaining the messages.

On one occasion Ruth and I had just returned from Malawi and I was asked to give a little talk at the retreat that Milona and a friend were leading. I spoke about Malawi and the birth of Mary's Meals, and showed a PowerPoint presentation I had put together. It comprised photographs of our work with quotes from people like Mother Teresa, Gandhi and Martin Luther King, and a haunting soundtrack provided by one of my favourite Scottish fiddle players. Afterwards, Milona asked me for a chat. She told me that when she was listening and watching the presentation she felt a call, as strong as the one she had first received at Medjugorje, to give her life to help the work of Mary's Meals. She asked me what she could do to help. I was overwhelmed yet again by God's abundant providence. If God had asked me to pick anyone in the world to help us spread the good news about Mary's Meals it would have been Milona. Very soon she was working for Mary's Meals as an ambassador, giving talks and introducing us to lots of wonderful people with huge hearts. Many of these were people she knew through Medjugorje; others were her relatives who became marvellous supporters of our work. Notable among these were the Prince and Princess of Liechtenstein. They invited me to meet them with Milona at their castle in Liechtenstein. I felt like a character in a James Bond spy film the first time I drove the steep, winding road through the Alps towards their ancient castle, perched on a rock overlooking the city of Vaduz, and passed over a drawbridge into their little courtyard surrounded by enormous, thick stone walls. The Prince and Princess greeted me with enormous warmth, setting my nerves at ease, and I thoroughly enjoyed my time with them, telling them about our work and answering their sincere, thoughtful questions. They became wonderful faithful supporters of our projects, spreading the word and hosting some spectacular events. The following year the Princess invited me back to speak to the Red Cross in Liechtenstein, as she was their patron and they had been fund-raising for our work. I mentioned that the date on which she wanted me to visit was our wedding anniversary and she immediately asked me to take Julie too! And so, along with Milona and her husband Charlie, who happened to be married on the very same day as us, we enjoyed a very special anniversary in a fairy-tale castle in the Alps.

On countless occasions Milona and I travelled together to give talks and do interviews with media. I never tired of hearing her speak about Mary's Meals and her own journey. 'In a way it is the logical consequence of a long search for the truth, the beauty of man and his value,' she once replied when asked about why she did this work.

'When Magnus showed one of the very first PowerPoint presentations about his work to a group of us on 26 September 2004, I met children. I did not meet an organization with high-achieving, successful, titled employees and directors. I saw children's faces and quotes of love, respect and service to these little ones. During that presentation, the children came out of their anonymity, and turned into the brothers and sisters I needed to commit to with all my life. It just became simple and obvious! I cannot describe that moment in other words than a calling.'

To this day we strive to ensure that our paid staff have a feeling of vocation, a sense of 'calling', when they work for Mary's Meals, regardless of their various personal faiths and beliefs. It is one of the reasons why our salaries will never compare well even with other similar-sized charities, let alone corporate organizations. People do not come to work for Mary's Meals as way to get rich or as a simple career choice. Of course, sometimes people go on from Mary's Meals to have good careers elsewhere, hopefully having learnt something in their time with us, and those of us who work for Mary's Meals need to be able to survive and afford to feed our own families too. But always to work for Mary's Meals as a paid employee will involve a sense of vocation and a sense of privilege that we are being paid to do this work when so many of our co-workers take part in this mission without any financial reward.

But most of our supporters didn't live in castles. In Vienna, an old friend of Milona's, Dr Christian Stelzer, had founded an organization called Oase des Friedens to spread the word about Medjugorje. When Christian learnt of Mary's Meals he started to write articles in his monthly magazine about our work. The response was astounding. Thousands of people in Austria began to make generous donations and hundreds of thousands of euros were given for Mary's Meals. Christian then invited me to give a talk at an annual prayer evening that they held in the enormous St Stephen's Cathedral in Vienna. I arrived early and was amazed to find the church already packed full with thousands of people and more arriving each minute. Maria, one of the visionaries, was also there and it was lovely to catch up with her after a long time. She had her apparition on the altar steps and then Cardinal Schönborn celebrated the Mass. It was a very special evening. Afterwards many wanted to speak to us about Mary's Meals, having heard the little talk I gave, which Milona translated. Among the many new supporters of Mary's Meals in Vienna was Cardinal Schönborn himself, who became a wonderful advocate of the work of Mary's Meals, which in later years he described as a fruit of Medjugorje. On different occasions he preached about our work and wrote articles on it.

The support in Austria has continued to grow in the years since. The way our work there developed was something hard to explain, certainly in terms of established fund-raising methods. For the first several years in Austria, there were no paid staff or full-time volunteers (although Christian, when he was not working long hours as a GP, spent hour upon hour, often through the night, writing about our work and organizing events) and yet the support base multiplied and proliferated way beyond the original Medjugorje network. As our work has grown around the world I am sometimes asked to give talks about fund-raising. I normally decline as I would never consider myself an expert in fund-raising; nor do I pretend to understand all that has happened with Mary's Meals. And perhaps those things that I believe have been most important in our growth – prayer and trust in God's providence as starting points – would not necessarily be received as helpful pearls of wisdom at fund-raising conferences. There were, however, things we learnt along the way, certain approaches and ways of doing things, which became dear to us. Our experience convinced us that it was important to concentrate mainly on supporting the growth of a grass-roots movement. Thousands of people making regular donations appeared a safer way to support a long-term intervention like Mary's Meals than becoming over-reliant on grants that would perhaps last only three years. And we felt that part of our core mission was to involve as many people as possible in this work, and to let people know that all could play a part no matter their circumstances, background, creed or race. Some, like my brother Mark whose health had deteriorated to a point where he could no longer help us in other ways, made prayer for Mary's Meals a personal commitment. He would come to me often and ask if there was anything particular that he should pray for. I was normally able to supply him with a long list! And at Craig Lodge House of Prayer at that time lived Brother Paul, a saintly ninety-five-year-old Marist brother. Every morning he prayed for Mary's Meals (and each day he was on his knees in our chapel before 6 a.m.) and the rest of the day he was the most incredible joyous advocate of our work, telling all who passed through the doors of the retreat centre about the marvels of Mary's Meals.

One day Brother Paul mentioned to me that his grand-nephew happened to be Sir Terry Leahy, the well-known CEO of Tesco, and although he hardly knew him he had started writing to him about Mary's Meals. He showed me one of the letters.

'Magnus is a very tall man, but not at all scary ... perhaps you would like to meet him?' he had written. I laughed a lot at his choice of words but a couple of weeks later we were surprised and thrilled to receive a letter from Sir Terry, asking me to lunch at their HQ in London. After a series of meetings with him, other staff and board members, Tesco began to support Mary's Meals very generously through their Foundation. And so the doors continued to open in all sorts of unexpected and amusing ways.

Another key philosophy that developed from this idea of Mary's Meals being a 'movement' was that there should never be a sharp divide between givers and receivers. We wanted to develop a deep understanding that we were all walking together with the same goal. Those who lived among the poorest of the poor and gave up their time to cook the daily meals were unified with those rattling collecting cans, or making donations, in their desire to see the hungry child receive that daily meal. We wanted to ensure that those involved in the programme delivery part of the work never saw fund-raising as just some necessary evil, but rather another crucial part of the whole process – with equal beauty and ability to change lives.

For similar reasons, we felt we should look for funding in Malawi too, even if that seemed unlikely to be fruitful. Through Gay and David we met members of the small business community, and before long large sugar companies, banks and estate agents were supporting our work. In addition to generous funding others gave us 'gifts in kind'. A sugar company shared their HR expertise and gave us a hugely reduced price on the sugar we required for our Likuni Phala, while a fuel company provided us free diesel for transporting the food. We organized high-profile events for these company executives in the cities of Blantyre, Lilongwe and Mzuzu, and a huge sense of pride and responsibility for

Mary's Meals was engendered. At one point in the early years of Mary's Meals 10 per cent of our required budget in Malawi was being raised from within that country.

We also became great friends with some prominent members of the Asian business community – both Hindus and Muslims – who supported us generously through their charitable organization called Gift of the Givers. Often they funded the provision of water wells in schools where we wished to begin cooking meals but where there was no clean water supply, and over the years we enjoyed some wonderful dinners together marked by fascinating discussions about our various faiths. Years later we teamed up with Gift of the Givers to fly and ship food from Malawi to Somalia during the terrible famine there in 2011. I made a short visit there that year to see bags of Malawian Likuni Phala, labelled 'Mary's Meals', being distributed to thousands of starving people in Mogadishu. It was the scariest place I ever visited. On my first evening, while unpacking in our makeshift accommodation, a loud close explosion made me jump. One of our gently spoken Somalian hosts, a young man with good English, turned to me and, as if soothing a small child, said, 'Don't worry. Don't worry. It was just a bomb.' For a few days I was surrounded by co-workers who at first light were on their prayer mats facing Mecca, while I sat on my bed saying my morning Rosary, and despite the stressful situation we were all in, there was something about that interfaith mission to bring food to those suffering hunger that I will always treasure.

Meanwhile, back in Malawi, we continued to meet children whose lives had been resuscitated by Mary's Meals. One day, Ruth and I visited a Mzedi school just outside Blantyre with Peter Nkata. The school was tucked into a rocky hillside, among little patches of cultivated soil, ready for planting and patiently awaiting the rains.

'Small Peter! He is alive!' exclaimed Peter Nkata, recognizing a boy in the crowd of children who surrounded us as we parked in the school playground.

'I was sure that child was dead,' he said as we climbed out of the vehicle. He pulled the little child, perhaps four years old, to himself and hugged him. Then he held him at arm's length and delighted in his appearance. An older boy stood beside him, with eyes that looked too large for his solemn face and legs too thin to support his frame.

'Your brother looks well, Lazaro,' Peter said to him.

The boy nodded his head and smiled. Peter then told us their story.

Some months back the teachers at Mzedi had noticed that Lazaro, who had previously been a very punctual boy, had begun to turn up late every morning without explanation. They investigated and discovered the mother of the family had died, leaving Lazaro and Small Peter at home on their own. Some distant relatives sometimes visited but gave little support. Lazaro, who looked about eight but was actually twelve years of age, became the head of the household and tried to look after his little brother. But they didn't have enough food at home and Lazaro depended almost entirely on his daily meal at school. Small Peter, inevitably, fell sick. As he grew weaker and weaker, Lazaro decided, literally, to take matters into his own hands. He knew that Mary's Meals were providing food not only in his own primary school, but also in an Under 6 centre half a mile away from their home. He started to carry Peter there every morning and only after he had deposited him there safely, knowing that he would be fed and cared for, did he continue to school himself – arriving late and tired. When Peter Nkata had visited some weeks ago he'd heard that the carers at the U6 centre had taken Small Peter to the hospital and were not hopeful he would survive. The weeks without food had taken their toll. But here, right in front of us, was a bright-eyed, smiling Small Peter, with the hand of the brother who saved him on his thin shoulder.

8

A Bumpy Road to Peace

> Poverty in the world is a scandal. In a world where there is so much wealth it is unfathomable that there are so many hungry children, that there are so many children without an education, so many poor persons. Poverty today is a cry.
>
> POPE FRANCIS

'What did you eat this morning before school?' we asked the next pupil on the bamboo bench.

'Nothing,' she replied, in the same way as all the others had before her.

'And yesterday – what did you eat?'

'Just rice.'

The answers were predictable. It seemed that each child, dressed in rags, ate 'just rice' or 'just cassava'.

But then a small boy surprised us.

'What did you eat this morning?'

'Nothing.'

'And yesterday?'

'Nothing.'

We repeated the question, thinking he had misunderstood. Again he replied, more softly, 'nothing'. He turned his head away, embarrassed, as tears began to form in his eyes. He didn't want the other children to notice.

'It's true. I saw him near my house yesterday rooting around for wild yams,' his teacher said to us quietly. We moved on quickly to question the next child, but the questions seemed pointless. We didn't need to complete this survey to know that the children of Biffany, a village in Liberia, would benefit greatly from Mary's Meals. Before we left the class I glanced back at the little boy who hadn't eaten the day before and saw tears were still trickling silently down his face. I felt so ashamed.

Soon after establishing Mary's Meals in Malawi we had developed a burning desire to put this project into practice in other countries as soon as possible. We could see it was transforming the lives of young people in Malawi and we were already stating boldly that our vision was 'that every child receives one daily meal in their place of education'. If we were serious about this global vision, and we were, we needed to prove to ourselves – and others – that the same approach would work in other countries, cultures and situations where children missed school because of poverty.

It seemed obvious that Liberia should be next on our list. We had been working there for many years and had a close relationship with the long-suffering people of Bomi County. In addition, it would have been hard to identify a country in greater need of Mary's Meals. The series of civil wars had at last ended in 2003 and the largest UN peacekeeping force in the world had just been deployed. There was a real opportunity to build a lasting peace but the people were suffering abject poverty and the children were hungry. Liberia had one of the lowest rates of primary-school enrolment in the world. If their young people could not access education and equip themselves to play a part in building a more prosperous Liberia, then other temptations would remain. Disenchanted, uneducated, impoverished young men (especially) would remain easy prey for future warlords looking for fighters who could be tempted by promises of power, status and loot. Meanwhile, in Bomi County, the children of the Gola were malnourished and dressed in rags. Once again families were taking the first steps towards rebuilding their lives. They had resumed their battle with the ever-encroaching rainforest and were clearing land to plant cassava and rice. Here and there little mud-and-wattle homes were being rebuilt. It would be months before their crops were ready for harvest – a harvest that could only be meagre because they had few seeds and few tools. In 2003, the *Economist*, which annually predicts the worst country in the world to live in the following year, had chosen Liberia for that dubious accolade. It was not difficult to understand why.

Among those rebuilding in Bomi County was Father Garry. As he drove me from Monrovia out to Bomi County and shared his latest news with me, I was struck by a depressing scene. At one time a rail track, built by mining companies to transport their iron ore to the port, ran alongside this road as far as Tubmanburg. Four years previously I had watched men rip up the rail lines and load them on to trucks as the country was looted and stripped bare of anything that could be sold. This time, along the same stretch, hundreds of men, women and children were now digging up the small stones that had formed the rail track's foundations. They were washing the stones clean before heaping them in little piles for sale beside the road. It seemed even the quality of loot had reached a new low.

Before long we had left the tar road behind and on the muddy tracks between the villages we saw more pitiful sights: mothers searching for fruit and berries, fathers hunting wild game and children wading in swamps with home-made nets trying desperately to catch fish. Many of the children were naked with swollen tummies. The Gola were no strangers to such suffering. They had the misfortune of living in an area close to the diamond, gold and iron-ore mines, and the armed struggle for these natural resources had repeatedly torn apart their villages and ruined their farms. For some, this was the third time they had returned to looted, overgrown, broken-down villages to pick up the pieces.

We began to visit some of the villages to carry out surveys and talk to the communities about the idea of Mary's Meals. The people knew us well because we had been working with them for many years and their welcomes were as warm as ever. The mobile clinic that we funded was still providing the only health care in the whole county and was hugely important for the returning people. When we talked to the community leaders we were clear that Mary's Meals could only start if the local people were willing to volunteer to do the daily cooking and serving of food. This would be perhaps an even bigger sacrifice for the embattled parents of these villages than for those giving up their time to do this in Malawi, but our proposal was met with an overwhelmingly positive and excited response. Once again the people told us they were ready and willing. Our survey meanwhile confirmed what we already knew – that many of the children here were malnourished and that hunger and poverty was often keeping them from school. It also revealed other sufferings.

In a village called Jennah Brown, we visited another school to assess the need for Mary's Meals. Here local volunteers were teaching the children in what must have once been a relatively grand house, overlooking the village huts below. Until 1998, it had been used by an American company that was extracting gold from the nearby river. Inside, in the absence of benches, the children sat on black rubber pipes that had been used in the mining process and left behind. In another room, a group of older children sat on a vast metal safe where the miners had once stored their loot. Curiosity got the better of us and the children helped us prise open the huge lid. There was nothing inside but a few shreds of paper and some old leaves. The loot had, of course, long since been carried overseas. The hungry children clambered back on to their unusual seat, oblivious to the irony and the injustice.

But when we talked with them we learnt that most of these children knew all about carrying a different kind of loot. When the armed fighters took this village the children were forced at gunpoint to carry away every single item of value – often from their own homes. All household belongings, tools and food supplies were taken in this way. Some of the children were then made to carry guns and ammunition and often progressed to become child soldiers. They had no real choice, their village having been emptied and sometimes their parents killed. The children in front of us were those who didn't become fighters – either because they escaped or were allowed to go. They spent the rest of the war with their families in displaced camps around Monrovia, or became refugees in Sierra Leone, before recently returning home. All had been traumatized in different ways. In one class Father Garry asked if anyone had seen someone being killed during the war. Every child raised their hand.

One of the villages that the mobile clinic visited on a regular basis was Massatin. Of all the villages that he knew and loved, it seemed Father Garry had a particularly deep affection for this one. It was a leper colony and those suffering the disease had been neglected for many years, prior to Father Garry's arrival and his determined efforts to help them. Our health clinic had been visiting every week, dispensing medication for leprosy as well as for numerous other ailments. We had also been providing food for the sick given the acute hunger in the village. We decided this should be the very first place in Liberia to receive Mary's Meals. They had recently built a few mud-wattle classrooms and in them 162 children were being taught by teachers – who again were volunteers in the absence of any government provision.

During April 2004 we brought the rice, vegetables and some 'boney' (small dried fish) – enough for the first two weeks' meals – to Massatin, and these were stored carefully in a little room at the back of the school. We were frustrated that there was no possibility of buying locally grown rice in a country completely reliant on imported food, but decided that, for now at least, the most important thing was for the children to be fed and in school. Again the local community had built a simple shelter to serve as a kitchen and two elderly women cooked the eagerly anticipated food in two large pots on an open fire. Eventually the children were invited to line up for the meals, which were served into colourful plastic plates. Within minutes 162 children were sitting silently in clusters under trees or in the shadow of the school walls, devouring their delicious meals. Their parents gathered beside the kitchen to clap and sing their joy.

Afterwards, I watched the children with big smiles file back into their classes. Through an open door I could read a question on the blackboard.

'What do you have to offer the Lord?' the teacher had asked his class that morning.

And below he had neatly written the children's answers.

'I have my hands.'

'I have my life.'

'I have my soul.'

'I have my heart.'

'I have my song.'

'I have my dream.'

Before long Mary's Meals was being served in a number of other schools in the town of Tubmanburg and the villages round about. And again the numbers of children enrolling increased quickly and dramatically.

Yousif Sheriff, the headmaster of an Islamic school just off Tubmanburg's little main street, showed us round his crowded classrooms. He explained with glee that since we began providing Mary's Meals here his school roll had increased from 302 to 425. That story was repeated in the community school just along the street, as well as in the villages where teachers told us happily that hunger and the search for food no longer prevented children attending school.

By the time we had satisfied ourselves that in Liberia Mary's Meals would produce the same positive results we had seen in Malawi, we had begun to receive many requests from hungry schools. We pondered which areas should be our priority.

In 2005, a close friend of mine, Alex Keay, who had grown up with me in Dalmally, and who was also a fish farmer, volunteered a year of his life to work in Liberia to support our fast-growing programme there. Not long after his arrival, Father Garry began to suggest we help the people of the Bellah district. They were a very small tribe, the smallest of the sixteen ethnic groups in Liberia, living in remote, virgin rainforest. Father Garry had a deep affection for them because when he had been kidnapped by child soldiers during the war and taken by them on a three-week trek to Guinea, their route had taken him through the villages of the Bellah, and the tribe's kindness to him during his short stay was something that moved him profoundly. He had promised that if he survived he would come back and help them one day. Father Garry used his considerable powers of persuasion on Alex, whose adventurous nature was only encouraged by the description of the arduous journey there. So Alex and some of our more experienced Liberian team members made the fourteen-hour drive to the Bellah on what could only loosely be described as a road. By the time I arrived on my next visit, the groundwork had been done with those communities, volunteers organized, and the first food deliveries made. Mary's Meals was now being served to three village schools in the Bellah district and I decided to travel there to see it for myself.

During the last six hours of our journey there we never passed one other vehicle. Our four-wheel-drive pickup slipped and strained along a dirt track, roughly gouged out many years previously by a logging company. They had constructed bridges by laying huge logs across streams and rivers, and as our driver inched slowly along these trunks we prayed his wheels wouldn't slip and that the logs wouldn't snap. On each side of us the rainforest towered towards the sky. Huge frogs leapt out of puddles as we approached and squirrels scuttled for cover. Now and again a 'chicken hawk' flapped off the road ahead of us and disappeared away up above the trees. Once we came upon a group of people who had been paid to clear this lonely overgrown road. These former fighters and their families, armed with machetes, had hacked down the trees on the edge of the road for many miles. Beside their makeshift camp, over an open fire, they were smoking recently shot deer and monkey. Alex – who seemed to have learnt ways of doing things here remarkably quickly – haggled to buy some meat.

'Why you white people not bring bread from Monrovia?' a laughing young man said to us as he handed over some prime cuts of monkey.

A little further on, at the top of a steep climb, we passed a burnt-out pickup. Inside was the skeleton of a government soldier who had been ambushed by rebels several years previously. The forest road seemed endless and I began to understand why no other aid organizations were working in these areas.

As the sun began to dip behind the tallest trees, we finally reached Belleh Balama: a cluster of thatched huts in a wide clearing. A crowd of laughing, waving children dressed in tattered clothes swarmed round us, screaming their welcome. A group of village elders met us and showed us into the mud-and-wattle hut we were to sleep in. The family of the house embarrassed us by moving out to make sure their visitors had a bed. The elders gave each of us a new name. For the duration of my stay here I became Mr Tanjo – 'the owner of the land'. After welcome speeches, in accordance with local custom, they gave us cola nuts to chew, a white chicken and a silver coin (an old Liberian dollar). Before long we were playing football with a group of local men, while the women played kickball in a field nearby. Later a thin, tall young woman called Helen, who had been assigned to look after us during our stay, warmed water on an open fire for our 'baths' (taken in a tiny wicker-panel cubicle behind the house), and cooked us rice and the monkey meat we had purchased earlier. Some of the locals gathered with us and together we drank 'God to Man' (a palm wine tapped straight from palm trees that requires no brewing). That night, sleep came easily in the beautiful, dark and silent village.

The next day the three schools that were receiving Mary's Meals were closed so that all the children could take part in a day of celebration and welcome for us. We were treated to beautiful songs written specially for us. 'You are welcome, Mr Tanjo! You are welcome! We hope that you bring good news!' sang the young choir.

A Bumpy Road to Peace

I talked to them about Mary's Meals. When they asked, I explained that Mary was the mother of Jesus and that when Jesus was very little they'd had to flee from men who wanted to kill them, and that they too had known poverty, hardship and hunger. Later, after several plays and the exchange of many speeches, it was time for Mary's Meals to be served to all 500 children present. As we made our way to a recently constructed thatched 'dining room', we were struck by an incredibly violent storm, which no one seemed to have guessed was coming. A roaring wind began to rip up the thatched roofing, the sky turned dark and thunder crashed around us. As we ran for shelter from the deluge we got an even bigger surprise as we bumped into a group of UN peacekeeping soldiers and two smartly dressed white civilians, who had appeared as if from nowhere and who were seeking the same shelter. After getting over the surprise of such an unlikely meeting, we began chatting. They had just landed by helicopter and were part of a security assessment team for West Africa. They had come to make an inspection as there had been a large arms cache here during the war. As we talked, the rain eased, and the serving of Mary's Meals began. The men from the UN looked more surprised than ever. One of them, Captain Alec from Kyrgistan, congratulated us sincerely on what we were doing.

'What you are doing will work,' he said. 'We are trying to prevent a return to violence by taking away guns. But if people want to fight they will hide the guns. How could we find them in this forest? But you, if you can feed the children and get them into school, that will build real lasting peace here.'

The next day we made a two-hour walk through the forest to the next small village, called Kanata, which could not be reached by road. At one point our journey involved wading through some swamps and Helen, still conscientiously looking after her visitors, led the way with a briefcase balanced on her head. This contained jotters, pens and pencils – gifts we had taken for school pupils in Kanata. As we walked she told us a little of her own tragic war story, describing how she was forced at gunpoint to carry loot all the way to Guinea, and left me with the impression that this was only a small part of what she had suffered. The children of Kanata stared especially intently at us as our unusual little group strode into their village. Alex explained to me that when he had visited here for the first time a couple of weeks previously, he had been told they had not seen a white man in their village since 1988. The children held our hands and stroked our strangely hairy arms.

As always, according to custom, we were greeted formally by the village elders and given the ceremonial gifts. We were then taken to their 'palava hut', the place for village meetings, and were served platefuls of rice and bush meat. I felt a little disconcerted by the crowd who pressed silently round to watch us eat. As I was about to tuck into my meal, Alex nudged me and said very quietly, 'Magnus, what kind of animal do you think these belonged to?'

I looked at his plate to see a pair of testicles – those of a deer or a monkey, I think – presented proudly, all alone, on a bed of rice. While the elders continued to stare intently at us we began, despite our most strenuous efforts, to laugh uncontrollably until the tears were streaming down our faces. We managed, eventually, to eat the testicles. Thankfully, no offence was taken. If the truth be told, I have never done anything particularly heroic in service of Mary's Meals, but that meal came closest.

Afterwards we began to discuss with the elders a plan to begin Mary's Meals in their village also. It was agreed that once a month the men of the village would walk to Balama (the furthest point a vehicle could reach) and carry back the food delivered there for them. They were eager to begin as soon as possible. Their children were hungry, they told us.

The following morning, back in Balama, I opened my bedroom shutter to see two small children carrying little wooden home-made chairs towards their school. They were followed by older girls carrying buckets on their heads – the water for Mary's Meals. After their classes had begun we visited the little bullet-scarred school.

I spent some time chatting to Nyango, who was standing with a giggly group of friends. She was thirteen years old but until very recently, like many other girls in the village, she had never attended school. Every morning while her brothers walked along the path to the mud-brick classrooms under the huge cotton trees on the edge of the village, she had stayed at home, working with her parents as they strove to feed, clothe and shelter their family. Her days had been spent carrying water from the river, collecting firewood, pounding palm nuts for oil and working on the land to grow rice and vegetables. In recent years, along with other villagers who chose not to flee, she had been forced at gunpoint to carry ammunition and arms for rebel soldiers as they waged war on Liberia's previous regime.

But three weeks previously, the day the first Mary's Meals were served here, her life changed. That day many parents, including Nyango's, decided it was now possible to send their children to school. While we talked, some of Nyango's younger classmates played in the dust nearby. Nearly all had distended stomachs and discoloured hair, the result of the daily hunger they had lived with.

After they had all eaten their meal, they resumed class. Nyango's teacher pointed to some arithmetic on the board and began asking questions. Next door I noticed Helen, the young woman who had cared for us during our visit, sitting at a desk among the smallest schoolchildren. We had just seen three of her children eat Mary's Meals in the school playground. And she, too, was a pupil here. The war might have robbed her of the chance to read and write, but now she was sitting in a primary one class with no shame, just a happy determination to learn. She beamed a broad smile at us through the open door when we looked in, and continued writing in her jotter.

Before we started our long journey back to Tubmanburg, the elders wished us heartfelt farewells.

'Remember your name is Mr Tanjo!' they shouted to me as we climbed into the pickup.

We continued to work hard to reach more schools. Our programme grew rapidly, and numbers of staff with it. We decided it was time to move out of the accommodation generously provided by Father Garry on his mission. The community leaders in Tubmanburg gifted us a generous piece of land only ten minutes' walk away on which to build a home for Mary's Meals. By now Liesbeth Glas, a lay missionary from the Netherlands, and someone who had lived for many years with Liberians – mainly in refugee camps in Ghana – had become our first Country Director here. She had a deep understanding and love for the local people – and for Mary's Meals. It was she who organized the building of our first office and staff house on the donated land. But even before it was complete she approached us with another request – one very close to her heart.

Everywhere in Bomi County, through the work of the clinic, or the setting up of Mary's Meals in schools, we met children who were deaf. The complete absence of even basic primary health care meant that many here suffered lifelong impairments caused by ailments that should have easily been treated. And the deaf children's suffering was acute. Unable to communicate with their family and community, they were often shunned and neglected. With no possibility of learning a means of communication, they were condemned to a life of isolation and rejection. Liesbeth had worked with deaf children in the camps of Ghana, from where she had recently returned along with some trained Liberian teachers who knew sign language and how to teach it.

'Why don't we start a proper school for these children? We have the teachers and we could build on the land we have been given beside the staff accommodation?' Liesbeth asked me.

Just as we were starting to be clear that we should concentrate all our efforts on school feeding, and amid my repetitive urging to all that we must now stay very focused, I had been hit with another proposal that was impossible to ignore. This particular suffering simply seemed too great, and our ability to help too real, to pass it by.

So in the centre of the little Mary's Meals compound, with our offices, warehouses and staff accommodation, is the Oscar Romero School for the Deaf. The Mary's Meals staff in Tubmanburg surprised me when they gave it this name in honour of the archbishop in El Salvador who was assassinated in 1980 while celebrating Mass, because he would not stop speaking out against injustice and oppression of the poor – Julie had recently stuck a copy of Romero's Prayer on our fridge at home and I had been deeply moved by the words. We had originally planned that this would be a residential school for forty but in the end it became home to sixty children, most of whom sleep there but return to their families in the villages as often as possible. But not all have families to return to.

Three days after we opened the new school some policemen from Monrovia arrived at the compound. They had with them a boy, about nine years old, dressed in a very scruffy T-shirt and shorts. They explained they had found him wandering alone on the city streets. Unable to hear or speak to them, they did not know what do with him and put him in prison for the night. Then they heard about our new school for the deaf – as the first of its kind in Liberia it was getting coverage in newspapers and on the radio – and so they had decided to take him to see us. We could only say yes when they asked if we could take him in. The young men learning carpentry at the deaf school were already working hard to make more bunk beds for us. We could find a place for him in the growing family. Of course the little boy could not tell us his name, or his story, but immediately began to take part enthusiastically in the sign-language lessons with the other kids. We called him Joseph and looked forward to the day he could tell us his real name and where he had come from – and where he wanted to go.

Another new initiative born in Liberia, which ran parallel to and complemented Mary's Meals, was our Backpack Project. In Malawi and Liberia we had begun to notice that many of the children coming to school because of the meals had nothing with which to learn – no pencils, jotters or any other basics. When we talked about this someone suggested that we adapt our 'Shoebox Appeals', through which children in Scotland had for many years been filling shoeboxes with gifts for impoverished children in Eastern Europe, in order to address this need. We began to ask schools to invite their pupils to fill school bags with basic educational items so we could ship these to Africa. The response from schools was overwhelming. The teachers loved the project because it allowed them to introduce a strong educational element about the places and people to which these gifts would be sent, and also because the filling of a backpack allowed a child to learn that they, personally, could do something to help a child in poverty. In Liberia, and then Malawi, the distribution of backpacks became the most joyous of events and another incentive for children to come to school.

'You know, there are more possessions in one of these backpacks than an entire household would normally own here,' Joseph, our Liberian Head of Operations observed as we bounced towards a village school with another truck of backpacks, part of a container-load recently arrived from Glasgow into the port in Monrovia. I marvelled once again at the excitement and unbridled joy of the kids who unpacked the backpacks in their classrooms, showing each other, with looks of disbelief, the exercise books, crayons, tennis balls and T-shirts that had just been given to them from someone they did not know in a faraway land. And later, when I visited some of their homes in the village, I did a little mental assessment and concluded that Joseph's startling statement was certainly no exaggeration. In the years to come many people – including primary-school kids (and others), all over the UK, Ireland, Germany, Austria, Croatia and Italy – took part in this project, selecting items from our list and placing them with love in their backpacks. When I last checked we had sent over 400,000 of these bags to children in Liberia and Malawi.

But our priority and focus remained the provision of school meals, and by this stage we were faced with a question. Should we continue expanding in the rural areas or try to help schools in the city also? The population of Monrovia had doubled since before the war to around 1.3 million. Many of those who had fled the bloody conflict in the countryside to the safety of the displaced camps around the city had never returned to their villages. Like millions of others in the developing world, they were chasing the urban dream. With a view to making an informed decision, we visited the bustling streets of Westport, one of the older slum areas, where hordes of children were working on little market stalls selling fish and second-hand goods. Others carried loads balanced on their young heads or pushed carts between stalls.

ABOVE: Emma and her children, including Edward, sitting at the back on Emma's right, November 2002. *Chris Furlong*

RIGHT: Magnus, Fergus, Ruth, Ken and cousins at an apparition with the visionaries in Medjugorje, 1983.

BELOW: The shed in Dalmally, where it all began.

BELOW RIGHT: Children from Dalmally Primary School help paint the shed, 2011.

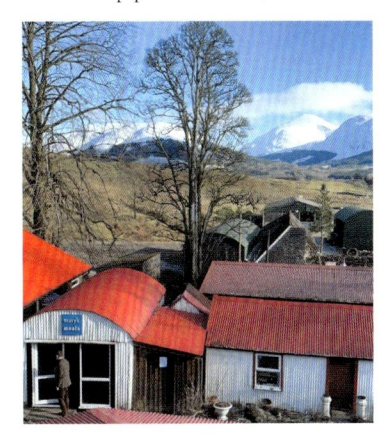

LEFT: Julie and Magnus consult their map en route to Bosnia-Herzegovina, 1993.

ABOVE: Attila, one of the first of the children in our homes in Romania to die.

ABOVE: Magnus visiting a school in Blantyre, Malawi, 2012. *Heathcliff O'Malley*

RIGHT: Another container of aid from Scotland received by Father Garry Jenkins in Liberia, 2004. *Colin Mearns*

LEFT: A child in Cité Soleil, Haiti, 2006. *Angela Catlin*

RIGHT: In a village school, Liberia 2004. *Colin Mearns*

BELOW: Servings for preschool age children in Blantyre.

BELOW: Children eating Mary's Meals in Cité Soleil, Haiti, 2006. *Angela Catlin*

LEFT: Gay Russell with the plane she flew for a sugar company.

ABOVE: A volunteer in Malawi carries a bag of Likuni Phala, made with maize and soya grown in the country. September 2014. *Chris Watt*

LEFT: Volunteers cook a pot of Likuni Phala for children in Malawi, 2015. *Chris Watt*

RIGHT: Gerard Butler visits a Mary's Meals school feeding programme with Magnus, Liberia, 2013. *Chris Watt*

ABOVE: Queuing for porridge, Malawi.

ABOVE: A girl in India, learning to write.

RIGHT: Annual Medjugorje Youth Festival, 2012.

ABOVE: Magnus and Julie (just out of shot, behind Magnus) meet Pope Francis, 2013.

RIGHT: A child in Myanmar eating Mary's Meals.

ABOVE: The iconic image, captured by drone, to celebrate the First Million milestone, Chirimba, Malawi, 2015. *Chris Watt*

BELOW: Niagara Falls turns blue in celebration of Mary's Meals, Canada, 2015

BELOW: Jimmy Belabre performs at Mladifest, Medjugorje, 2016

RIGHT: Magnus is presented with a signed football shirt – a gift from Luka Modrić – at an event in Zagreb, 2019.

ABOVE: Lunchtime in Kenya, 2018. *Chris Watt*

LEFT: Felix during his fundraising challenge, 'Felix Runs for Mary's Meals', Germany, 2020.

RIGHT: Magnus signs copies of his second book, *GIVE: Charity and the Art of Living Generously*, in the shed, Dalmally, 2020.

ABOVE: Providing daily meals to internally displaced people in Tigray, Ethiopia, 2021.

RIGHT: A woman collects take-home rations during school closures, Haiti, 2020.

ABOVE: Community distribution of take-home rations, South Sudan, 2020.

RIGHT: Handwashing station at a community distribution, Malawi, 2021.

And while doing so, they were missing their chance of an education and an escape from that grinding poverty. In one of the schools there the head teacher, Mr George, shared his struggle with us. He was doing his best to reach as many children as possible by running two schools in the same building, one in the morning and one in the afternoon. But still many children were not in school because they had to work, and many others attended too hungry and too weak to learn. At least the teachers here in the city schools were being paid, but their monthly salary of sixty US dollars was the price of one large bag of rice.

'We are desperate. This poverty is one of the things that causes families to break up,' Mr George told us.

After the tour of the school and further sharing of information, he asked us when we could begin Mary's Meals in his school. I told him that I could not give him an answer to that because we were just starting to look at possibilities and had not even decided if we would set up in Monrovia.

'Do you know what it is like to have a daughter who you cannot afford to feed?' he asked me with some anger in his voice. 'How do you tell your teenager daughters to behave and stay at home when you cannot even feed them? How can you blame them if they go on the streets and do not respect us? How can you blame them if they go their own way and misbehave?'

I did not know the answer to any of his questions. I had never been unable to give my children food to eat. I do not know how it feels to be tormented by a fear that my daughters might have to sell themselves for food. I knew I could not even begin to understand what this father standing in front of me was going through and I found it difficult to look him in the eye.

'I'm sorry. I just can't give you an answer now. We need to think about this. We will do our best and I promise you we will let you know when we've decided,' I offered him, feebly, as we took our leave.

In the end, having weighed things up, we decided to continue our efforts in the rural areas rather than the city. We could see that most aid efforts were happening in the city while villages were neglected and even poorer. We wanted to do all we could to encourage a return to the farms rather than adding to reasons for people to stay in the city. Not that we doubted for one second that there was a huge pressing need for Mary's Meals in places like Westport; it was rather a case of recognizing we could not do everything at once.

But Mr George's questions bothered me. How easy it was to pay visits to the poor, ask them questions and take photographs, before climbing back in our cars. And how difficult it was to understand for even one moment what it really felt like to be so poor. Because I believed I had learnt a lot from the poorest of the poor – especially in matters of faith – I was at risk sometimes of almost romanticizing poverty. But there was nothing romantic at all about the kind of poverty that was destroying Mr George and his family. It was a destructive, evil thing that no human was created to endure. But perhaps it was good also to find myself in that situation and to be powerless too. By admitting to Mr George that I might not be able to help him with his desperate need, I was also admitting to myself that my efforts and ability to help were very limited too. And that was good – at least for me.

Over the next few years we were able to expand into Grand Cape Mount, another large forested district in Western Liberia, bordering with Sierra Leone, whose mainly Muslim population lived in small villages connected by dirt-track roads. One by one, we began to serve eighty-two schools in that county, having built a satellite warehouse where we could store bulk-food supplies.

I was hugely impressed by the bamboo-pole kitchens the communities constructed here, and even more so by the school gardens that were now becoming a key part of our model in Liberia. These little farms belonged to the school communities, and by now we had decided that if a school wished to be considered for the Mary's Meals programme in Liberia it had to make a commitment to having such a project at the school. Huge amounts of work had gone into clearing large areas of bush adjacent to schools, and head teachers proudly showed us rows of cassava and other 'greens' which they were adding to the meals we supplied, as well as pineapples and other valuable produce they could sell to provide desperately needed support for the schools. Another enormous benefit of these gardens was the opportunity to teach farming skills to a generation of pupils who had spent much of their childhood in displaced camps away from their farms.

One day in 2012, on the way to a school in Cape Mount, we crossed a neatly constructed concrete bridge. Joseph explained that when they first visited this school after receiving a request for Mary's Meals, they had been forced to tell the community we were unable to include them because it was impossible to reach them with a delivery vehicle. A few weeks later the village elders came back to Joseph and asked if he would send one of our team to reassess the road. This time they discovered the previously impassable small river had been spanned by a new concrete bridge built by the community. The enormous desire for Mary's Meals in these communities was prompting many good works. At each school we met queues of children with colourful bowls, women cooking on open fires and teachers telling us about all the new children coming to school for the first time. On average, enrolment increased by a staggering 40 per cent in the schools in Cape Mount after the introduction of Mary's Meals.

On our return journey from visiting some of those schools, we stopped for a meeting with community leaders involved in the delivery of Mary's Meals in this area. An Imam who had worked tirelessly to mobilize the communities here – and who had organized for the donation of land on which we had built our warehouse that served the county – met us on his motorbike beside the road, all smiles despite us being over an hour late. He led us to a village hall full of other patient people who welcomed us warmly. The Imam opened the meeting with a prayer, and then before inviting them to speak to us about their experience of Mary's Meals, we told them our plan to try and reach all the other schools in Cape Mount before the end of the year. They broke into prolonged applause.

An elderly man with a white beard and prayer cap spoke with great emotion, saying, 'We are so grateful for this news. It is pitiful to eat when your neighbour is going without. When I saw the children round here hungry I would feel hungry too. Now that I see them fed every day I am no longer hungry.'

9

In Tinsel Town

> Baloney is flattery laid on so thick it cannot be true,
> and blarney is flattery so thin we love it.
> FULTON J. SHEEN

All over the world new doors began to open and a bewildering assortment of people invited Mary's Meals in. In ornamented Austrian churches, on historic Roman squares, round a pool in Palm Beach, at a football stadium in Calabria and inside a Young Offenders Institute in Glasgow people gathered with open hearts to hear the Mary's Meals message. The diversity of people I talked to was staggering, almost comical, and I discovered so many unexpected things when I went to meet them. In a synagogue I discussed why our work was named after a Jewish mother; at a global conference on education in Abu Dhabi I was asked to give my talk immediately after a presentation on Exocet missiles given by someone who manufactured them. At a party in Los Angeles I met a professional beach volleyball player and a retired stuntman, both of whom seemed as genuinely fascinated by my work as I most certainly was by theirs.

Of course, not all my talks were in exotic faraway places. I spoke to hundreds of schools and church groups in Scotland and was able to reach many people just a few yards from my office, by talking to the groups of faithful who continued to come to Craig Lodge on retreat. When I had first reluctantly begun giving talks, the ones I found most terrifying of all were to schools. But eventually these became my favourite. I especially loved the part when they asked me questions, which were normally very sincere and heartfelt but sometimes wonderfully surprising.

'Have you ever seen a killer bee?' was just one that left me floundering for something more than a one-word answer.

But the thing I liked most of all about the schoolchildren was their lack of cynicism and the very short gap between them deciding they would like to do something and them actually doing it. To them it seemed obvious that no child should go to school without food, and clear that they personally should and could do something about it; procrastination was something they left to adults.

But while the grassroots support at home continued to flourish, the international support was growing even faster. Mary's Meals Germany was registered as the first of several European affiliates in 2006, and then, in the USA, Mary's Meals was born in 2008 through a group of wonderful people in Miami, a city that by now I often travelled through on my way to Haiti. Milona told me she had good friends in Florida, whom she had met in Medjugorje, who were offering for me to stay with them. Thus it was I came to know Lourdes

Guitierez, her daughter, Lourdes Fanjul, and their good friend, Lourdes Diego. Having never even met anyone with that lovely name before, I found myself asking what the plural was – especially as they all became not just good friends but founding board members of Mary's Meals USA, along with another couple called Michelle and Albert Holder. Together we worked hard to start raising awareness of Mary's Meals in the USA, without knowing that something was about to happen that would make that task a whole lot easier.

In the spring of 2010 we received a call from CNN in New York, saying I had been selected as one of their 'CNN Heroes'. They explained this would involve them featuring me and the work of Mary's Meals in some short films they would broadcast, and asked if they could send a film crew over the following week. After recoiling at the 'hero' label, we took stock and realized this was the most incredible opportunity we had ever been given to raise awareness of our work, particularly in North America, where supporters of Mary's Meals had already spoken to us of CNN Heroes. So we said yes, and within a few weeks the story of Mary's Meals was being broadcast into millions of homes around the world. A couple of months later I received another call from CNN, this time to tell me I had been selected by a panel of esteemed judges as one of their 'top ten heroes' of the year. I was particularly thrilled to learn that Muhammad Ali was a member of that panel! So we were invited to Los Angeles for a very glamorous, star-studded event that would be televised. And so another film crew arrived in Scotland, and then travelled to Haiti with me to make a short film that would be broadcast with the event. A couple of weeks later Julie and I found ourselves arriving in Los Angeles, feeling rather nervous and a little bit excited too.

At our hotel they introduced us to the other nine 'heroes' who we had by now become familiar with on the CNN website. Some of them did indeed already feel like heroes to us. We had read all about Evans Wdongo, a young Kenyan man who had designed a simple solar-powered lamp so children in Africa could read and do homework at home in the evenings; Anuradha Koirala who was working to prevent the trafficking and sexual exploitation of Nepal's women and girls; and Dan Walrath, a Texan, who was building homes for injured Iraq and Afghanistan war veterans. It was lovely to meet these remarkable people, most of whom seemed equally uncomfortable in the environment in which we all suddenly found ourselves. As the big event drew closer I kept reminding Julie that she would need to point out any famous people who we might come in contact with; my lack of awareness of celebrities had been causing some hilarity among my colleagues within Mary's Meals for some time and I was nervous that I might offend someone with my ignorance. In the lead-up to the event, our team in Scotland had done their research and explained to me that at the award ceremony CNN would pair each 'hero' with a celebrity who would present them with an award. They had discovered that Gerard Butler, the Scottish Hollywood actor, was one of the celebrities and they predicted I would be linked with my compatriot on the night.

The CNN people took us all to the venue, the famous Shrine Auditorium, where televised awards ceremonies such as the Oscars and Grammys have been previously held and gave us a tour. They explained more about the event and took us through some stage rehearsals. They informed us that in addition to the 3,000-strong, star-studded audience that would be attending the show the following evening, a further 16 million were expected to see it on television around the world. They also told us we had 45 seconds exactly for our acceptance speeches and if we went over time at all they would simply edit it out. Then they told me they wanted to put me on first. They said the film they had made about Mary's Meals was spectacular and they wanted me to make the first acceptance speech. I did at this point become very nervous indeed. As soon as I had understood the magnitude of this opportunity some weeks before, I felt that any acceptance speech should be used to give thanks to God and Our Lady for this work. I suspected the editors at CNN might not let that go but I had a conviction that this is what I should do.

Arriving at the theatre the next evening with Julie squeezing my arm, dressed in my kilt and my dad's fiercest sporran, I felt a little better. Then came the first of several bizarre experiences. I was taken backstage for 'make-up and hair styling'. This was a new and uncomfortable experience for me. I sat back as the friendly lady put gel in my hair, and thought of windy days back on the fish farm, of sea spray and oilskins and woolly hats and not having to talk to another human being all day. Then we were being shown to the front row. Julie looked even more beautiful than usual. I felt braver. Sitting a few seats along from us was Jon Bon Jovi, who was there to perform, and I felt very comforted that I at least recognized this famous person – and even more so when he talked to me in a warm and friendly way.

The show began, with Anderson Cooper presenting (I recognized him too!), and first up was Gerard Butler to introduce me. Our team in Scotland had called that one right which was great because it meant I also knew who he was. This was going well. He read a very flattering little introduction speech, and then they showed their film about Mary's Meals – which was indeed beautiful and even more flattering. Then I went up to receive the award – a rather nice inscribed block of wood. I swallowed to try and get my impossibly dry throat working and told the people in the theatre and the 16 million at home how happy I was to receive this award on behalf of the thousands taking part in this work, that I believed that this vision of ours is possible to achieve – that every child can receive one meal every day in their place of education – and I thanked God, then Mary, the mother of Jesus, who herself brought up a child in poverty and knew what it was to be exiled, for her inspiration and her love. I must have made it within the forty-five seconds because they broadcast it all!

As soon as we left the back of the stage Gerard shook hands with me vigorously, saying, 'I need to tell you something really funny! Yesterday I was in here rehearsing for this. I got halfway through the script about you and said, "wait a minute, this is the guy my mum keeps telling me about!" My mum keeps phoning and saying I need to meet you. She heard you talking about Mary's Meals at some event in Glasgow a few months ago and has been on about it ever since!'

His agent shook my hand and laughed. 'Yes, I will be in some serious trouble if we don't get a photograph of you and Gerard together to send to her!'

Thus they turned the whole situation hilariously on its head. After posing for some pictures, during which we discovered we both supported the same football club – Glasgow Celtic – we rushed back to our seats for the rest of the show.

At the interval things got even funnier. Gerard came over to meet Julie and for some reason with him was Demi Moore. Now for many years Julie and my little brother Mark had teased me about her. I think I must have said something about her beauty while watching a film with Mark, and he had mischievously repeated the comment to Julie. They never missed an opportunity to laugh at me whenever Demi Moore appeared on television – or even if her name was simply mentioned. And here she was being introduced to me. She was crying about the Mary's Meals film she had just seen, kissing me on the cheek and congratulating us on our work. I can't remember what I said to her, but it was certainly incoherent. Julie laughed so hard when we got back to our seats for the remainder of the show. At the end of the evening Anuradha was pronounced the overall winner, which I was delighted at because her cause was such an important one – and she herself a very dignified and impressive lady.

Next we were led to an 'after party', where each of us was given an area to sit with our friends and where people had the opportunity to come and talk to us if they wished. All the other celebrities had left immediately at the end of the show, but Gerry and his agent came along, much to our delight. A little queue formed of people waiting to speak to me. Actually, I discovered quite quickly that it was not so much that they wanted to speak to me, more that they wanted a photograph with me wearing my kilt. For the next few hours we never got to the end of the queue, photo after photo was taken with all kinds of people. One unexpected encounter was with a group of miners from Chile, who were at that point world famous. They had been trapped in a mine deep underground for sixty-nine days while the whole world watched and prayed. My own children had been praying for them every evening for weeks prior to their recent rescue, and so it felt very wonderful to unexpectedly be talking with these men whose suffering and bravery and wonderful escape we had watched unfold.

That evening gave me a very little taste of what life must be like for a famous person. For those few hours it was mainly fun, but only because I knew that I could go back to normal the next morning. It made me think stardom must be an extremely dangerous thing to live with every day. Even after a few short hours it began to make me feel a bit disorientated – like I suddenly wasn't very sure who I was because everyone around me was behaving as if I was someone else. Apart, that is, from Julie and our good friends from Florida, Iowa and New York, who had joined us there. Maybe that is the only way that famous people can stay sane and happy – if they have good loving family and friends around them reminding them who they really are. Actually, perhaps that is partly true for all of us, famous or not. Anyway, it felt so very good the next morning to be back in my jeans, strolling through the streets with Julie, up to the 'Cathedral of the

Angels'. I had suggested we go and see Hollywood, but Julie felt we had had enough 'star dust' for one weekend. So instead we sat together in silence in the church, thanking God for our rather unusual weekend break and trying to process it a little before heading home to tell our kids all about it.

A few weeks later, not long before Christmas, Gerry called me out of the blue. He had promised in LA that he would take his mum over to see us some time when he was back home in Scotland, but I hadn't taken him seriously.

'I am just on my way over now – we'll be there in a couple of hours,' he told me and hung up. Never had I seen the girls in our office so excited! And sure enough, before long, he was posing for photographs with them and all who met him. He has been a friend ever since, helping raise awareness of our work in lots of ways.

A few months after the CNN event I was emailed by a lady in Canada who had watched the show. She said she was very interested in the fact that I had mentioned Mary, the mother of Jesus, in my acceptance speech and this had led her to investigate our work further. Since then she had been handmaking rosary bracelets and selling them to raise funds for our work. Each sale provided one child with meals for a year. She also explained that she was recently retired as a teacher near Toronto and wondered if we were interested in setting up Mary's Meals Canada as a fund-raising organization there. She was very confident that our work would be well received and supported there. Over time Bridgid and her husband, Mike, became good friends. The first time I travelled to meet them I was struck by Bridgid's unusual gift of deep peace and joy. She had invited a large group of her friends, and other Canadians who had been supporting Mary's Meals, to a barbecue so that they could meet me. It was a sunny afternoon and her back garden was filled with laughter. By the end of the meeting it was clear to me that Bridgid, who was clearly loved and respected by those who knew her, was the perfect leader for our work in Canada. I was struck by her determination to turn the talk into meaningful action. Later, when the others had dispersed and the house was quiet, Bridgid explained to me that she had terminal cancer.

'I don't know how long I have, but right now I feel great,' she said, smiling brightly. 'I want to do this for Mary's Meals – in the time God gives me – and I know Mike wants me to do this too. He's taken early retirement just to be with me and to help me.'

Later that year we held a meeting in Scotland for the fund-raising groups around the world. Bridgid and Mike came over for their first visit to Dalmally. As always we started the meeting with a short prayer and introductions. Bridgid stood up and told us a remarkable story. She explained she had decided to travel to Scotland via London so she could visit a long-lost aunt there. She phoned the aunt just before boarding in Toronto to tell her the arrival time and mentioned that she was only going to be in London briefly as she was on her way to a Mary's Meals meeting in Scotland. After hanging up, her aunt looked up the Mary's Meals website. Her window cleaner was there and she called over to him.

'Have you ever heard of Mary's Meals? They look amazing!'

'Heard of them?' replied the startled young man. 'Heard of them? I would not be here if it was not for Mary's Meals. I am from Malawi. I would not have gone to school if they had not been providing the meals there. And so I would never have ended up at university here in London. That is why I am here.'

Our gatherings of the dispersed Mary's Meals family often seemed to be marked by remarkable stories and connections which confirmed a sense of belonging and calling to this work. Sometimes we had held such gatherings in Medjugorje. As the work grew and the number of Mary's Meals groups proliferated, we wanted to make sure that, regardless of our various backgrounds and different faiths, we all shared the same vision, mission and values. The end results of our work were not all that mattered to us; the way we did this work was just as important, and for this reason we wanted to come together in the village where the work had been born many years previously and learn from each other. The little store where Fergus and I had first unloaded gifts from our Land Rover in 1992 still stood at the corner of the street, not too far from the hall in which we had gathered for one such meeting in 2009. And what a colourful and diverse family we had become in the years since.

In addition to a big team of staff, volunteers and supporters from Scotland, we had representatives from Malawi, Liberia, Croatia, England, Wales, Ireland, the Philippines, Uganda, Italy and Germany. Among those who gave talks about their involvement with Mary's Meals were businessmen, missionary priests, a visionary, a reformed gangster and an archduchess. We encouraged all to tell their personal stories, not just to talk about the current work. It was very rich and deeply moving.

John Pridmore spoke to us as the Chairman of Mary's Meals Ireland. He was once a well-known gangster in London, who had experienced a profound religious conversion after nearly killing someone in a pub. He had spent a year with us in Dalmally in the youth community at the House of Prayer and thereafter devoted his life to speaking to young people about God's love. Along the way he had written several books, including the bestseller *From Gangland to Promised Land*, and had become an internationally renowned public speaker. He and the community he founded in Ireland had decided to take Mary's Meals on as a special project. Despite the fact they survived themselves on divine providence, mainly in the form of collections taken for them in parishes where they gave talks, they decided to ask that these collections be instead given entirely to Mary's Meals – trusting that God would look after them in other ways. He did indeed, but meanwhile amazing support and awareness of Mary's Meals was raised all over Ireland through the words and example given by John and his friends.

Another profoundly moving and important talk was given by Željka Markić about Mary's Meals Croatia. Željka was another old and dear friend, the daughter of Dr Marijo Živković, the amazing man who we worked with in the early years of delivering aid to refugees in Croatia. Along with her friends in Zagreb at that time, Željka used to tell us that one day, when things were better in Croatia, they too would work to help people in need in far-off lands. We had lost touch after the war but then, after a few years, she visited us in

Scotland with her family. Željka was now a successful businesswoman and, along with her husband Tihomir, a doctor, and their four sons, she wanted to know all about our work and to understand how it had evolved into Mary's Meals. They drank in the story.

'Now it is time to keep that promise,' Željka said. 'Things are better now in Croatia and there are many people who could support this work for hungry children. We should set up Mary's Meals Croatia so that they can.'

And that is exactly what she then did, together with some close friends in Zagreb. In time, thousands of Croatians became supporters of Mary's Meals. And when I listened to the talk she gave us at our little gathering in Medjugorje, I realized that Željka had a unique perspective on our work.

'I remember when Julie and Magnus came to Croatia with their little truck. We used to help organize the distribution of the baby clothes and nappies that they would bring. Many of my friends – and me too – benefited from this ourselves. And today we are the ones running Mary's Meals in Croatia, so that others in need might be helped.

'It is really important for us to know how to both give and receive when we do this work. It is important we treat those who receive our aid with as much respect as those who give to us.'

At some sessions during the week-long gathering, pilgrims who happened to be in Medjugorje would come in and join us. One of these was a lady called Ellen Miller from Iowa, who had a chat with Julie over a coffee between meetings. She explained that she and a friend were organizing a conference called 'Christ Our Life' in their city of Des Moines.

They were determined to fill a basketball stadium with thousands of people and were looking for speakers.

'Do you think your husband might come over next year? We'll look after him, we promise!' said Ellen, having identified very quickly that the best way of persuading me to agree to do something was to get Julie to ask me.

And so it was that in September 2010, I found myself being met at Des Moines Airport by Ellen's smiling son, Mike, who had been assigned to look after me for the weekend. The following morning I arrived at the stadium along with 4,000 other people who had gathered for the conference. I was struck by the numbers of young people there and the prayerful atmosphere. In the afternoon I had the chance to tell them the Mary's Meals story and afterwards hundreds of people came to our stall to tell us they wanted to help. I left soon afterwards, very impressed by the Miller family and the good people I had met there, but without an understanding of what we had just ignited in Iowa. In the months and years following that conference, the most incredible Mary's Meals grassroots movement spread across Iowa and beyond. Numerous schools and parishes began supporting. Thousands there joined our mission by becoming donors, volunteer speakers or people who prayed for our work. Lots of spontaneous fund-raising campaigns began. Ellen and her friends designed T-shirts and schoolkids sold many thousands of them, with each sale feeding a child for a year. There were other surprising fruits from that first brief visit too. I had enjoyed chatting with Mike, Ellen's friendly, cheerful son, as he drove me around that weekend. He told me he was just finishing university where he was studying finance, and planned to join the supermarket chain that his father had worked for. He seemed excited about the prospect. He also asked a lot of good questions about Mary's Meals. A few weeks after my visit he called me, said he had been praying and thinking since we met, and asked if Mary's Meals might need any help from someone with a finance background. I was amazed by his offer. I talked about our need for someone like him to work with our teams in Haiti or Liberia. He said he would love to volunteer in either of those places. Initially we planned for Haiti, but then because of staffing changes in Liberia we asked if he might go there instead. He said yes immediately, and soon found himself based in Tubmanburg and an important part of our team there. In time he became a paid member of staff and has been working for Mary's Meals ever since.

More and more I began to notice that it was often young people who were leading the most amazing fund-raising efforts. Another sitting among the audience in Iowa, unbeknown to me, was a twelve-year-old called Allison Ockenfels, from a small farming community in the north of the state. She learnt it was possible to fund-raise to provide one specific school in Malawi with Mary's Meals, through our 'Sponsor a School' campaign. Unfazed by the target of $12,000 required for one school, she set about fund-raising in her village. By the time I heard of Allison, she had already reached her target and was working on the next school! She asked if I would visit her family when I was next in Iowa, a request I was happy to say yes to.

The Ockenfels lived on a dusty farm track in rolling fields of corn, far from any town. I stayed with them for a night, learning that Allison and her two brothers were home-schooled. Her dad sold enormous, used combine harvesters – a whole row of them were parked near their house. I enjoyed their home-made food and the simple loving family life they had worked hard to create. In the evening they took me to their little wooden parish church a few miles away. It was packed. Every person there – and they had come from many miles around – knew about Mary's Meals and had been supporting Allison's fund-raising efforts. This farming community, these growers of food, had taken the Mary's Meals message into their hearts in a very special way.

The next evening I had to give a talk in downtown Chicago, at the home of some people I knew there. Despite the fact this would be a five-hour drive, my new friends, the Ockenfels, insisted on driving me all the way there. I learnt on the drive that Allison and her brothers had never even visited the 'Windy City' before and it felt good to be on this adventure with them. My hosts in Chicago had been among the very first to fund-raise for Mary's Meals in the USA and had been faithfully fund-raising for a specific school in Malawi for three years. They lived in a very fashionable apartment among the famous dazzling skyscrapers of Chicago. My audience could not have been more different from the previous evening. Instead of speaking to God-fearing farmers, I explained the work of Mary's Meals to a group of masseurs, vegan chefs, beauticians and politicians. Instead of a collection basket, money was raised through the auctioning of donated art, special books, massages and meals in restaurants. All these people showed great kindness, and they too ensured that one more school would be able to receive Mary's Meals.

It seemed like people in every situation imaginable were finding ways to support us. A man called David in a prison in Kansas wrote to Patty in our New Jersey office with a donation of $5:

> Dear Patty,
> I hope and pray the good Lord blesses you and the Mary's Meals programme. For me to give the little I have has changed me immensely. Now, when I have money sent to my account I make it a priority to send five dollars to Mary's Meals. Funny though that when I was in the outside world I never once thought about donating to the needy. Again thank you for allowing the impact on other people's lives. Truly it is me who has been impacted by Mary's Meals. God does work in mysterious ways.

And David did continue to give regular donations and even started to make collections from other prisoners that he would pass on.

Back in my shed, we took calls every day with more invitations. It became increasingly hard to know which to accept. By now we had developed an amazing network of volunteer speakers who were always ready to go and speak on our behalf but sometimes, especially for overseas invitations, the expectation was that I would come myself. I was intrigued one day to receive an invitation to visit Abu Dhabi. We had been receiving very sizeable donations from a parish there, and because I wanted to thank whoever was responsible I decided to go.

I made my way to a shopping centre in Dubai where I had agreed to meet my host. I was early, and was talking on the phone in a coffee shop. It didn't cross my mind that the lady sitting at the table opposite me was the person I had arranged to meet until I noticed that one of the two small girls with her was wearing a T-shirt with *Mary's Meals* written on it. At that same moment the lady heard my Scottish accent and extended her hand with a smile.

'I'm Catherine. I thought I'd recognize you from the CNN thing,' she said, 'but it was in black and white.' While I tried to figure that one out, the very sweet excited girls gave me a whistle-stop tour of the rest of the Ibn Battuta shopping mall, during which I learnt a lot about the explorer of that name and they bought me a lovely frozen yogurt, before we drove across the desert to their home in Abu Dhabi. On the way they reminded me that Mary's Meals had been brought to the United Arab Emirates by Sister Ligouri, an Indian nun who had made a retreat at Craig Lodge House of Prayer, while living in England several years earlier. Having learnt about Mary's Meals while staying with us she introduced it to St Joseph's parish in Abu Dhabi when she had moved to work there.

'We should just make it in time for the evening Mass and you'll have a chance to thank the people,' said Catherine as we entered Abu Dhabi.

It was midweek and I imagined an evening Mass attended by a few faithful elderly daily Mass goers. I wondered if, perhaps, among the little group, might be a wealthy benefactor responsible for the large sums we had been receiving. When we drew up at the church there was an enormous crowd in the courtyard. I presumed at first this was nothing to do with us, or the evening Mass, until Catherine explained that this was in fact the congregation. Over 1,500 people had turned up, far too many to fit inside the church, so Mass was outside tonight and while the opening hymn was sung fervently, the call to prayer from a local mosque echoed beautifully from somewhere nearby. Those singing in the courtyard around me were nearly all immigrants from India, the Philippines and Africa.

At the end of Mass I was able to thank the congregation, who applauded warmly when I told them that Mary's Meals was now feeding more than 500,000 children every day. Afterwards I spent time with some of the people and learnt that the sizeable donations from Abu Dhabi did in fact represent thousands of little gifts from these hard-working, low-paid people who had left their homelands to find jobs. I also discovered that most of the fund-raising had actually been organized by the children of the parish, who led various initiatives such as collecting coins in bottles during Lent. Nyapthala, the girl with the big heart who bought me the frozen yogurt ahead of our hot desert drive, was most prominent among them, they told me.

Allison, Nyapthala and children all over the world were fund-raising for Mary's Meals in extraordinary ways. Milona returned from a trip to Italy where she had been giving talks to our new fund-raising group. Gleefully, she told us how in Modena children were planting pumpkin seeds in a field near their school and after they had grown large and tasty, they were selling them to raise the funds that would mean another child in a faraway place might eat.

In Brighton, meanwhile, a seven-year-old boy called Charlie Doherty began to tell his mum he did not want birthday presents and that instead he wanted her to give the money to Mary's Meals. And then he began to fund-raise in other ways. He organized a group of friends to swim the length of a marathon, and, not content with that, persuaded his mum to do a sponsored cycle ride with him from their home on the south coast of England to Glasgow. Like Allison in Iowa, he then decided to sponsor a school in Malawi and, in time, raised the funds required to provide over 1,000 meals every day in a large school there.

In 2012, perhaps the most spectacular example yet of a child leading a Mary's Meals initiative began, when a nine-year-old girl called Martha Payne started a blog called *Never Seconds*, to write about her school dinners. She wrote her opinion on each meal in the format of a restaurant review, scoring it on its quality, health rating, number of hairs and marks out of ten based on a 'Food-o-Meter'. Her blog began to gain a huge following and I first heard of Martha when her grandfather, a very committed and active Mary's Meals volunteer in Edinburgh, asked if I might let Martha interview me, explaining that she was now using her blog to raise money to sponsor a school for Mary's Meals. I agreed but explained it would need to wait until I returned from a trip I was about to make to America. A few days later Argyll and Bute Council, annoyed by what they saw as her criticism of their school meals, banned her from taking photographs of the food she was served at school. An enormous storm of protest and media interest ensued. The story went viral and overnight Martha became a global Internet star. All over the world, newspapers and TV stations picked up the story. I couldn't believe my eyes when I read about it in the *New York Times*. Before the council's ban Martha had already raised about £2,000 for Mary's Meals. A few days later that total stood at £130,000, and all over the world we had a new wave of supporters. Martha's family took every opportunity to use the situation to support Mary's Meals, telling the media if they wanted an interview they would need to include something on our work. In the following months, we were often asked by admiring marketing professionals from larger charities to explain to them the secret of how we had engineered this spectacular social media event. We had to explain that it had nothing to do with us. If only we were that clever! A few months later, it was a thrill to see a smiling young Martha travel to Malawi with her family in order to visit one of the schools where her funds were being used to provide meals – and the fact that the BBC went with them to make a documentary helped us gain even more supporters.

Children were showing us how to fund-raise in all kinds of incredible ways, but the sheer speed of growth meant we desperately needed other kinds of help too. I had no experience of running a large organization. The numbers of staff were growing in proportion to the size of our work, but our determination to keep our overheads very low and our conviction that we should never pay high salaries meant we could not just go out and hire people who had years of senior management experience and qualifications that we were lacking. We prayed that God would send us some new helpers.

We had just found a wonderful new board member called David Clayton, a former PwC partner, who later became our Chairman. I invited him to come to an international gathering in Medjugorje as a way for him to get to know the people involved in Mary's Meals. He immediately accepted this invitation, but feeling a little nervous about visiting this place of 'Catholic' pilgrimage (David is a Scottish Presbyterian) he phoned an old friend to ask if he might join him. That old friend was Jim Kennedy, who indeed joined us in Medjugorje for the week. Just before we flew home, he asked to speak to me. He explained that he was recently retired from a long career working in very senior positions with Hewlett Packard and Compaq, and that his intention on retirement had been to give his time to help some charitable organizations. He now felt that rather than helping a number of organizations he wanted to devote his time to just one, Mary's Meals. Having listened to the speakers during the week, he was on fire in regard to our mission and he could also see that we were in need of his help. Less than a week after our return from that conference, Jim made his first visit to my 'shed'. We set up the flip chart and began to discuss priorities. For the first few months Jim mainly listened. He had a huge respect for the way we were doing things and wanted to be very cautious about introducing business methodologies that might be in conflict with our values and current systems. He had an incredibly sharp mind and began to help us enormously with the development of a senior management team, strategic planning and robust working practices. He would challenge my starting positions vigorously, but respectfully, in a way that I found extremely helpful, and all of us with positions of responsibility learnt things from him about the importance of rigour and attention to detail. For the next five years Jim, as an unpaid volunteer, worked as hard as any member of staff. Sometimes his serious, almost fierce, demeanour would suddenly dissolve into laughter for no apparent reason as he stood with his pen poised at the flip chart.

'When I worked for Hewlett Packard we used to have a standard phrase if someone got a bit carried away and became over-ambitious in their thinking. We would say to them, "Calm down! We're not trying to solve world hunger!"

'And what am I doing now? Standing in this shed with you lot in front of this flip chart trying to do just that!' he roared.

Like Ruth, Milona and several others, Jim's contribution made a huge lasting impact on the evolution of Mary's Meals and the way we work. While Ruth developed much of our language and the particular way we articulate what we do, and Milona taught us much about how this work should be rooted in love always, Jim showed us how to be very effective stewards indeed with the resources entrusted to us. Sometimes those involved in our work, who believe in divine providence, are challenged and worried by the introduction of more planning and procedures and talk of strategies, but the ability to do these things well can be God's gifts also, I believe. And so too are those people who make dramatic decisions in their lives to become part of this mission.

10

Reaching the Outcastes

> Education is not the filling of a pail,
> but the lighting of a fire.
> W. B. YEATS

Out of the first rays of dawn, which streamed through the poplar trees and along the cobbled lane, some children appeared. In groups of three or four they came, wearing uniforms and carrying school bags. As they made their way past the little sugar-cane plant, some of them waved to their fathers, who were just finishing their night shift, before they continued on into their little school playground. Outside her mud-brick house on the edge of the lane, a mother was hurriedly trying to smooth her son's hair with water as he frantically looked in his school bag for something. Finally he found it and ran out on to the lane to catch some passing friends. As I watched, I thought of Julie and my own children and our very similar routine at home. But then a horse trotted past, pulling a cart in which a man with a white turban stood holding the reigns. The morning had begun to unfold much like any other in Kuwakhera, a small, backwater village in Uttar Pradesh, north India. But for some that unfolding was not such a happy one.

While the school bell rang and neat lines of pupils were forming in the playground for morning assembly, eleven-year-old Devand and his ten-year-old sister Gemina were just beginning their twelve-hour shift in the sugar-cane plant. They were the youngest members of a family of six who were all employed here. In a flat area behind the rickety old machines that noisily pulped the sugar canes to extract the sweet juice, the brother and sister started to spread the leftover shreds to dry in the hot sun and thus become fodder for local farmers. The adults who worked in this plant as casual labourers were being paid about 55 pence for each twelve-hour shift they worked, while the family of six were employed on a permanent basis and received a lump sum between them all.

Behind the school, we walked into the fields where the sugar cane was being harvested and where more children were working while they should have been gaining an education and the possibility of an escape from poverty. Crouched among the stubble and tangle of cut cane, a young boy dressed in rags was gathering the stems into bundles. He was filthy and had a face as sad as I've ever seen. He was reluctant to talk to us. Perhaps he had never seen people with white skin before or perhaps he had not had a conversation for a very long time. But slowly, without lifting his eyes from the ground, he began to answer the questions posed by my Indian friend.

His name was Kailu, he told us, and he was fourteen years of age. He came from a small village in the forests of Bihar.

'We had elephants and we ate deer from the forest,' he whispered when we asked about his village.

Slowly he began to grow a little more confident, even raising his gaze to look at us.

'I think I have been here for about six months. A "contractor" came to our village and recruited 200 boys. We were put on a train. I was taken to this village where a farmer paid the contractor £15 for me. He said he would deduct this from my wages. I have not been paid anything since I have been here.'

By now he seemed happy to answer our questions.

'I rise at 7 a.m. and I go to bed at midnight. I have not had a day off since I got here. After I finish in the fields I do household chores and I clean the cow sheds. But I am lucky because my master never beats me or abuses me. They give me two meals every day. I am not allowed in their kitchen so I eat them on my own. I have nothing apart from these clothes I am wearing.'

I looked at his old top, jeans ripped at the knees, and his flimsy flip-flops.

'Do you know anyone else here?'

'I do not know anyone.' And he turned to look at the school on the edge of the fields from where we could hear children's laughter.

'And do your parents know what your life is like here?'

'No, I am not in contact with them. I cannot write and they cannot either. Our village is very poor – it is why they sent me away for work. I only saw a telephone once, in the railway station when I got off the train. Sometimes, when I think of my parents and my life here I sit and I cry.' He was looking at the ground again.

'Will you return home?'

'Yes. After one year, on the feast of Holi, I will receive my year's wages. I will go home and never return here,' he replied.

By now Kailu was looking anxiously across the fields towards some houses, worried that his master would arrive and see him talking to us. We took our leave. As we walked through the cane, I asked my companion, Father Joson, if he thought Kailu would ever receive any money for his work and whether he would even know how to get back home if he did. He shook his head sadly at both questions. I wonder if Mary's Meals had been served in a school in Kailu's village whether his parents would have made the same choices.

It was 2004 and I was making my first visit to India. I had been introduced to Father Joson the previous year when he was working for some months in a Glasgow parish. He was from Kerala and was a trained lawyer as well as a priest. He had told me about his work in India with the Pragati Social Service Society, an organization that had been set up to serve the poor and marginalized. They worked mainly with Dalits, who make up more than 15 per cent of the population and who are deemed 'untouchable' by the caste system in India.

Although discrimination according to caste was now illegal in India, the caste system which had evolved over thousands of years still pervaded every aspect of life in the rural areas. The kind of job you had, the people you associated with, your access to the village water pump – all these things could be decided by which caste you had been born into. The Dalits continued to be oppressed, enslaved and humiliated as they carried out the tasks that no one else in society wanted to do. They worked with bare hands among the rubbish, they disposed of human waste and they worked as 'human donkeys', pulling heavy loads. They often became bonded labourers. ('Bonded' refers to those who have fallen into debt to a landowner who deducts repayments from their wages and for whom they are obliged to work until the debt is paid off. Those landowners normally charge extremely high interest rates and often, when the bonded labourer dies, the remaining debt is passed on to his children who are thus bonded to the landlord in the same way.)

Father Joson impressed with his serious and thought-through approach to development in India, and his love for the suffering Dalits was very evident. The Pragati Social Service Society (PSSS) concentrated much of their effort on the formation of self-help groups in villages and slum areas, with the main aim of empowering women and girls in those communities. Among other things, these self-help groups set up initiatives to pool their savings and provide loans so as to help people avoid falling into inescapable debt. They also ran Balawadies (nursery schools), aimed at encouraging children into education. And it was in these Balawadies that we had begun to work with PSSS in 2004 in order to serve Mary's Meals to the poorest young children. Before long we also started to provide meals in little 'non-formal' schools being set up by PSSS in slums and villages, so that working children could for the first time, benefit from an education. Five years later, in November 2009, I once again travelled to northern India by train with Father Joson, to revisit these non-formal schools and to help plan the support of new ones.

In a village in Haryana, we visited a small cluster of homes made out of plastic and cardboard in a place known simply as Slum Area Sector 7. Maybe the people who lived here had never given it a proper name because they had no legal rights and could be moved on at any time by developers. This had happened to them four years previously and nice new houses now stood where they had once lived in huts. Among their pitiful homes, in a patch of waste land, a sheet of tarpaulin had been suspended between four poles and underneath a teacher was introducing a little huddle of children to the Hindi alphabet. A circle of curious parents looked on. Ten-year-old Biba arrived late, carrying her baby sister. She had been working all morning in one of the 'rich people's houses', she told us. She would return there that evening to continue working, but meanwhile she was looking after her sister while her mum continued to work. I noticed a young woman standing near us, transfixed by the sight of her child learning to write, and I asked her why she had never before thought of sending her daughter to school. She looked at me as if I was mad and eventually answered, 'Why would we? We are poor.'

Under the tarpaulin sheet the teacher was doing an admirable job of keeping order, given that sitting still and reciting the alphabet for hours was a new experience for these children. Suddenly, though, the children leapt up, screaming with delight, and despite the teacher's protestations they raced off down the path leading back towards the main road. Eventually I realized that they had sprinted to meet their lunch, which was arriving in metal pots carried on a pedal rickshaw (lunch here was cooked at a nearby orphanage). Soon the children were back sitting in orderly rows as rice, vegetable sauce and chapattis were dished out to them. Before she began eating herself, I noticed our friend Biba tearing her chapatti up and feeding small bits of it to her gurgling baby sister. Silence descended as many little hands scooped up every last morsel of food served to them. Before the lessons resumed, I noticed out of the corner of my eye that one of the fathers, who had been watching earlier, was sitting with his boy and was painstakingly copying out the alphabet letters from his textbook; his first attempts to write taken under the proud gaze of his young son.

When we arrived at another centre in Ghaziabad, near Delhi, a high-caste Hindu lady and a Catholic nun were trying to teach the alphabet to around thirty Muslim children crowded into a tiny dark room. Three world religions, in a nation scarred by bitter sectarian divides, were brought together in their desire to see the hungry child fed and educated. When we had recently opened this centre, the children had come straight from their work as rag pickers, sometimes with huge sacks of putrid garbage over their shoulders, attracted by the hot meals on offer. Some of the young boys in the little class were street performers and monkey charmers, and for a little while they showed us their tricks. Ten-year-old Saroja then arrived with a broad grin, and explained she had been working in rubbish 'since before the sun rose this morning'. Her friend Moni told us that she looked after the family's goats and how one was stolen by a man on a motorbike the previous day.

'I screamed but no one came to help me,' she said indignantly.

From there we travelled into the countryside of Uttar Pradesh, and as we went we passed more children working among the sugar cane. We were welcomed into a little mud-hut village, which had been home for forty years to a Bangladeshi refugee community. Every year the village was flooded. The previous year the entire community had lived for one month on a nearby canal embankment until the waters subsided. I asked them if they ever thought of moving and in reply they asked me 'But where could we go?' They had no electricity and one handpump served the whole village. Here our little centre was operating under a thatched 'lean-to' shelter adjoining someone's house. The children sat in a circle in the village courtyard and it began to rain gently as the food was being served to them. Chitaranjan Khan, one of the older men, who could still remember life in Bangladesh before they fled, told me proudly that his three daughters 'had grown wings' in our little centre and had now moved on to mainstream schools nearby.

In nearby Vagra, the children were being taught under a huge old tree in the centre of the village. Two water buffalo were looking at the scene with interest, and while I chatted to the teacher one of his pupils put up his hand to inform us politely that a goat was eating the alphabet chart behind us. The conditions were not ideal for teaching, but the teacher was delighted with the progress that his thirty-one Hindu pupils were making.

The light was fading fast by the time Father Joson and I arrived at Kear Colony, a small slum on the edge of Karnal, two hours north of Delhi. Nineteen families lived there in makeshift tarpaulin and plastic tents erected among enormous piles of rubbish. Outside some tents people were brewing their evening meals on cow-dung fires, while in a space behind the tents a few boys were playing cricket. In the shadow of a high brick wall two elderly women sifted methodically through shreds of paper, plastic bottles and an endless variety of other refuse, patiently placing in piles the items they could sell. Everyone in this community played a part in this recycling process on which their survival depended. As I watched, two men arrived on their rickshaws (three-wheel pedal carts) on which were tied huge sacks of unsorted rubbish. This they had gathered from the streets and bins around Karnal and it was added to the piles to be sorted through.

A family invited us to sit with them outside one of their tents to share their Chai (sweet milky tea) and to hear their story. They had left their homes in Chattishaghar, a state 700 miles to the south-east, about twenty years previously when drought and lack of paid work had forced them to move in order to survive. All of the men spent each day on rickshaws collecting rubbish, but they explained that none of them had ever saved enough to buy their own (a rickshaw cost about £60); instead they had to hire them on a daily basis. On a bad day the value of the rubbish they collected did not even cover the cost of the hire, and then they also had to pay the local landowner for the right to pitch their tents there. Each day was a desperate struggle for survival and none of the fifty-five children in Kear Colony ever attended school. We discussed the idea of setting up an outdoor school there and providing Mary's Meals so that their children could attend. There was much delight at the idea. It was now quite dark and they refilled our cups. A young man held a little home-made kerosene lamp beside me so that I could write notes as together we formed a plan, while a huge orange sun began to set behind the mounds of rubbish where the two women continued to work.

Finally, we visited Somalaka, where we had opened one of the first of these 'non-formal' schools five years previously. Here most of the children were Sikhs, belonging to a caste that made and repaired keys. No one here had even thought of school as a possibility before the centre opened. The children, wearing turbans, sat peacefully in rows, and the difference in their behaviour and that of the more rowdy children in the new centres I had just visited was marked. Lunch was a little late and while we waited Father Joson asked them if they would be upset if the food did not come. A little boy thought about for it for a moment before he said solemnly, 'No, not upset. But we will be hungry.'

Before we left, the teacher told us astonishing news. She explained that of the forty children they had begun teaching here five years ago, twenty-five had now moved on into formal education. Five of those children, now teenage girls, had come back to the centre today and, after helping to serve the food to the younger children, they sang us a song which offered us a 'hearty welcome' and told us that in their hearts they had 'love like a mountain and peace like a river'.

More than ever, the startling power of one daily meal served in a place of education became evident in those oppressed communities in India, where previously people had not even dared hope their children could go to school.

And so we went on, meeting all sorts of communities in all sorts of countries, to discuss the possibility of them serving Mary's Meals to their impoverished children. We began to work with the semi-nomadic Turkana people in the desert lands of northern Kenya, in a landscape that overwhelmed me with its terrifying scale and remote beauty, among a people whose lives depended upon their herds of cattle, goats, donkeys and camels. Endemic malnutrition was a feature of Turkana life. A government survey just before my first visit revealed that of every 1,000 babies born in Turkana, 159 died almost immediately. In little thatched nurseries, malnourished young children began to eat daily meals, served by women whose necks were stretched by colourful beads. Climate change here was making their traditional way of life unsustainable and many Turkana needed to find a new way to live and support their families. The education of their children – starting with the youngest – was becoming more important than ever.

Meanwhile, 400 miles further south in Kenya, we began serving meals in sprawling urban slums around Nairobi and Eldoret, where many children who previously lived on the streets and sniffed glue to stave off the pain of hunger began to come to school, drawn in by the promise of a good meal.

And in neighbouring Uganda we also began to meet children enduring a very specific and acute suffering. Here we were providing meals for children who had been forced to flee the atrocities of Joseph Kony's infamous Lord's Resistance Army. One evening, in 2005, I visited some of those children who had become 'night commuters', in a place called Layibi, on the edge of Gulu. We arrived after dark and our headlights shone on the gates of a church compound, which swung open as we approached. Inside a tiny courtyard they sat huddled in tight rows; hundreds of small children and a few adults. They stared at us in curious silence, blankets draped around their shoulders. Some of the smallest children were already asleep, curled up beside their older brothers and sisters. We had some whispered conversations and then, a little later, before they entered the security of the church for the night, the people prayed together and sang a song to Our Lady. Their quiet harmonies rose unexpectedly through the silent evening like wind rustling through trees. Then the older children shook their younger siblings awake and helped them with their blankets and rolled mats into the church. Inside they lay down in rows beside the pews that had been stacked to one side. These children were among 40,000 'night commuters' who, every evening, left their homes to seek security in the centre of towns such as Gulu. To stay at home would have meant running the very real risk of abduction by the Lord's Resistance Army (LRA). Over 1.4 million people had been forced to flee their homes and were living in terrible conditions in huge displaced camps. Many of those people were now heading south to Kampala to start a new life away from this terror in a place where their children could go to school – and in some of those schools we were now providing Mary's Meals.

The next day, in Kampala, I visited a place called Kireka on the edge of the capital city. Here, men, women and children spent their days quarrying gravel to survive. From a cleft in the rock on the steep hillside, black smoke billowed upwards. Men hammered out large chunks of the scorched stone and carried them in adapted plastic jerrycans to hundreds of women and children sitting on the slopes below. With little home-made hammers – pieces of lead attached to a rough stick – they spent their days smashing the lumps of rock into small pieces. From all over the hill came the sound of lead cracking against rock, while way above, from a little church clinging to the top of the highest cliff, the sound of a choir practising their hymns floated over us. I approached a group of young mothers and their children, who sat hammering among piles of dusty rocks. When I said hello, they invited me to try breaking the rock. I began hammering as I talked to them and felt the sharp splinters in my face, and wondered how they could possibly do this all day without losing their sight. They told me they were nearly all Acholi from the north – but some of them were Sudanese refugees. They were paid three pence for each small jerrycan of gravel, and they produced about eighty of these in a week. Most of their children now attended the nearby primary school, where we had just begun providing Mary's Meals, and so at least received one good meal every day. There were less children working here now, but there were still far too many, like the three orphans they pointed out to me, who worked nearby beside their elderly grandmother in the shadow of an overhanging cliff. One of the women, called Stella, told me how she had very nearly been killed recently. She had been trapped under a rock fall and screamed until other workers rushed to pull her out. Seconds after they had freed her, a huge rock, 'the size of a bus', fell from the cliff above, landing exactly where she had been. But all of them agreed that even this was better than life in camps. And then they laughed as they noticed a speck of blood on my finger and made jokes about my soft white hands as they took the hammer back from me before I did any further damage.

'Life here is very hard,' said Stella, becoming serious again, 'but at least now we can try to provide for ourselves instead of surviving on handouts in the camps.'

That was one of the more common misconceptions or prejudices that I encountered while fund-raising; that progress in Africa was not being made because there was a handout culture and that people preferred to do nothing and wait for aid. In my own experience that was very rarely the case. I have not met, anywhere, more hard-working people than some of the farmers I spent time with in Liberia, or those working all day in Delhi for pitiful pay in order to feed their families, or those like Stella working in that quarry to survive. And most of them had a burning desire to be free from dependence on aid. That is why those parents I met living in poverty almost invariably craved for their children to be educated, for they knew, ultimately, that was how their children could become independent, and they were willing to make extraordinary sacrifices for that to be possible.

And who knows when any of us, however hard-working, might be in need of some aid. Certainly there were many living on the southern coasts of India, Sri Lanka and Indonesia who had never before required aid until, during a few awful moments on Boxing Day 2005, their lives were ruined. In the early hours of that morning, off the west coast of Sumatra, beneath the ocean floor, the Indian Plate was subducted by the Burma Plate, triggering the third-largest earthquake ever recorded. The series of tsunami waves that were produced killed over 230,000 people in fourteen countries around the Indian Ocean. It was one of the worst natural disasters ever, and even before that scale could be fully understood, the world was stunned by the news woken up to that Boxing Day morning. Later that day, Father Joson phoned me to explain that the Tamil Nadu coastline of south-east India had been devastated and that he and his co-workers were trying to provide immediate emergency aid – indeed some of his colleagues living near the affected areas had already started helping. He pleaded for Mary's Meals to raise funds and for me to travel to join them and help plan a response. My first reactions were selfish. I had been desperately looking forward to my Christmas break with my family as I had been travelling a lot, and initially, I said to Julie, I felt it would not be fair for me to go. She felt strongly otherwise, saying that I should be with our friends in India, and that I should make a quick visit there immediately so we could launch a public appeal for help with a concrete action plan that could be supported. Ever since Julie and I had taken emergency aid to Bosnia-Herzegovina during the war, we had been cautious about rushing to get involved in every emergency reported by the news. We had seen in that situation, and others since, that some charitable organizations used such events to fly their flag and raise a lot of money, without necessarily being the best placed to work in the given area or being well-equipped to meet the specific needs. So we had formed a policy, whereby we would only respond and launch an emergency appeal if we were already working in the country where the disaster took place and believed we had the ability to deliver a well-designed, focused response. If not, we would suggest that people donated to other, better-placed organizations. On this occasion, because our partners in India, PSSS, were already in the area and had years of experience of working in those communities, we were convinced we should act.

So it was that a few days after the deadly wave had struck, I once again found myself travelling with Father Joson, this time southwards from Chennai towards some villages on the Tamil Nadu coastline.

The little fishing village of Arriyanattu, on the edge of Nagapattinam, must have once looked like a picture postcard. With its thatched cottages amid palm trees on the edge of a sandy beach dotted with colourful fishing boats, it had all the ingredients. In the space of a few awful hours, that idyllic image had been chewed up and spat out by an enormous wave that roared out of the glistening sea without warning. When we arrived nothing was how it should have been, or where it should have been. At the top of the beach, in a sandy space where the railway station used to be, a large wooden fishing boat lay beside the track. The row of cottages nearest the sea had been replaced by a pulverized mess of smashed boats, bricks, plastic cups, outboard engines, fishing nets, school bags, books, tree stumps and human remains. The stench that had begun to invade our nostrils even a few miles inland, as we approached the village, was now almost unbearable. Amid this wreckage, a young man sat crying on the concrete foundation of his home; all that was left of his house. We began speaking to him. His name was Kennedy Raj and he told us he had lost his father and they had not yet found his body.

Behind him a team of volunteers, wearing masks over their noses and mouths, were working to clear up the mess and recover the bodies. They were using their JCB cautiously.

Already that morning they had found 100 bodies. As the remains of a young woman were lifted from beneath a squashed house, her brother, Thennarson, and his wife, Malathi, sat nearby crying quietly. For them, though, the horror had only just begun. Within the next hour the bodies of their two dead children were found. As the volunteers covered their remains in white disinfectant powder and carried them out on a stretcher, Malathi became hysterical. She screamed at the sea and the sky, and began to hit herself until she fell sobbing on the beach. She was joined by other mothers who held each other and, in turn, clawed at the sand and screamed as their loved ones were placed beside a huge hole that the JCB had dug in the beach, which would become their final resting place. Here and there, amid the carnage, people sat on the places where their homes used to be and stared at the ocean. Three young boys perched on a fallen tree, with scarves pressed across their mouths and noses, watched with fascination and horror as the JCB worked its way through the wreckage of their village.

We found most of the survivors from Ariyanatta a few miles away in a Hindu temple called Nilathachi Amman. When they had fled the village they ran there and had since slept in the courtyard enclosed by the temple walls. Washing lines were strung between ancient, ornate pillars, round which peeked little smiling children, apparently oblivious to the horror through which they had just lived. As the late-afternoon sun dipped behind the walls, a few boys played cricket in a dusty corner, while three women sat huddled together on some stone steps. They were three generations of the same family and the younger two had both lost children to the tsunami. They began to tell me about living conditions there in the temple, explaining they desperately needed powdered milk for some of the babies. Suddenly the grandmother screamed and began crying. The other two held her tight and together they rocked back and forth, sobbing.

'If the government had given us some warning this wouldn't have happened!' said a woman beside them. She pointed up at the thirty-foot-high temple wall, saying, 'The wave was that height.'

A group of children gathered round and began to tell us their escape stories. Some had climbed swaying palm trees and clung there until the water had subsided. A little girl told me she was watching television when she heard this funny noise and saw water appearing. She ran as fast as she could and just managed to escape.

'I have lost my brother, though,' she said.

'Yes, we've been looking for him everywhere,' her little friends told me.

Beside them was a young blind man with a very small baby. They explained he had lost his wife and his two other children. His baby had been found unharmed by his neighbours, miraculously floating among the debris. I wondered who was left to help the blind man care for his baby.

I asked their mothers when they might think about going back to Ariyanattu (without telling them about the horrors we had witnessed there that morning).

'We are getting some food and medical care here – what have we got to go back to there? Only mud!' answered a lady in the crowd.

'We feel helpless, though,' said another voice.

Reaching the Outcastes

'We can't stay here sleeping outside like this, but we've got nothing ... nothing left. All we knew was fishing, but ...' her voice trails off and she looks ashamed, 'we're scared to go near the sea now.'

The next day back in Chennai I discussed with our partner organization, PSSS, about how we could best help. We decided to concentrate our efforts on that village of Ariyanattu, starting with the immediate needs of those who had lost their homes, their livelihoods and their loved ones, while we assessed how to help them recover. We provided the funds for two nuns, connected to PSSS, to live among the homeless of Naggapattinam for a few weeks. They would help the people with their day-to-day needs and carry out an assessment of how we could help them take the first steps towards recovery.

Our planning meeting ended after 10 p.m. and Father Amil, a local priest who had been working flat out since the wave hit, announced he was off to load another lorry of rice for a coastal village. I asked him where they were buying the rice from and he explained that they weren't buying it. He had been out on the streets with a loudspeaker, asking people to donate rice. Hundreds of people were responding and tonnes of donated rice were pouring in – even schoolchildren were turning up with cups of rice. The people of India desperately needed help from people in other countries, given the almost unprecedented scale of the disaster, but they were certainly not just waiting for Western aid to arrive. The kindness was a sign of hope that I clung to amid the horror of those few days; as was the support that began to be provided from all over the world in response to our latest appeal. This allowed us, during the next year, to provide health care and temporary shelters, and to replace fishing boats so that people here could once again venture out to sea to earn their living.

To witness the horror of Arrayantu was traumatic. Even though we had come to help, and we certainly did over the coming months, I felt as if I had intruded in their unimaginable grief. Like others around us who had come to help there, I took photographs. But later, when I looked at them, I felt ashamed that while people screamed for their lost loved ones I had been there taking pictures. I decided then that sometimes, even when you felt pictures were essential to help with the raising of desperately needed money, it is better to leave your camera in your pocket.

After that hellish day in the village, having watched over a hundred bodies laid to rest in the gaping hole in the beach, without anyone there to identify or even count them, we headed on south. We arrived exhausted at an unlikely place called Velankanni, a vast shrine, with churches and huge basilicas. It was like an Indian version of Lourdes. I was incredulous. Father Joson explained that there was a tradition here that some time during the sixteenth century, Our Lady with her infant son appeared to a lower-caste Hindu boy who was carrying milk to a customer's home. She asked him for some milk for her son and he gave her some. On reaching the customer's home, the worried boy apologized for his lateness and tried to explain the reduced amount of milk by relating the incident that had occurred on his way. As he did so, the milk pot became full and started overflowing. The man, another Hindu, realized something miraculous had happened, and accompanied the boy back along the street and also saw

Our Lady. Many other miracles began to occur there in the years that followed – most famously the saving of some Portuguese sailors whose boat was sinking in a violent storm off this coast and who, after praying to Our Lady, ran aground safely at this very spot. So convinced were they that they had been miraculously delivered from drowning, that they built a chapel in honour of Our Lady and she became venerated here by Christians and Hindus alike as 'Arokia Matha' – Mother of Good Health. During the celebration of her feast each year over a million pilgrims – both Christians and Hindus – gather in Velankanni, and each year hundreds of miraculous cures are reported.

Sleep did not come easily that night despite my exhaustion, and I prayed to Our Lady that she might intercede for those suffering at the hands of a storm much worse than any that afflicted those Portuguese sailors and that, in the same way she had used that small offering of milk, she might, too, use our little acts of kindness and make with them something beautiful.

11

Friends in High Places

> Not what we give,
> But what we share,
> For the gift without the giver
> Is bare.
>
> JAMES RUSSELL LOWELL

Lucy MacDonald, who was my PA for several years, had a wonderful knack of passing on messages to me in amusing ways. Her desk was in the 'new shed' next door to mine. Normally she was able to transfer incoming calls directly to my desk, but sometimes if something urgent came up when I was already on the line she found other ways to let me know. One day, in 2010, while I was deep in a telephone conversation, I glanced out of the window above my desk to see Lucy standing there with a big grin, holding a piece of cardboard on which she had written with a thick marker pen: 'The Pope wants to meet you and the Queen will be there too.'

Pope Benedict was about to make an historic first state visit by a Pope to the UK, and he was to be received at the beginning of his trip by the Queen at Holyrood Palace in Edinburgh. I was thrilled to be among the guests invited to the historical meeting. And it became a very special day for Mary's Meals when we were also invited by the Catholic Church in Scotland to be present on the streets of Edinburgh, among the crowds, in order to raise awareness of our work and collect donations. Many volunteers from all over Scotland, Ireland and England arrived to help us for the day. On a bright sunny morning, with the eyes of the world watching as the 'popemobile' made its way along Princes Street, blue Mary's Meals T-shirts were visible everywhere among the crowd.

I had met Queen Elizabeth before. About a year previously, someone from Buckingham Palace had called me to say the Queen wished to invite me for lunch. I really was not entirely sure if one of my friends was playing an elaborate hoax until I received a written invitation some days later. A few weeks afterwards I turned up at the front gates of Buckingham Palace, approached one of those famous guards, in his red uniform and huge bearskin hat, and showed him my letter of invitation. He ushered me in, along with ten other guests, and before long I was being introduced to the Queen and the Duke of Edinburgh. The Queen surprised me by being so well informed about our work. She had a warm and sincere interest in Liberia and our work there, and shared some vivid and amusing memories of a visit she had made there some years previously. At lunch I found myself sitting beside the famous actress Joanna Lumley. She was incredibly gracious and kind to me, noticing that I was having a bit of difficulty with the correct order of assorted cutlery in front of me. Every now and then she would nudge me discreetly and point. I still don't know why I was invited. I looked at the other nine guests round the table and could not figure out anything in particular that we all had in common. I asked one of the aides afterwards what the purpose of the lunch had been and he said, 'No reason at all apart from the fact the Queen and the Duke of Edinburgh like to invite people to lunch with them now and again.'

Afterwards my mum and Julie were desperate to know what I had eaten at lunch, but I could not remember a single item on the menu. I have no doubt it was delicious but I must have been so nervous it was entirely wasted on me. Ever since then, whenever I have been invited to do something in a social setting that makes me very nervous, I remind myself of that lunch and tell myself that I should now be able to take anything in my stride.

We continued to receive all sorts of wonderful invitations to meet and speak to groups of interested people all over the world. It became increasingly hard to keep track of how these invitations came about and sometimes I would arrive a little confused about why I was there and what exactly was expected of me. One winter's evening I arrived on a delayed flight into Chicago and took a taxi through deep snow to the address in my diary. In a lovely warm and spacious apartment I found a crowd of people waiting for me, wine glasses in hand, perched on sofas and tabletops. I hardly had time to put down my suitcase and take off my jacket when my host (who I now remembered I had met at a previous event in this city) had introduced me to the assembly and asked me to speak about Mary's Meals. Afterwards I had just begun to chat to some of the guests as they departed (I had kept them late due to my delayed flight) when the kindly host gave me an address on a slip of paper and told me she had vacated her apartment for the night so I could go and stay there. Once again I was humbled and embarrassed by an act of startling generosity, and before long my taxi was depositing me outside one of those landmark Chicago skyscrapers. I remember waking in the middle of that night and staring out of the window at a breathtaking view of thousands of twinkling lights against an ink-black sky, and for a few minutes wondering where in the world I was.

It was becoming harder to make judgements about which invitations to accept and which to decline. It was impossible to know who might be at one of these gatherings or how receptive their hearts would be.

In 2010, having said yes to a warm invitation from a friend of a friend, I travelled to meet another group of people I did not know – this time in New York – having no idea that I was about to encounter some people who would come to play a very special role in the Mary's Meals story. The connection had been made by our friends in Miami, who had founded Mary's Meals USA. They told me their friends, the Laffont family, would love me to come and meet them next time I was in New York, and so we arranged a date. Usually, if I had meetings in the New York area I would stay at a rambling old friary in Newark, New Jersey, that was home to the Franciscan Friars of the Renewal. One of the friars, Brother Francis, was an old friend of mine. He had lived in the Craig Lodge community as a young man just at the time when I began collecting aid for Bosnia-Herzegovina, and had often accompanied me as I drove around Scotland with my truck to pick up donations of aid. He was the perfect co-worker for this task, being one of the tallest and strongest people I have ever met. It was like having a human crane in the back of the truck. For some years now he had been a Franciscan and it was a special blessing for me to stay in their community where I could enjoy some peaceful prayer time in the early mornings and evenings, before heading into New York for meetings. On this particular trip I was accompanied by Milona, and Brother Francis kindly offered to drive us into Manhattan, a place that neither of us were very familiar with, to the home of the Laffonts. They lived in a wonderful house on the Upper East Side and we were warmly welcomed into their home, which was packed full of their friends. We were perhaps a slightly unusual sight – Brother Francis at six foot ten inches tall in his Franciscan habit always tended to attract attention. Ana Laffont was perched on the stairs with some small children who had the excited expression of those avoiding bedtime, while their dad, Philippe, asked us to tell them the story of Mary's Meals. After we did so there was a flurry of questions and we chatted to a number of the guests who wanted to get involved. Philippe had to leave, but before he did so he announced to the room that he would match any donation that any of them cared to make to Mary's Meals. I began to realize that we were meeting some very unusual people, who had enormous resources at their disposal and hearts to match.

This was the beginning of a wonderful friendship with the Laffonts. Over the coming months and years Ana devoted an increasing amount of time to our work, eventually becoming the Chair of Mary's Meals USA. She threw herself into learning about every aspect of Mary's Meals, including trips to Africa, Dalmally and Medjugorje. And this deep understanding of all that was involved allowed her and Philippe to help us in very particular and thoughtful ways. They formed a deep appreciation that Mary's Meals was first of all a grassroots movement – that this was an intrinsic part of our mission and that all who supported were of equal value no matter the type or size of donation. They loved this approach and wanted to help us protect it and help the movement grow by enabling us to tell the story in new ways to bigger audiences. In addition, given that they had enormous experience themselves of managing fast-growing organizations, they saw that the fish farmer from Argyll and his co-workers could use a bit of help in that area too.

I began speaking to Ana about an opportunity we had to make an amazing film about Mary's Meals. For some time I had been a fan of a film-making company in Brooklyn called Grassroots. Ruth and I had watched one of their films a couple of years previously and commented that they would be the perfect people to make a film about Mary's Meals one day. I had almost forgotten about them until Patty, who worked in our New Jersey office, asked me at the end of a call one day if she could finish work early to go and do an interview with an organization called Grassroots, who were making a film on a different topic.

'Absolutely!' I said. 'As long as you mention Mary's Meals to them! I have always wanted them to make a film about our work.'

To my amazement Patty came back to say that Grassroots already knew about our work and would love to make a documentary about Mary's Meals. I began talking to them and realized that they were very serious indeed about this, but I also learnt that making such a film was not cheap and not something the Mary's Meals low-cost approach could support. When I mentioned it to Ana and Philippe they immediately saw this as a wonderful way to help us tell the story of Mary's Meals to a much bigger audience and they offered to fund the film.

So, a few weeks after those initial chats, I found myself with the Grassroots film crew on a whirlwind tour of Malawi, Kenya and India. In each of those places we spent time with children whose lives were being changed by Mary's Meals. We wanted their stories to be the basis of the film. We did a lot of hard work to plan it all, setting up places to film and people to meet, but in the end the most amazing parts of the film were things we could never have set up.

In Eldoret, Kenya, we had organized to film in a rubbish dump where many children spent their days scavenging for items to sell to recyclers, sniffing glue to stave off the pain of hunger. We were providing school meals in Eldoret and could see this was helping many children leave the streets and go to school for the first time. We arrived at 5 a.m. at the dump and began filming. As well as children there were many adults, some obviously high on glue, and many bore wounds on their faces and limbs. It was a frightening place. As they filmed, a crowd surrounded them – some friendly, others not. At one point Cliff, one of the crew, called over to me.

'Magnus, there is a small boy here you should meet.'

He led over a little boy called Muksi, perhaps eight years old, who was saying over and over again, 'I want to go to school. I want to go to school …'

I talked to our Kenyan colleagues, asking their advice about the best thing to do.

'Well, we can take him to a school here and he will receive Mary's Meals,' said Abel, with his hand on the boy's shoulder, 'but we really need to find somewhere for him to live.'

'There is a children's home on the other side of the city,' said Charles. 'Who knows, they might be able to take him in.'

Before long we were driving across the city with Muksi and found the home, with a neat, brightly painted play area outside. A couple of us went in and introduced ourselves. When the people who ran the home learnt we were from Mary's Meals they became very animated.

'Oh, you are from Mary's Meals! We have always wanted to meet someone from Mary's Meals. You have started providing meals in the school across the street from us. All the children who live with us here go there and so are now eating every day at school, thank God! We want to thank you with all our hearts!'

I felt this was a really good moment to tell them about the little boy in the car outside.

'Yes, we have space. We can take him – we are happy to!'

Thus it was that Muksi's life was transformed in front of our eyes. I couldn't believe it when I glanced at my watch and noticed it was still only 10 a.m. After Abel and Charles had sorted out arrangements at the home, and ensured we could check up on his welfare, we invited Muksi to hang out with us for the day as we continued to film at schools in the area.

By the end of the morning he was behind the camera. I even saw him laugh for the first time. By midday, we realized we had been working for eight hours without eating and called in at a restaurant by the roadside. It happened to be rather formal with white tablecloths and suited waiters who looked distinctly unimpressed as we walked in with the dirty little boy in rags, who did not smell at all good. We took him to the bathroom and scrubbed him as best we could before sitting down to some chicken and chips. At one point during lunch one of us asked Muksi when his birthday was. Of course he didn't know.

'Well, today is your birthday!' we all told him together.

The film that Grassroots produced, *Child 31*, is a wonderful, moving representation of Mary's Meals. It has become the most effective tool I have ever had to help us tell the story and explain what Mary's Meals really is. We encouraged supporters all over the world to organize screenings of *Child 31* and the response was amazing. Over 1,300 people showed up for the 'premiere' at our Open Day in Glasgow. Former Prime Minister Gordon Brown, who had by then been appointed United Nations Special Envoy for Global Education, attended the event and introduced the film. I had got to know him a little and was struck by his genuine long-held passion to help eradicate extreme poverty. As we chatted before going on stage in Glasgow, he asked me to tell him more about the work of Mary's Meals. Afterwards he made an extremely powerful speech, ending it by saying:

'Ensuring every child has the opportunity to go to school and learn is a long-standing passion of mine. Education breaks the cycle of poverty and unlocks better health and job prospects.

'As I travel throughout the world on this mission, as the UN Envoy for Global Education, I don't need a calling card. I will just leave a copy of *Child 31* and show what can be done to encourage children into education.'

Over 600 screenings of the film, which we had subtitled in seven languages, were organized in many different countries. In many European countries, as well as the USA, Canada, the United Arab Emirates, Australia, Liberia, Malawi and India, people gathered to watch the film in all sorts of venues – cinemas, palaces, sitting rooms, schools and universities – while in several countries the film was broadcast on TV. I had hoped this film would allow me to cut down on travelling to give talks, but that was naive – the initial screenings provided opportunities to speak to many new audiences. Given how often I watched the film in venues far from home, the fact that three of my own children – Bethany, Toby and Anna – appear fleetingly in the film was a special little treat for me at times. Grassroots had filmed at a fund-raising event in our local Dalmally primary school and as there are only about forty children in the school, it is not surprising my children and their friends appeared in the final edit. Often, at the part when Anna, among a crowd of classmates, smiles and waves at the camera, I would surprise the person beside me in the audience by nudging them and saying proudly, 'That's my daughter by the way!'

When the film was aired on a national TV station in Croatia their website crashed as it became inundated with people wishing to donate, and over the following months

Mary's Meals doubled its income in that country. Everywhere our work grew like never before because of *Child 31*, and to this day it continues to move thousands of people to help. Various celebrities, including Celine Dion, provided sincere video endorsements after watching the film. Annie Lennox said:

> If one fact should resonate in our minds after viewing *Child 31*, it might be that the average cost of a lunch in the United States could feed a child in a developing country for an entire year.
>
> Mary's Meals feeds over half a million children every single day, encouraging them to attend school and receive an essential education at the same time. It's not rocket science and it really works.

I particularly liked her last sentence. Some development experts criticize Mary's Meals (and advise the governments and institutional donors whom they work for not to fund us), suggesting we make it all sound too simple and that this approach of feeding children cannot be sustainable. The environments we work in, the challenges we need to overcome to ensure the schools have food every day, and the problems that people in poverty battle with, are certainly anything but simple. But our core approach is. Annie Lennox, like everyone else who has met us and visited a Mary's Meals project, certainly knows we are not rocket scientists, but she is also in no doubt that we don't need to be. The tens of thousands who support us with small donations all over the world and the thousands who cook for the kids in their communities are generally not rocket scientists or 'development experts' either, but they immediately see that this approach is necessary and life-changing.

And the question about sustainability always bewilders me because I am not sure what can be more essential in creating long-term sustainable solutions than ensuring children receive the nutrition they require and an education. The word itself – 'sustainability' – can be problematic because I notice that people tend to use it in various and often vague ways. I once asked a room full of MBA students who had raised the subject of sustainability to define the word for me, and the spectrum of answers put forward was startling. Actually, 'sustainable development' was defined in 1987 by the Brundtland Commission, which was established by the UN to do just that, as 'development that meets the needs of the present without compromising the ability of future generations to meet their own needs'. I cannot see how Mary's Meals could ever be accused of falling short against that definition and I can only suppose that the issue is much more about timescales. These sorts of funders normally expect an 'exit strategy' after three to five years of funding. It seems the perceived wisdom in development circles is that if a project is not complete after that length of time, then it is flawed. We chose to take a different view of how long it takes to build something that will really last and fundamentally change things for the better – and can make that choice because our work is supported by a global movement of people who agree. We choose to create a sustainable approach based on their generosity.

But there are connected conversations that are harder to reconcile and more disturbing than a difference in opinions about timetables. Once I met with people from an organization running schools in Haiti who realized that many of the kids coming to their schools were chronically malnourished. They asked us about our model and we expressed interest in expanding our project to their schools, so the children would be fed. But they did not want to partner with us because they did not think our approach was 'sustainable'. I asked them to suggest how they would do this in a 'sustainable way' and they said they wanted to work on some things related to micro finance. That was several years ago and to my knowledge the kids attending their schools have never received school meals. I would rather approach this the other way round. The first imperative is the hungry child in front of us. They need food today, not in ten years' time.

It makes me sad, when people in development almost talk like these children are the 'problem' rather than the principle builders of a new and brighter future. Children of today should never be sacrificed to the Moloch of a future that none of us can know. And the future belongs to those children at least as much as it does to any of us who think we are experts in development.

But the seeking of celebrity endorsements for *Child 31* also prompted some laughs. One day a team of us brainstormed and wrote up a list of famous people. One of the names we agreed on was Pamela Stephenson (the comedian, writer and wife of Billy Connolly). When someone retyped our list they accidentally wrote Pamela Anderson (it wasn't me, honestly) and one of the team then duly contacted the agent of Pamela Anderson (as in star of *Baywatch*) to ask if she would endorse *Child 31*. It was only after she had come back and said that she would love to do this that we realized the mix-up. We were reassured anew of the universal appeal of Mary's Meals.

Meanwhile, in addition to *Child 31*, the Laffonts suggested another precious gift to Mary's Meals, but this time I needed some persuasion. They told me about the Bridgespan Group, a consultancy firm that specialized in helping charities develop strategies to expand and replicate their successes. Bridgespan had grown out of Bain, the very prestigious, international management consultancy firm that advised many of the world's largest corporations and governments. Ana and Philippe believed that Bridgespan – who worked only with organizations they felt had potential to replicate their success on a larger scale – might be interested in working with us to help plan for the future, and if so they would be willing to fund this gift also. A lot of this was very new to me, including the language. Terms like 'scaling up', 'tipping points' and 'enhancing effectiveness' all sounded foreign and a bit scary. While I certainly recognized the need to prepare for further growth by strengthening our organization, so that we might continue effectively to feed growing numbers of children, I was concerned about doing something that might undermine our values. I found it hard to believe that these high-powered consultants, hugely respected by very successful businessmen in the USA, would be able to take seriously our aversion to setting monetary targets or our related desire to recognize that ultimately we were not in charge. And I suppose I was a little intimidated, too, by the thought of working with these highly trained, academically gifted people. The thought of them sitting in my shed to discuss strategy with us embarrassed me a little. But by now I knew and trusted the Laffonts enough to agree to meet with Bridgespan, who indicated they would indeed be happy to work with Mary's Meals, believing they could help us at our stage in development.

At a second meeting I spelt out my concerns, stating several things relating to our values that were not up for debate. The respectful way they listened and responded left me convinced by the end of the meeting that this was something we should do. The Laffonts' generosity gave us the opportunity to work with Bridgespan for six months, during which time they helped us form a robust 'growth plan'. During this time we had some wonderful conversations and found ways to reconcile the 'divine providence approach' with the need to plan thoroughly and carefully. Through this work I became good friends with all in the Bridgespan team that we worked with, and today two of them continue to be very involved in Mary's Meals as board members. A few months after that work with them was finished I visited Boston for the first time, to do a TV interview. When Bridgespan heard I would be in their hometown they invited me to their offices to chat with their staff. They surprised me by having their entire team in a room waiting for me, as well as their people in New York and California on video link-ups. They invited me to talk to them about my experience of leading Mary's Meals and how I had felt about working with them. After I did that quite briefly, we spent the rest of an hour having a fascinating discussion, developing the theme of reconciling planning with divine providence. By the end of that conversation it was very clear to me that many of them were also motivated by their own deeply held faiths and all were genuinely respectful of the Mary's Meals approach. This meant an enormous amount to me. I had understood by then that this work with Bridgespan did not undermine or threaten any of our dearly held values; rather it strengthened them and gave us a greater confidence to share, protect and live them. One of the approaches we explored and articulated more clearly than before, was our belief that the Mary's Meals family should be guided by the principles of 'solidarity' and 'subsidiarity'. While a new central organization – Mary's Meals International – would work to ensure all the Mary's Meals entities were bound by our common vision, mission and values (solidarity), it would only carry out tasks that could not be carried out more effectively at a local level. This would allow Mary's Meals to take on a life best suited to the various situations, cultures and opportunities in which we worked. It also addressed a long-held concern of mine that those of us 'in charge' of Mary's Meals could very easily become the limiting factor, and supported a view that, ideally, Mary's Meals should be more like a 'movement' than a strongly centralized organization. The work with Bridgespan was another gift and another piece of learning that enabled us to work harder than ever to gain more support and remain confident that we would translate new kindnesses into many more meals for hungry children.

And then, unexpectedly, yet another opportunity to raise awareness of our work appeared. I had continued to stay in touch with Gerard Butler after meeting him at the CNN Heroes award ceremony in 2010. Early in 2013, he got in touch to say he wanted to follow through with his promise to travel to Africa with me to see first hand the work of Mary's Meals. We discussed where would be most suitable and eventually chose Liberia. We felt it received very little media attention, had desperate needs and was a place where we were determined to reach more children as soon as possible. We knew that the publicity a visit by Gerry would generate could help us to do just that.

We based ourselves at our compound in Tubmanburg where our Country Director kindly vacated his little two-bedroom house. Things were very basic there – electricity only provided for a few hours a day by a little generator, no air conditioning in the extremely hot and humid climate and nowhere to eat out nearby. But Gerry seemed to love every single moment of it, never once complaining about a single thing. Not even my terrible cooking. He worked from dawn to dusk every day of our stay, travelling to remote villages, spending time getting to know people in each one and making everyone, including me, laugh continuously until our sides ached. It was also wonderful to be able to hide behind him a bit and relax. The welcomes we received in the villages were warmer than ever, and while Gerry delighted our hosts by dancing exuberantly with every one of the dancers in the village – and even some who weren't dancing – I was able to stay in the background. Dancing while being the centre of attention was never something I enjoyed! We had some good laughs in the evenings about how our personalities were polar opposite – the ultimate extrovert and introvert. I was fascinated by his wonderful gifts. Within seconds of arriving in a village, everyone was smiling and laughing at him despite the language barrier. The children clung to him and he wanted to know everything about their lives. I began to notice that he would remember the name of every person we met in a village. I mentioned this to him and then he began to show off by going back round to each person we had been introduced to, repeating their name. He was also someone who was thinking very deeply about what he was seeing and experiencing. On our last evening, ahead of one long final day's filming, he produced copious notes that he had been writing: his thoughts on the beauty and importance of Mary's Meals and the best ways to articulate these. He wanted to choose every single word with painstaking care. His meticulous preparation amazed me, as did his hard work. I had hoped when we set out on this adventure that we might return with a few nice soundbites from Gerry; instead he had gifted us many hours of incredible footage.

'One of the things I have been struck by during this visit is the strength of the people's dignity, and what I love about Mary's Meals is that it is all about retaining this. They don't operate a free system where people are just taking; instead it is all about respecting and promoting the lives of people, their culture and what they are capable of,' said Gerry to the camera on our final day.

'I see communities full of resilience, integrity, warmth, love and hope. All of that is already here but Mary's Meals is like a switch that helps flick it on. Magnus believes this is a work of God, and so do I.'

There were many who agreed with that assessment of who this work belongs to, gathered behind the church in Medjugorje one baking hot summer's day in 2014. From the stage, I looked out at where vineyards and fields used to be, at a crowd of over 50,000 young people, many waving their national flags. I had been invited again to talk to the youngsters who had assembled for the annual youth festival here. When we had first visited Medjugorje in 1983 as teenagers, we had been among only a handful of pilgrims from other countries. Today it was astounding to look out over this enormous, happy sea of humanity, consisting of people who had been moved from every corner of the globe to gather in this obscure, difficult-to-get-to place. At a time of year when most of their generation were heading to beaches and music festivals these young people had chosen to come here. Most of them were wearing headphones and listening to the translation of our talks on short-wave radio. Lidija, standing beside me, was translating my words into Croatian and, in rows of cubicles in the yellow building where we sometimes held Mary's Meals conferences, a row of people sat at desks translating the Croatian words into a further nineteen other languages: Italian, German, French, Spanish, Polish, Lebanese, Arabic, Korean and many more. I was used to having talks translated, but today it was a little disconcerting to realize that my words were being translated twice and that the young people in front of me were listening to me on their radios. But I had been joined on the stage by a huge group of supporters wearing Mary's Meals T-shirts and felt reassured by their presence. After my little talk the crowd watched *Child 31* on the huge screens. Much of the rest of that week of festival I spent in our little information point, with Milona, chatting to a never-ending stream of happy young people, from China, Mexico, Lebanon and many other countries, who wanted to know more about Mary's Meals. Some were existing supporters and others were learning of our mission for the first time. A group of Swiss teenagers chatted to us for a long time, asking how best they might fund-raise. As they left one of them turned to me and said, 'You know, for the first time in my life I really understand that to be a Christian means that you really have to *do* something!'

Another memorable conversation I had was with one of the local priests. I mentioned to him the fact that some believed the whole story of apparitions here was a carefully created hoax of the local parish.

'Have you seen all the young people here on their knees in prayer? Queuing for confession? Unable to fit in the church? Have you seen their joy? Have you heard their stories and the talks, like the one you gave, describing some of the fruits of this place?' he asked me.

'If we made this whole thing up for this last thirty years, if we actually know how to do that, then we should adopt it as a pastoral plan for every parish, every diocese across the world!' he chortled.

Maybe I should have suggested that to Pope Francis when he walked with extended arms to greet Julie and me in St Peter's Square on a scorching hot day in the summer of 2013, but somehow I think he knows more about pastoral plans than I do. A few weeks previously I had answered the phone at home while holding my son Gabriel, who was two years old and crying loudly. It sounded as if the person at the other end of the phone said he was from the Vatican and was asking if I would like to come to meet Pope Francis.

After hurriedly handing Gabriel to Martha, his older sister, I asked the man at the end of the phone to repeat himself. But I had indeed heard correctly the first time. It was appropriate then that the first thing that Julie did when a beaming Pope Francis reached out and clasped her hands, was to give some cards our kids had made for him, in an envelope marked *Pope Francis!* in red felt-tip pen. He grinned and asked us how many children we had, before we talked to him a little about Mary's Meals and I handed him a blue Mary's Meals mug and a copy of *Child 31*. He passed these on to one of his aides and continued to clasp both our hands. Then he placed my hand on top of Julie's and with his still on top he blessed our marriage, his smile growing bigger and more beautiful all the while. I have never been smiled at like that – with such love – by anyone, and I will never forget it. Of all the unexpected encounters and undeserved treats I have received doing this work this one was the most amazing. After only a few months as Pope he was already my hero – Julie's too – and for us both to have been blessed by him like that was more than we could have ever hoped for. As always I was painfully aware that there were many around the world involved in Mary's Meals who should have been further ahead in the long queue waiting to meet this remarkable man.

Since his election Pope Francis had repeatedly highlighted the 'scandal of poverty'. Not long before we met him he said that to address this, 'We all have to think if we can become a little poorer, all of us have to do this.'

I know that the blessing we received that day was for all who have done just that, while they have shared the bread that belongs to all, with Mary's Meals and the hungry child.

12

Friends in Low Places

> I do not despair of happier times, considering that at the
> helm of the universe is He who overcomes the storm
> not by human skill, but by his fiat.
> ST JOHN CHRYSOSTOM

Our work in Haiti also began in Medjugorje. On a warm sunny morning in May 2006 I was part of a crowd listening to Jakov, the youngest visionary and now in his mid-thirties, speaking about Our Lady's messages from the front steps of his house. As always he finished his simple and moving talk with a prayer and then, as I turned to leave, someone in the crowd tapped me on the shoulder.

'I've been looking for you everywhere!' said the smiling, middle-aged lady in front of me excitedly. 'I'm Anka – remember we met at the youth festival last year?'

Of course I remembered. She had been the translator for the talk I was asked to give at that event and I had a vivid memory of how she had embellished everything I said, making the crowd of young people laugh in a way that was a little disconcerting. For a while I felt like a stand-up comedian except that I didn't understand any of my own jokes.

'I've just been to Haiti doing some humanitarian aid work – I really need to talk to you about it!' she said. 'It is terrible what is happening there. Everywhere I went I kept thinking "what these children really need is Mary's Meals".'

We walked over to the Mary's Meals Centre, our little cafe in the heart of the village, where we served tea and coffee to pilgrims and told them about our work. This was Milona's base and here people from every corner of the globe learnt about Mary's Meals and often became the people who returned home to start Mary's Meals fund-raising organizations. As usual we arrived to find a hive of activity where several concurrent conversations were taking place in different languages. Once again I marvelled at Milona's ability to flit from one language to another and give her full attention to every single visitor who turned up. Over a coffee Anka asked me if we might be interested in setting up Mary's Meals in Haiti, showing me her pictures and pointing out it was now the poorest country in the western hemisphere. I explained to her that we would love to help the suffering children there but our available funding was already committed to other projects.

'Let's pray about it and think about it and see what happens,' I suggested to her as I took my leave before heading to the airport. I said this sincerely as I already knew a little about the extreme poverty in that Caribbean island and certainly felt moved by Anka's graphic descriptions of suffering children there, but I travelled home without any great hope that we could do anything in Haiti soon. Almost every week we received new requests for help, more than we could ever keep up with.

When I arrived home I popped into my shed to check my emails. In my inbox was a message from a lady called Cecilia from the north of England, who had just returned from a holiday in the Cayman Islands in the Caribbean. At that point I had never met Cecilia, but had heard of her because she was one of those tireless volunteers who seemed to spend her life telling every person she met about Mary's Meals! Often new supporters from the north of England would contact us and tell us that Cecilia had introduced them to our work. Her email to me explained that while in the Caribbean, she and her husband got talking to a man in a restaurant and, of course, she told him about Mary's Meals. He was very moved and explained that he sat on the board of a grant-making Foundation that was currently looking for the best way to help the poorest children in Haiti. I realized that about the time they were having this encounter in the Cayman Islands, I must have been in the cafe listening to Anka's request to start Mary's Meals in Haiti. The email ended with a phone number and a request for me to phone this gentleman. When I did, he confirmed Cecilia's story and asked in-depth questions about how Mary's Meals worked. He told me that if we sent a funding proposal for setting up Mary's Meals in Haiti, he would present it to the board of his Foundation, who were likely to regard it favourably. By now I was in no doubt that we were meant to do this and we began serious research on the needs in Haiti – child malnutrition rates, school enrolment data, current providers of school meals and so on. It was clear there was an overwhelming need for Mary's

Meals in the country. Then we began to look at various organizations working in Haiti – particularly those working in education – that might be potential partners for us, and we began talking with some of them.

By September I made my first visit to Haiti, accompanied by Maria Byars, a bright young member of our now growing team who had spent much of the previous two years working with us in Malawi and Liberia. I had known Maria since she was a young girl, first because she used to come with her parents to Craig Lodge on retreat, and then later when she joined the little youth community there. She developed a passion for the work of Mary's Meals and, after completing her Masters at the London School of Economics, she came back to join our small growing team – something that delighted me given she was one of the most thoughtful and intelligent people I knew. She had started to write down our model as it developed, articulating things such as community engagement and our approach to long-term sustainability, as well as leading our first efforts to monitor and evaluate our projects in a meaningful way. She was also a deeply spiritual and private person who, after a few years of working closely with me, left me speechless by announcing out of the blue one day that she had decided to become a nun. Today she is a Franciscan Sister of Renewal, working with the poor in New York.

We travelled first of all up into the central plateaux, climbing on very bumpy roads over two mountain ranges to a town called Hinche. Much of what we saw reminded us of West Africa, but there were many differences too. Donkeys were the most common form of transport and the little houses by the roadside were painted in pretty blues and greens. The crumpled mountains were extraordinarily beautiful, although totally denuded of trees. In places the erosion was so severe they looked as if they were about to crumble and disintegrate completely before our very eyes. And a crushing, ugly poverty was all too evident. Men pulled crude wooden carts piled high with heavy loads. Under a wooden market stall by the road, I noticed a dreadfully skinny child squatting in the dust and realized that he was painstakingly picking up tiny shards of charcoal and placing them in a little plastic bag.

Before my visit I had been reading about Haiti's appalling history of tragedy and injustice. The French colonialists had once administered a particularly brutal slave regime here. A third of the slaves, imported in huge numbers from West Africa to work the lucrative sugar plantations, died within a few years of their arrival. In 1791 the slaves rebelled, and by 1804 they had won a victory against Napoleon's France that shook the world. In 1825, the French, supported by the USA, Britain and Canada, demanded reparation payments for their 'lost property' such as slaves, land and equipment. To attain international recognition, and escape political and economic isolation, Haiti was forced to pay 150 million gold francs. This would be the equivalent of around 12.7 billion US dollars today, and although that amount was later reduced, Haiti was unable to finish paying this debt until 1947. After that date Haiti suffered at the hands of a series of notorious dictators such as Papa Doc and his son Baby Doc. I also read some other depressing current facts about Haiti and the legacy bequeathed by that horrible history. Around 80 per cent of the population now lived on less than two US dollars per day, 50 per cent of children under five were malnourished, while eighty of every 1,000 babies born did not live to see their first birthday. And less than half of the kids ever enrolled in a school.

Our first day in Hinche, 5 September 2006, was a happy one. Four months after that conversation with Anka in Medjugorje, we witnessed the first ever serving of Mary's Meals in Haiti. In a little orphanage called Maison Fortune, smiling children, in startling pink school uniforms, queued under towering green trees to collect their plates of rice and vegetables. Later that day we met some Missionaries of Charity (Mother Teresa nuns), who reminded us it was the anniversary of Mother Teresa's death. I was delighted that we had begun our work in Haiti on this day as I had a very deep devotion to Mother Teresa, whose words and approach to serving the poor had a huge influence on the way we worked. Her sisters, in their striking blue and white habits, invited us back to their house where they introduced us to the malnourished children they cared for – stick-thin, shockingly shrunken kids, only just clinging to life, so tiny and fragile-looking that at first I was afraid to hold them. But when eventually I did so it was hard to let them go, and by the time I placed the last one back in her cot I felt almost envious of those nuns who spent their days caring for those beautiful, precious little human beings. We also spent some time with another local organization, Caritas Hinche, discussing the desperate need for meals in the many schools that they were running in the central plateaux, and we agreed to form a partnership with them too. In time, they became our largest partner in Haiti and across many village schools in the central plateaux – some of them very remote and accessible only on foot or by donkey – volunteers began to cook rice and beans every school day for their children.

From Hinche we travelled down to Port-au-Prince to meet a Father Tom Hagan and, with him, visit a notorious slum called Cité Soleil. Since arriving in Haiti, every time we had mentioned our intention to visit that place, we had prompted laughter and then, after a realization that we were serious, a solemn statement that this, in fact, was just not possible. The situation there was currently in daily news bulletins. A UN peacekeeping force was positioned round the edge of Cité Soleil, effectively placing its 400,000 inhabitants under a kind of siege, while skirmishes with the 12,000 armed gang members who controlled the slum were ongoing. These gangs had been kidnapping people recently on the roads leading to their territory and most in Port-au-Prince were wary of travelling even into adjacent areas of the city, let alone Cité Soleil itself. Our 'pass' into Cité Soleil and our reason for wanting to visit, was Father Tom Hagan, an American priest who had been working there for many years. I had been in regular contact with him for some months after learning about his work in Cité Soleil through his organization, Hands Together. In particular I was interested in the schools he had built there and the desperate need the children had for school meals.

We arrived at his house in Port-au-Prince and very soon the diminutive streetwise Philadelphian had us laughing. Over a cold drink he began telling us his story and the situation in which he was working, but each time he started to explain a serious, troubling and often macabre situation that he was dealing with, he would make a sudden diversion into a hilarious anecdote. Given the amount of violence and death around him I wondered if it was a way to cope – or at least to help us cope – with the reality of his life. He was humble, and disarmingly insecure, often questioning whether he had done any good at all for anyone in the time he was in Haiti.

Father Tom explained to us that after leading a group of students from Lafayette College to Haiti in 1986, he felt called to give up his post as Chaplain to Princeton University and eventually moved to Port-au-Prince in 1997, where he founded Hands Together. They set up education, agriculture and health projects in an area called Goniaves, but their biggest focus became Cité Soleil where they built eight large school campuses to provide free education for the first time there. He also described the current, extremely tense situation in Cité Soleil. He knew the various gang leaders well and was trying to find a way to broker peace there. Once again, while recounting some recent atrocities that had taken place, he veered off to a hilarious anecdote about the Indian Missionaries of Charity who lived nearby, and for whom he said Mass every morning.

'Many days when I go to say Mass for them they will have written on a little blackboard in their chapel a prayer intention for me to announce. Very often this will be one of the sister's birthdays or an anniversary of some sort. This one morning I get there and on the board they've written "Sister Horshit's birthday!" I composed myself and tried my best to pronounce it in a less obvious way. "Let's pray for Sister

Horseeeet on her birthday," I said, but no, they all immediately corrected me.

"No, no, Father! It's Sister Horshit ..."

By now he had us doubled up in laughter, and moved back to finish a story about a gang leader who had recently beheaded a rival. He answered our many questions and reassured us that it was safe for us to travel with him to visit the schools in Cité Soleil the next day.

And so, the next morning, after Mass with the Missionaries of Charity, feeling relieved that no one had introduced me to Sister Horshit, we headed for Cité Soleil. The main highway that led there from Haiti's international airport was alarmingly empty. Eventually a colourful bus roared past us, down the central lane, its horn blaring an unremitting message that this terrified driver was going to stop for no one. Like everyone else in Port-au-Prince, he was presumably aware of the kidnappings that had taken place on this stretch of road in recent weeks. As we turned off the highway on to a smaller road leading towards Cité Soleil we passed a huddle of white UN tanks, out of which peeked soldiers who trained their guns directly upon us. I thought of the incredulous reaction we had provoked since arriving in Haiti, every time we had mentioned to someone that we planned to visit Cité Soleil, and I glanced at Maria to see if she was OK. She looked a lot calmer and less troubled than I felt. I had in fact begun to ask myself how wise I was to place our lives in the hands of this eccentric priest who we had only just met the previous evening. Meanwhile Father Tom gave us a running commentary, explaining that since 2004, when the elected president, Jean-Bertrand Aristide, was ousted from power by a coup, a UN force had been controversially present. Ostensibly here to keep the peace, many Haitians saw the 6,000 UN troops as agents of international powers, who they believed supported the overthrow of Aristide. Many of the gangs within Cité Soleil remained loyal to the former president and accused the UN of brutalities against them and the impoverished people of Cité Soleil. In July 2006, the UN failed in an attempt to 'invade' Cité Soleil but up to eighty civilians were killed in the process. Since then they had become entrenched round the perimeter from where they launched sporadic attacks. They stood accused by local inhabitants of turning Cité Soleil into a concentration camp. A recent article published by the *Lancet* claimed that 8,000 people had been murdered and 35,000 women sexually abused in Haiti in the twenty-two months since the deployment of the UN force. It became clear by now that we had driven into what was in effect a war zone. The shelled buildings and walls riddled with bullet holes were no different from scenes I had become familiar with in Bosnia-Herzegovina and Liberia.

'That's the Daughters of Charity house,' said Father Tom, pointing at another war-scarred building. 'They had to move out last week when they started to be fired at which is really sad because those nuns were doing great work here. One of the Mother Teresa nuns was also shot in the arm but is making a full recovery, thank God.'

Apart from the Red Cross and Médecins Sans Frontières, it seemed Hands Together were the only humanitarian organization still functioning in Cité Soleil. We were now passing burnt-out buildings on which sat rows of young men who stared sullenly at us. I read the remains of a sign on a particularly bullet-scarred empty building and realized I was looking at what was left of a police station. I understood more clearly now that this place really was ruled by the gangs. There was no other authority here any more in this little autonomous state.

Did Father Tom really have a 'safe pass' into this place or was he perhaps completely mad? I asked myself again. I felt reassured when we finally arrived outside one of seven school campuses and passed through a gate in its high security walls. Inside was a little oasis of peace. Some men were making little wooden chairs in one classroom in preparation for the new school term, while a UN helicopter buzzed angrily overhead. Father Tom pointed to a neat bullet hole in the blackboard and explained that the children had been in class when it whistled over their heads.

We walked out into the little alleyways and were surrounded immediately by naked skinny children. The smell of sewage and putrid waste was overpowering. Everywhere there were piles of rotting rubbish and pools of stinking black water, through which the barefoot children walked. Tiny, flimsy homes made of rusting tin sheets lined concrete channels full of raw sewage. The children pointed to their mouths and distended stomachs, asking us for something to eat. Many times I had been asked by children for money, but not for food in this way. Huge black pigs rooted in the rubbish as we walked towards the old docks, and here and there children could be seen squatting amid the squalor to do their toilet. The stench and filth and lack of dignity were overwhelming. I could not believe what I was seeing. A small baby was crawling face down in the putrid grime, trying to make its way into a tin shack. I had never anywhere witnessed such a living hell. And I was scared too. Every now and then as we walked, young men would approach Father Tom and ask to speak to him. As soon as we stopped a crowd of men would start to form round us, many of them wearing angry stares. 'Time to move on,' Father Tom would say and on we went. How could anyone live here, like this, and remain human? Around the old wharf men sat mending their fishing nets, while in the harbour old cutters and fishing skiffs bobbed, with their huge sails framed by the emerald sea. The sudden glimpse of beauty startled me. Behind them enormous, hulking cargo ships were moored at the dockside. Nearby I noticed a little boy standing at the edge of the water where the water lapped gently against mounds of plastic detritus. He was flying a home-made kite, made out of thin sticks and plastic bags. He stared up at it, transfixed, as it hovered in the azure sky, oblivious to the foul muck, decomposing waste and the particularly large pig rooting beside him. In fact he looked serene as he marvelled at the beautiful flying machine that he controlled above his head. After watching him for a few minutes we made our way back through some different alleyways, passing a man with a home-made guitar singing while his wife breastfed a baby. She gave us a huge smile. Yes, of course it was possible to live even here and retain your humanity.

And then another unexpected surprise as Father Tom led us into a little, heavily guarded house, inside which was a fully operating radio station. He explained that a group of young men had come to him with the idea and he had helped them get it up and running. We found ourselves looking through the glass wall of the studio, as a young enthusiastic DJ introduced another track. Father Hagan whispered something in his ear and the DJ interrupted the song to tell his listeners he wanted to welcome some unexpected visitors from England. (We teased Father Tom afterwards about the fact we were Scottish not English, and a couple of years later, long after I had forgotten that incident, Father Tom took me to revisit the radio station. This time the DJ dramatically announced his visitors from SCOTLAND and played to his bewildered listeners a recording of 'O Flower of Scotland' complete with bagpipes.)

Outside we continued our tour and before long we bumped into some of the gang leaders, including the dreadlocked, sunglass-wearing, ultimate leader of all the gangs, who talked earnestly to Father Tom in Creole. Eventually Father Tom said something to him which made him laugh loudly and all the young men round him followed suit. As we walked on Father Tom explained to us that he was trying to persuade the gang leaders to hand over their weapons and negotiate an agreement with the government and the UN. He was exasperated because last week President Preval had a secret meeting with them, after which some of the more naive gang members had talked to the press, claiming the president was being forced to accommodate their views. Headlines embarrassing the president resulted, and Father Tom was now telling these gang members that they needed to make some kind of gesture to repair the damage. He feared it might be too late and worried that the UN were perhaps preparing to mount an invasion that would result in a huge loss of life. The relationship between these gang leaders and

Father Tom was an interesting one. During our few days with him, they phoned him constantly asking for his advice. They had a very obvious respect for him, the man who almost alone was feeding and educating the starving children of their territory. For his part Father Tom knew his relationship with them was vital in order to be allowed to work here, while it was equally important not to get too drawn into their web. He was walking a moral tightrope: trying to retain their permission to work here while not vindicating their methods of leadership. He explained to us quietly that a few weeks ago a man had thrust a gun through his window as he parked his car in Cité Soleil, demanding he take the keys from the ignition and hand them over. He managed to escape because the man turned away for a moment, not realizing that Father Tom had another set of keys in his pocket which he inserted in the ignition before speeding off. To Father Tom's horror, he learnt later that the people here had been so angry when they heard of what had happened that they killed the man responsible.

The leader of the gang that controlled the wharf area offered to show us around his patch. This was an important part of Cité Soleil, given the fact that Haiti is a transit point for drugs being smuggled from South America to the US by boat and that the gangs were probably heavily involved in this industry. He was perhaps thirty years old, small and dressed in a scruffy T-shirt. He was hardly intimidating and I wondered how he managed to rise to the position of gang leader. He walked with us around the hovels standing among the mounds of rubbish and pointed pitifully at the most emaciated children who surrounded us. I asked him what could make things better here. He pointed at Father Tom and said, 'food and school for our children'. Father Tom noticed that I was filming this little compliment and for the camera pretended to punch him on the chin in slow motion.

By now I knew that Father Tom was anything but mad. Eccentric, hilarious, courageous, reckless maybe, but certainly not mad.

As we walked back, Father Tom pointed out two men working on a flat rooftop and encouraged me to climb up to witness what they were doing. I'm glad I did, because if I hadn't I would never have believed it. In neat rows they were laying out little cakes made of mud to dry in the baking sun. Into the mud they were mixing a little margarine and salt. In Creole these mud cakes are known as 'terre' and traditionally are eaten by pregnant Haitian women in the belief that they contain minerals that are good for their unborn children. Now, though, it was not just expectant mothers who ate these cakes. The producers of 'terre' were perhaps part of the only growth industry in Cité Soleil as people took desperate measures to fill their empty stomachs. The people of Cité Soleil had been reduced to eating mud.

Later that evening we said a Rosary together on the roof of Father Tom's house, from which we could see Cité Soleil about 2 miles away. As we prayed, we could see the rockets and hear the dull explosions as the UN troops once again attacked the gangs. Father Tom wearily made some calls to organize for his ambulance to go down and park nearby. He had earlier shown us the fully equipped surgery he had set up in his house, the workplace of a surgeon who had become a specialist in gunshot wounds.

By now I knew that Haiti would be an extremely difficult place for us to work. Without a secure safe environment or even the availability of locally grown food it would not always be possible to implement our ideal model. But I had no doubt that this was somewhere we should be providing Mary's Meals, even if we had to make some compromises. While it was always our strong preference to buy food grown in-country, it was very clear that the children here would not complain if we needed to import their rice at this stage. Before leaving Haiti we agreed with Father Tom that we would begin providing the 4,500 meals he needed every school day for his pupils. He was overjoyed.

But I had another task before heading home. I had made this pledge without yet having secured the funding from the Foundation in the Cayman Islands. I had told them what we wanted to do in Haiti, including the support for 4,500 children in Cité Soleil, and while they had made encouraging noises they had not yet made any promises. So from Haiti I travelled to the Cayman Islands to make a presentation to the board of the Foundation and to seek their support. They were based in surroundings that could not have been more different from those I had just left behind in Haiti. In their offices hung expensive art and the men I was invited to speak to were smartly dressed gentlemen who I found hard to read, and they seemed devoid of emotion as I made my presentation. I explained what I had just seen in Haiti and our plan. I described to them the experience of seeing the first Mary's Meals served in Haiti and, for some reason, mentioned the encounter with the Missionaries of Charity and the fact that those meals were served on the anniversary of Mother

Teresa's death. To my great surprise they looked startled and moved by this piece of information. I finished my presentation and asked them for the large sum of money we required to provide all those daily school meals for the next year. After some probing questions they eventually, to my enormous relief, said yes. I thanked them profusely and asked them about their reaction to my story of Mother Teresa.

They explained to me that all the funding that their Foundation had at its disposal was donated by one wealthy lady. Three years previously she had had a vivid dream in which Mother Teresa appeared to her and asked her to feed her children in Haiti. This dream had such an impact on her it led her to provide the funding to the Foundation. Mary's Meals in Haiti was the first project they had ever funded in fulfilment of that request. Sometimes I felt God just wanted to remind us who was setting the strategy. Certainly I have never doubted in the years since that we were meant to be in Haiti and do our best to see more children fed, no matter how difficult that might be.

And certainly there has been no shortage of difficulties. By the time the earthquake struck on 12 January 2010, 12,000 children in Haiti were eating Mary's Meals every school day. A few hours before the earthquake I was on the phone to Father Tom and Doug Campbell, who called me from Miami Airport on their way back to Port-au-Prince from the US. We were confirming a plan to begin feeding the 'barefoot kids' – the children on the streets of Cité Soleil – after regular school classes had finished, and to begin introducing them to basic education. Father Tom, whose idea this was, was excited to tell me they were ready to begin the next day. A few hours later I heard the news of the earthquake and my heart sank. Unable to contact them, we called their families in the USA to learn that their house had collapsed on top of them, killing two young men who lived there, but that Father Tom and Doug were alive. But all the phones were by now down and no contact was possible. For the next two or three days, as the media reported to us the unprecedented scale of the disaster and the horrors that were unfolding in and around Port-au-Prince, Doug's family were beside themselves with fear about what had become of them. By now we had launched a full-scale appeal, working through the night to get word out to our supporters and through the media, and almost instantly we began to receive a tidal wave of donations. Meanwhile, I was trying with the help of my friends in Miami to find a way into Haiti. With no scheduled flights operating, there was an enormous demand on small charter planes but eventually we managed to book one. I began my journey to Miami and between flights in New York I received some good news and some bad news. First, to my huge relief, I spoke to Doug Campbell who explained that he and Father Tom had managed to get out of Haiti via the Dominican Republic – but having licked their wounds and hugged their loved ones, they were now determined to get back in as quickly as possible and wanted me to come with them to help. However, I also received a call from our friend and founding board member Albert Holder, in Miami, to say the charter plane arrangement had fallen through but he was desperately trying to find another option. I decided to go on to Miami anyway, and by the time I arrived at Albert's house I had heard of an unlikely breakthrough with some distant connections arranging for two seats on a flight if we turned up at the airport the next day – as long as we never ever revealed any details!

And so it was that we landed in Haiti four days after the earthquake, on our mysteriously arranged flight. Much of the terminal building had collapsed and we walked straight from the runway out on to the streets, which were swarming with people, among them many children begging for food. On the pavements and central reservations of busy roads, under the canopies of abandoned filling stations and beside the remains of their homes, hundreds of thousands were trying to find somewhere to sleep. Everywhere was rubble and twisted debris. Huge cracks ran through the squint walls of buildings that looked about to topple over at any moment, the president's palace looked like a pathetic smashed wedding cake, and the broken cathedral's roof lay mangled where the congregation used to sit.

Entering Father Tom Hagan's little courtyard from the dark, devastated city, I was struck by a sense of order and calm. His two-storey house had been reduced to a remarkably small pile of rubble. The courtyard was now a temporary home for some of the Hands Together staff and neighbouring families. In one corner a makeshift shelter of tin and tarpaulin had been erected to act as the new head office of Hands Together. Outside in the yard, people were settling down to sleep despite the incessant roar of planes and helicopters flying in and out of Port-au-Prince. Some families were sleeping in an old minibus and truck parked in the corner of the yard. Beside the shelter Father Tom had created a little 'chapel' out of things salvaged from his ruined house

– a rocking chair, a smashed crucifix, a little statue of Our Lady and a picture of the two seminarians who died beneath the broken concrete. Their graves, marked by simple wooden crosses, were a few yards away. We gathered to pray at the chapel before settling down on the hard dusty yard, under our blankets, to try and get some sleep.

The night was punctuated by sporadic gunfire from surrounding streets, as well as people's screams, moans and angry shouting. I was acutely aware that one of the four walls of this previously secure compound no longer stood to protect us. At one point a dog nuzzled me and curled up to sleep at my feet, and for a while I did too.

The next morning we travelled down into nearby Cité Soleil with some of the Hands Together team. Many of them had lost family members. The wife and daughter of Nelson, the Hands Together general manager, had been killed by their collapsed house, and I was amazed that he seemed able to concentrate on the work that needed doing. Our grim and emotional tour of the schools revealed that each had been damaged, perhaps beyond repair. Some of the team, strong macho men who had grown up among the gangs in Cité Soleil, broke down and cried for the first time in my sight, when they saw the state of the schools they had helped build. Children who usually benefited from our daily meals were sitting outside among the debris, but the dangerous cracked buildings were deserted. As we picked our way carefully through St Francis de Sales School towards the kitchen, the stench became unbearable and I braced myself for what horror we might find there. I was hugely relieved to find only a large pot of rotting beans. Outside we met Vaneesa and

Marie, two local Mary's Meals cooks. They explained that they 'had been up to their elbows in those beans', cooking Mary's Meals for the following day, when the ground began to shake, but that they had managed to crawl to safety. They showed us their scraped arms and legs.

In many ways the lives of people in Cité Soleil had been affected less dramatically than others in the city. Most here were already without enough daily food, and water. Already here many children died of hunger-related causes each week. They had no running water or sanitation in the first place. And homes made of flimsy tin are less likely to kill you when they collapse. But the need for aid was still desperate indeed, and the insecurity in Cité Soleil meant that most agencies could not set up an effective way to help.

Back in Father Tom's little compound we had a meeting with the teachers and community leaders, who had been living on the streets since the earthquake. One team was tasked with making an immediate assessment of needs in each school community; who had died, who had lost their house, what were people's current situations? Another team was to begin picking out reusable bricks from the debris around each school. As soon as possible they would rebuild the school campus walls in order to create secure bases to resume an effective food distribution programme. Meanwhile the water tanker truck used each day by Hands Together to bring clean water to the people of Cité Soleil was filled up and ready to begin distribution again. And even while we talked some men were already rebuilding the collapsed compound wall and a group of women were cooking a pot of rice for our evening meal.

As we talked, Doug realized that unless we could get a fuel supply very little would be possible. He and I sped down to the huge UN tented city that had formed near the airport, where many of the NGO workers were based. We began asking for fuel – even just one large barrel – and were passed from office to office. No one seemed to want to take responsibility for giving us what we urgently needed, despite accepting that we represented an organization that had a very legitimate need for this and admitting that they had a huge supply of fuel in store. One young man from Sweden pointed at a nearby marquee and said we should join a co-ordination meeting that various NGOs were having. We noticed very quickly that there was not one black face in the crowded tent, and as we listened it became clear most of them had only just arrived in Haiti. I couldn't help but make a comparison with the meeting we had just had in Father Tom's yard. After some time a man stood up and introduced himself as belonging to a very well-known global NGO. He talked at length about the poor accommodation that he and his colleagues had been provided. He was indignant about this and some others began to raise their voices in support. Doug and I looked at each other. I was genuinely concerned that he was going to hit somebody. While a lively debate about their accommodation continued we walked out of the tent, straight over to the depot where we could see barrels of fuel stacked high, and told the startled man in the stockroom that we needed one right now, and could he please have it placed immediately in the back of our pickup as we were in a big hurry. He didn't even put up an argument and a few minutes later we were heading back through the pitiful streets with our precious cargo.

I learnt a lot from working with Father Tom and Doug. In the days after the earthquake they began to speak a lot about 'humility in action' as a guide to our decision-making and approach; an emphasis on remembering how very small we are in a situation like this and the importance of recognizing what we could and could not do. It gave us a focus and allowed us to do some things very well in extremely difficult circumstances. But it was not just their words that taught me things. On a visit six months later, after they had rebuilt some temporary accommodation at their compound for the team, I noticed that Father Tom was still sleeping in a one-man tent in the compound. I asked him why he hadn't moved into the accommodation where there were proper beds.

'Today there are hundreds of thousands of Haitians still sleeping in pathetic tents. It is a scandal. And as long as they have to do that, then so will I – and anyway, I quite like it actually,' he laughed.

In all we were donated £1.3 million for our emergency appeal for Haiti. Within two months of the earthquake, temporary classrooms had been built and all of the children were once again receiving a daily meal. The next phase became the repair and rebuilding of the damaged schools. Within a year we had spent all of the money raised and the amazing Hands Together operation was up and running once again. We were able to account for and report to our donors on every pound spent. And then we resumed our day job, working to bring daily meals to more hungry children in Haiti. In fact, even by the end of that year after the earthquake, the number of children receiving Mary's Meals in Haiti had risen from 12,000 to 15,000. Again I saw what was possible when we worked in the right way with local communities, and repeatedly I was humbled by the spirit of the Haitian people and their resilience.

I eventually found my way out of Haiti after the earthquake by hitching a ride with a small cargo plane that we had chartered to transport a precious consignment of urgently needed medicine into Hinche from Miami. The evening before I departed we sat round the outdoor chapel, once again in the dark. Father Tom saw me looking at his mangled crucifix hanging on the tree. The plaster figure of Jesus had been smashed and wires protruded from the broken plaster limbs. He explained that this was his family's crucifix, which had hung in his house in Philadelphia as he grew up. After he became a priest he had always kept it in his home and so was delighted when it was salvaged from the rubble of his fallen house here.

'I won't ever repair it. I will keep it just like this,' he says. 'It reminds us that Jesus is broken too, with us.'

13

Generation Hope

> The philosophy of the school room in one generation will be the philosophy of government in the next.
>
> ABRAHAM LINCOLN

Just before the sun rose over the hills to the east of Gay's home, we began our journey to Edward's village. It was June 2014 and I had not met him again since our only encounter twelve years previously, when the fourteen-year-old had sat beside his dying mother and answered my question about his hopes and ambitions: 'I would like to have enough food to eat and I would like to be able to go to school one day.'

I had been repeating those words that sparked this mission of Mary's Meals, ever since, to thousands of audiences all over the world. They have appeared in renowned newspapers and been broadcast in many languages. And, strangely, I have never tired of repeating them. Even on the crazy occasions when I have given seven or eight talks in one day, they feel fresh and vital each time.

Gay was driving and I felt very glad she was with me. It was she who had managed to arrange this meeting and who, indirectly, had been responsible for my first meeting with Edward too. In fact, she had been responsible for just about every amazing thing that had happened these twelve extraordinary years in Malawi. My oldest son, Calum, who was making his first trip to Malawi (I had always promised my children I would take them here for their first visit when they were sixteen years old), was also in the car and Gay and I regaled him with tales about the early days of Mary's Meals as we drove north under skies clear and blue. Gay's husband, David, who featured in many of our stories, had died in 2010, but not before he had delighted us all by joining us for a Mary's Meals meeting in Medjugorje. During that week he chose to climb the steep rocky path up Krizevac, the Hill of the Cross, with Gay, where together they had a very deep experience of grace and healing. One year later, to the day, while laughing in Gay's arms as he arrived home at their front door, he had died of a massive heart attack. As we continued our drive I had a strong sense of the passing of the years and together we prayed the joyful mysteries of the Rosary together.

Sometimes, after I gave public talks, people asked me what had happened to Edward and his brothers and sisters. The question pained me because the truth was that I had no idea what had become of them. I had met him during a whirlwind tour of villages during the famine of 2002, in a fleeting visit to a village near Balaka, and it was not in this area that we began serving the meals. In fact Mary's Meals only reached Balaka nearly ten years later. At that point we had tried to find Edward and been told he had left the area. I presumed I would never see him again, but a few weeks before this visit I had asked Gay Russell to try one more time. She talked to the Italian priest at Balaka, Father Gamba, who had first taken us to meet Edward's family, and showed him a photograph that we had taken in 2002 of the children with their dying mother. To my amazement I received word back from Gay that this time they had found them, back in the very place we first met. The mother had died a few months after our meeting, but some of the children still lived there, and Edward, now married with a child, lived in a village only a few miles away. Father Gamba offered to set up a meeting with him.

It was appropriate that this day happened to be the feast of the Visitation and early that morning, before setting off on our journey, I had felt challenged when reading the day's scripture passage.

'Do not let your love be a pretence,' St Paul had written to the Romans. 'Work for the Lord with untiring effort and with great earnestness of spirit ... If any of the saints are in need you must share with them ... Rejoice with those who rejoice and be sad with those in sorrow. Treat everyone with equal kindness; never be condescending but make real friends with the poor.'

'Make real friends with the poor.' That was difficult sometimes. The barriers between the rich and the poor, between the educated and uneducated, between the Malawian and a person from a country that had once made them part of their empire, often felt impossible to break through. As we drove towards Balaka I was asking myself about my relationship with the poor. And part of me was not looking forward to meeting Edward because I knew, that for him, Mary's Meals had come too late.

Father Gamba's long hair and beard had grown white since I last met him. My previous brief meeting with him all those years ago had left me with a vague memory of someone who looked like Jesus. The Italian missionary priest was now much older than the crucified Jesus, but his smiling eyes and crinkled tanned face more than ever exuded holiness. It was a Saturday morning and before we went on to our appointment with Edward he led us to the nearby parish youth club where hundreds of kids met every weekend to play games, dance and sing, and also to do works of charity in their local community. As we arrived the children clapped and sang their welcome.

'Keep the fire burning!!' was their slogan and they sang it loudly to us, before we chatted with them for a while. They told us about some houses they had helped build for destitute families in the town and about a very remote village on a nearby mountain, two hours from the nearest road, which they had started to visit with Father Gamba. They were helping the children there to set up a youth club like their own and were building a nursery with them for the younger kids. I asked them if any of them knew about Mary's Meals and every child raised their hand, laughing and saying they ate Mary's Meals every day in their various schools. Before we left they asked earnestly if we could try and bring Mary's Meals to the village on the mountain. They explained they would visit there again the following Sunday, the feast of Pentecost, and asked if we would come. I told them we would try.

We travelled on from there on dusty tracks to meet Edward. We parked outside a simple home by the road, outside which some teenage girls and young women sat with babies and children around them. Some of the children looked malnourished. One small child lay under a blanket shivering with a fever. We said hello and two of them shyly introduced themselves as Angelina and Maya, Edward's younger sisters and called over their youngest brother Chinsinsi to say hello. They pulled out some chairs for us to sit on outside the house and they explained that the parish had built this home for them as they were all orphans. Various people greeted us and after a few minutes a skinny young man arrived and shook my hand. He frowned anxiously.

'I'm Edward,' he said after a moment of awkward silence, taking me by surprise because he looked absolutely nothing like the Edward I had in my mind. He had a sad tired face with a prominent nose. He also seemed nervous and I guessed he was unsure and perhaps fearful about why we had asked to meet him.

I asked him if he remembered our meeting twelve years earlier and he said that of course he did. He led me to a neighbouring little mud-brick home where that meeting had taken place. I was amazed to see it standing just as I remembered it. It had not looked like it had been built to last so long. I began to talk to Edward about his life.

'Since my mother died I have only had problems and because I could never go to school each one of those problems is doubled.' He looked dejected and perhaps a little angry too.

I asked him about his life, hoping he would say something happier.

'I grow some maize. But it is difficult.'

'How was your harvest?' I asked him.

'I got four bags of maize.'

'How long will that last you and your family?'

He shrugged and thought about it for some time. 'Between two and three months, I think,' he finally answered, but seemed unsure and stressed by the question. 'But I am worried about my brothers and sisters. They don't have enough to eat here either.'

I turned to Maya and Chinsinsi, the two who still attended a local primary school. 'Do you receive Phala at your school?' I asked them, having already checked that Mary's Meals was now being served in this district.

They smiled broadly for the first time since I had arrived. 'Yes, every day we get Phala at school!'

Maya explained she was just finishing primary school and had been sitting exams.

I asked Edward if he had heard of Mary's Meals.

'Yes, they are a group who are feeding children in schools around here.'

And so I explained to him the story of Mary's Meals and the part our first meeting had played. I told him how the meals were not just being served around here, but to children all over the world. While I talked, his wife arrived with their two-year-old child.

'This is Blessing,' said Edward, proudly holding his son. And now he was smiling for the first time too.

'Will Blessing go to school when he is older?' I asked.

'Yes, of course I want him to go to school. Every father wants what is best for his child. Every parent wants their child to go to school,' he replied with feeling in his voice.

'And at the school in your village, is there Mary's Meals also?'

He smiled at me. 'Yes, there is. Blessings will receive Phala there every day.'

There were many thoughts going through my mind and a jumble of emotions in my heart as we drove in silence back to Blantyre: sadness at the poverty of Edward's life, joy that the lives of his youngest siblings and son would be helped by Mary's Meals, and a nagging guilt that I had been using his words all these years while he continued to suffer in the very trap we were trying to help people escape from. But more than anything I felt a desire, more intense than ever, to reach more children with Mary's Meals as soon as possible. The glaring contrast between Edward's life and that of Veronica, who I had met the previous day, was also in my mind.

We had gone to meet her at her little brick house in Chilomoni, the township on the edge of Blantyre, whose children had been the very first to receive Mary's Meals twelve years ago. We walked between market stalls teeming with colourful life, silver fish dried on tabletops, multicoloured flip-flops hung in bundles and translucent pink tomatoes neatly stacked into pyramids. Some ladies sat among a pile of black charcoal, bagging it for sale. Veronica was waiting for us at her door, wearing a colourful dress. She welcomed us with a huge smile and invited us into her simple, tidy home, explaining that her two sisters, who raised her, were out at work. She was eighteen years old and had just completed secondary school, an incredible feat for a child from this community who had grown up without the support of parents. We began chatting and asked her about her childhood.

'I lost my father when I was eleven months old and then my mother when I was nine years old,' she said, looking at her hands. 'Sometimes I would go the whole week without food. I was weak. Back then my brothers and sisters weren't working and we used to share the food between us.

'Then I got the porridge in 2005, from Standard 5 onwards. I was doing my best before the porridge, but the food improved my performance. When I was going to class I was full in my stomach so I was able to concentrate and listen as I had more energy than before.'

She brightened and became animated when we started to enquire about her life now. 'A lot of my old schoolfriends are married now. But I want to concentrate on my education because I have suffered a lot and I think education is the only way out. So that's why I work hard.'

And an enormous grin spread across her face as she told us some very special news. 'I have been selected to go to the Polytechnic University!'

'That is incredible!' I yelped. 'Amazing! What will you study?'

'Business and education. I am not sure if I want to work in a bank or be a teacher!' she laughed, unable to contain her excitement at the life unfolding in front of her.

Veronica's effervescent optimism and Edward's gloomy toil were on my mind, the following day, when I joined a very different meeting in the atmospheric upper room of Mandela

House in Blantyre. Believed to be the oldest standing building in Malawi, it was built by the Moir brothers from Glasgow in 1892 as the base for their African Lakes Company. While the ground floor is now an art gallery and restaurant, the upper floor has become a library and conference room, the walls of which are adorned with faded historic photographs and slightly uncomfortable reminders of a Scottish-flavoured colonial past.

Anastasia Msosa, the Chief Justice of Malawi (and the first female in this country to hold the post), apologized for arriving a little late. We were amazed she was able to come at all considering the country was in the midst of a post-election crisis, with allegations of serious vote-rigging by the outgoing president delaying the announcement of a new president. Anastasia took her seat beside the Honourable Justin Malawezi, a slightly built, bespectacled elderly man, who, as the former vice-president of Malawi also had some deep insights into the current political situation. Other trustees round the table included David Haworth, the former Managing Director of Illovo Sugar, one of the largest companies in the country and, of course, Gay Russell, who has been attending these meetings with me since the very first ones that took place in her own living room. Hitesh Anadkat, a leading member of the Hindu Asian business community in Malawi, had sent his apologies for being unable to attend this time.

We had a busy agenda to get through before lunch, starting with reports from our new Country Director Chris MacLullich and our Head of Operations Panji Kajani. We noted the fact that Mary's Meals was now serving nearly

700,000 children every day in Malawi – nearly 26 per cent of the primary-school-age population – and discussed the best ways for us to engage with a new government in order to encourage them to support our work and eventually provide an extensive school-feeding programme themselves. The government in recent years had adopted a policy of universal school feeding and begun to provide meals in a small number of schools, while stating the impact of Mary's Meals in their country was one of the main catalysts that prompted this. While all of us round the table were greatly encouraged that the government had recognized that school meals were essential, we also recognized that the meagre resources at their disposal, and the fact that their education and health budgets were already horribly short of the requirements for basic needs, meant the Malawian government was very unlikely to provide meals on a large scale any time soon. We discussed how we could support them by sharing our skills and methodologies while always retaining our own independence. Meanwhile, we reconfirmed plans to continue expanding Mary's Meals to schools on our waiting lists as fast as our funding would allow. Please God, one day, the government here will be in a position to take over our programme and make us redundant in Malawi – that would be success for us, leaving us to concentrate our efforts in other areas of need – but we agreed that until that becomes a realistic prospect we will continue to work as hard as ever to reach the next hungry schools on our list.

Next we learnt that we are having much success in encouraging the school communities to begin tree-planting projects. Deforestation is a huge problem in Malawi, and while we had long been committed to using the most fuel-efficient stoves in the school kitchens, we also wanted the school communities, who are responsible for the provision of their own firewood, to plant trees so that their source of fuel would become self-replenishing. We then heard an update on the imminent launch of Mary's Meals in neighbouring Zambia. We had travelled to Zambia a few days previously – my first visit to that country – and had visited schools around Chipata, near the Malawian border, which would be the first to receive the meals. It was clearly an area of very great need with large numbers of local children not enrolled in school. I had been surprised to see just how near those villages are to schools which are already receiving Mary's Meals on the Malawian side of the border, and was amazed to learn that Zambian children were currently migrating across that border each day to attend those schools where they would receive a meal. Chris and Panji told us they were confident that the new Mary's Meals programme in Zambia would stop this cross-border traffic.

Justin Malawezi then explained to us that this area of Zambia could just as easily have been part of Malawi. On both sides of the border the people are Chewa, as are most of the people in Malawi, including himself. He is a special advisor to the King of the Chewa and has deep knowledge of the traditional structures that are in some ways at least as important for us to understand as the current political ones. Justin's insights and informative comments in this area were always something I looked forward to at these meetings.

'I am happy that Mary's Meals is expanding according to the Chewa kingdom rather than the modern-day borders of

Malawi!' he observed with a smile. 'Maybe we should start in Mozambique next! There is a large Chewa population there too, you know!' he laughed.

We finished the final points on our agenda – a review of our Under-6 centres, current food prices, currency fluctuations – before heading our separate ways.

During the meeting I had been a little distracted by the invitation we had been given by the youth club to climb that mountain on Pentecost Sunday and to meet their friends on its summit. It was an invitation that proved impossible to resist and so, very early the following Sunday, Calum and I met Father Gamba and his youth group at the foot of Chaoni Mountain. We were joined by Chris MacLullich and his Liberian wife, Mercy, along with her six-year-old son Tony. The well-worn, red path climbed very steeply through the forested slopes of the mountain. The members of the youth club, clambering with us, carried various bags and parcels – gifts for their friends who lived 3,000 feet above. We passed some girls, perhaps twelve years old, resting beside huge bundles of firewood which they were carrying up the path. As we climbed higher I began to notice that those we passed did not reply with the standard response when we said 'Muli Bwanji', the common Chichewa greeting of 'How are you?' Father Gamba explained that those living on the mountain were of the Yao tribe with their own language. Over streams and round enormous boulders we climbed, until above the forested slopes we found ourselves amid neat fields of maize and sweet potatoes and clusters of banana trees. The views across the plains beneath us were exhilarating. After two hours of hard climbing we reached the plateau on top of the mountain where we began to find clusters of houses. A group of little children who had been pounding maize outside their home stopped and stared open-mouthed at us as we waved to them on the way past. Eventually we arrived at a bigger village with a church, from which we could hear drumming and beautiful harmonized songs of praise. People were already arriving for Mass, among them several elderly Muslims, wearing prayer caps, who took their seats at the back of the church. It seemed appropriate on this feast of Pentecost, the day when the Holy Spirit had allowed people divided by many different languages to understand each other, to be sitting in a church beside my Scottish, Liberian and Chewa friends, listening to Mass in a language that I had never even heard or spoken before. And as always the Mass was very familiar and very new at the same time.

As soon as we left the church we were ambushed. Father Gamba had obviously let the people of Chaoni know that their visitors were from Mary's Meals. On a football field nearby several hundred people had gathered to welcome us. Some of them, including the paramount chief, had even travelled from the neighbouring mountain to be there. We were invited to sit on a row of chairs and were entertained by singing, dancing and tug-of-war competitions. The elders made a series of speeches and presented us with gifts. I was given a beautiful black polished staff by the chief. And then, having captivated us with their welcome, they read us a plea to bring Mary's Meals to the community here. We learnt there were over 5,000 people living in the villages on the plateau and that their one school had 917 students. Many children were not attending school and when we looked at their records we could see that the dropout rate of students was horribly high. A class of well over a hundred children in Standard 1 had dwindled to just thirteen pupils by Standard 8. Poverty and hunger were taking their usual distressing toll on the isolated children of the mountain.

Having learnt all this, and heard their speeches and received their gifts in front of hundreds of expectant children, it was with some awkwardness that I finally rose when invited to respond to the request they had just made us. While part of me felt a little annoyed by their carefully orchestrated 'ambush', which had taken me completely off-guard, I also could not help but admire their determination and planning. They clearly wanted Mary's Meals for their children very much. After thanking them for their welcome and gifts, I told them that we had only climbed the mountain to celebrate Pentecost with them and that their request had surprised me. I explained that we had many schools on our waiting lists and for each one we went through a careful process of discussion with the community to agree a partnership. And besides, for Chaoni, we would also need to figure out how to transport the food on the steep two-hour walk from the nearest road to their school. They immediately responded by telling us that they would happily come and carry the food from a village at the bottom of the mountain, if we could only deliver it there for their children. We agreed we would return very soon for more formal meetings with their community leaders. We said our goodbyes, and with the children of the youth club, who had led us here and who were now happy that their hilltop friends might receive the Mary's Meals, we descended the mountain.

I felt as if I had seen two worlds collide happily that day on top of the mountain. In some ways the whole story of Mary's Meals is a series of collisions or meetings, between individuals and communities, with ears to listen to each other. An irresistible force for good is created when disparate peoples move towards each other with a shared desire and willingness to see hungry children fed. The idea of the people of Chaoni, descending to meet us at the foot of their mountain, in order to take possession of gifts sent by people in faraway places and then carry them up steep paths in order to cook them for their children is a poignant one. And I especially loved the fact that in this case it was children who had led us up the mountain so that other children, even hungrier than them, might eat.

It seemed that everywhere I looked a bright new young generation was now leading the way. Not far from Gay's house is the wonderful Jacaranda School for Orphans. I first met Marie de Silva, the remarkable founder of this school at that CNN Hero event in Los Angeles (she, too, had been named a 'top ten hero' in a previous year). We became great friends with Marie and her husband Luc. The orphans in their school receive Mary's Meals every day, and in return we receive much more. Here they sing gloriously and the songs they have written about Mary's Meals, such as 'One Cup of Porridge' and 'Let Us Be Educated', make me cry whenever the children sing them to us, which is exactly what they do as soon as Calum and I arrive to say a quick hello. A few months previously we had invited two of their most gifted singers, Vanessa and Joyce, over to Scotland, where they delighted a crowd of over 1,000 people at our annual

Open Day, before we travelled on to another Mary's Meals event in a beautiful palace in Vienna where they sang in front of the Prince and Princess of Liechtenstein and many other distinguished guests. It was great to see them again, this time back in the more familiar setting of their classroom. They were still buzzing about their trip of a lifetime, and many of the kids were asking how they could help Mary's Meals in Malawi. Incredibly, four of their former schoolmates, who have recently graduated from Jacaranda, are now paid employees of Mary's Meals. There is something deeply gratifying about reaching the stage when we can employ staff who have themselves eaten Mary's Meals at school.

Recently, in Liberia, I had spent some time with Boakai, now a Mary's Meals monitor and vital member of our team there. He amazed me by telling me that he was among the little children who queued up to eat the very first plates of Mary's Meals served in his country. I remember that day vividly. Boakai explained that as a child he had lived with his grandmother near Massatin, the leper colony where we had chosen to serve those first Liberian Mary's Meals, and he described walking 3 miles every day to receive the meals and attend school. After our chat I watched him climb on to his motorbike, and head off down the rough road, slaloming round the deep potholes, towards the remote schools he was due to visit and write reports on that day. Just round the corner he would pass Bomi Radio Station, where Meloshe, one of Liberia's rising stars, works. He is the director of news at the widely listened-to regional station, and manages a team of twenty-two people. This independent radio service is fearlessly holding the government to account, with lively political phone-ins and topical debates.

Ten years ago, Meloshe's life had been in tatters after he was driven from his home by rebel forces during the civil war. Later with the help of Mary's Meals he regained the chance of an education.

'Mary's Meals helped me to get where I am now,' he proudly states.

Many of his generation, having enjoyed Mary's Meals, are now starting to build a new much brighter future for their countries. On my last visit to Haiti I was given an overwhelming welcome at one of the Hands Together schools in Cité Soleil. I arrived to find an entire campus bedecked in home-made posters that made statements about Mary's Meals. On a balcony above the central courtyard three boys were leaning through the railings to attach a banner that that read, *No Education without Food*. Flowers adorned a doorway on which was written *Welcome Magnus and Mary's Meals*. And in the kitchen a team of cooks wearing Mary's Meals aprons were working under a huge painted sign that said *Thank you Mary's Meals*.

I was enjoying their hugely impressive and entertaining school concert, when, to my great surprise, Jimmy climbed on to the stage and took the microphone. I had first met Jimmy in 2010, a few months after the earthquake, when he was head boy of this school. I had interviewed him about his life. He impressed me hugely with his intelligence and his positive approach, despite the fact that he lived in a pitiful, tiny, broken tin home in one of the poorest parts of Cité Soleil. He had told me then about his passion to study agriculture so that he could help the people of Haiti grow more of their own food and escape dependence on aid. From the school stage he addressed us and the assembly of pupils with passion and confidence. He told us how he had received Mary's Meals for many years.

'I have figured out now that Mary's Meals helped me physically, morally and spiritually; it gave my body strength, it made me think about sharing with others and it led me to think about the "yes" of Mary and the "yes" of all those who serve Mary's Meals.' For a moment his smiling swagger dropped and he became choked with emotion. As he left the stage his audience clapped loudly and roared their approval. Jimmy, who was by now working for Hands Together, was clearly popular in these parts.

Later, after school lessons were finished for the day, I witnessed something that moved me even more deeply. At long last a special project, which had been originally planned to begin the day the earthquake struck, was up and running. The 'barefoot children' who live on the streets of the slum were now invited in for a daily meal, after the end of the regular school day. Some of those children had initially arrived naked, a few weeks previously, but by now Father Tom had given them all a T-shirt and shorts. I watched as 1,353 of these little barefoot ones queued for their plates of rice, fish and beans. They devoured them in silence, before making their way, laughing and chatting, into the school classrooms where they have started to receive their first school lessons given by young volunteers, recently graduated from this same school. François is one of those who has returned to give something back. Wearing a white shirt and blue tie, he cuts a handsome animated figure as he points at the letters on the blackboard and speaks to the ragged skinny children in front of him. François knows the taste of Mary's Meals. He knows that for him, and the children in front of him, education is their only hope – the only way out of the squalor and violence and hunger all around them. And so he happily gives up his time for these children without financial reward.

As we finally leave the school I notice one more poster among the hundreds of carefully handwritten signs that proclaim gratitude and love for Mary's Meals. The handwriting and the little spelling mistake suggest it has been written by one of the younger pupils, perhaps even one of the 'barefoot kids'. It says simply: *Food maks it better.*

Old Epilogue

It is summer and the Orchy has grown ponderous and narrow and warm enough for my kids to swim in her. I saw them through my shed window earlier, trotting down the farm track with their towels and lunchboxes, heading for the pool at Corryghoil. For a moment I was tempted to join them but there are some things I need to do.

Over a million children are now eating Mary's Meals every school day in over 1,200 schools. New pictures drawn by some of them are on my wall. The extraordinary ways in which all this has grown and developed have continually surprised me and filled me with a sense of mystery and awe. It would not be true, though, to say that I never expected our work to grow so big. I have long felt that the vision of Mary's Meals is so compelling, and people of good will so numerous, that it must be fulfilled. That is why we are celebrating this landmark as 'The First Million'. The fact that there remain many more millions without daily meals, and that thousands die each day because of hunger, is a scandal that screams this mission of ours has only just begun.

When we first reached a million I asked our clever team in the Glasgow office to provide me with some information about what it would take for the rest of them to eat at school. I mean all the children of primary-school age in the developing world. But it was a mistake. The spreadsheet they sent me told me that to provide Mary's Meals to every child in Malawi, based on our current costs, would require an annual budget of £22 million. I was not able to resist typing that value into Google. I saw there was a house for sale in London with that asking price and a rare orange diamond had been recently sold for the same amount. I am not sure if orange diamonds are the sort they mine in Liberia, but the figures showed that actually we would only need a little more than half the value of that diamond to feed all of the primary-school children in that nation each year.

I notice, too, that the annual whisky sales from Scotland are worth a similar total to the sum needed to feed all the primary-school children in the whole of Africa who are currently without meals at school. But then I close the spreadsheet, deciding that this is not a particularly good use of my time. I know already that our vision is eminently achievable. It would require the world's governments and international bodies to devote only a tiny fraction of the resources at their disposal to make this happen and thereby transform the future of the world's poorest nations. And it would require all of us to share only a tiny fraction of our own resources in order to make it happen too. The purchaser of that house in London is not obliged to share their bread any more than I am.

Old Epilogue

The shed is heating up now in the midday sun and I begin writing a letter to our supporters, those who are indeed sharing what they have in generous ways. I thank them on behalf of Veronica, Boakai and Jimmy, and those other young people whose lives they have saved and transformed. I tell them about the schools currently on our waiting list (including that one on top of Chaoni Mountain). And I remind them, too, of the relatively small cost for us to feed another child for a year. As usual, I feel the letter falls well short of what those people deserve and once again I wish each of them could meet those children, watch them eat their meals and listen to them talk of their hopes and dreams. The fact that our donors continue to share what they have without ever knowing that privilege humbles me.

Seeking some inspiration for my letter, I head into the chapel next door at Craig Lodge. It is my favourite room in the world. The sun is streaming through the bay windows. In the far corner is a statue of Our Lady, under which sits another huge, fresh, beautiful bunch of flowers, grown, picked and arranged by my mum. A message given by Our Lady at Medjugorje many years previously pops into my mind.

'Open your heart to Jesus, like a flower opens itself to the sun,' she had once advised us.

On the altar table (on which a snooker table of my childhood once sat) is a roughly carved wooden crucifix. I remember the dark, frightening evening when it was given to me by Father Tom and his friends as we huddled praying in the rubble of his courtyard after the earthquake. They had salvaged it that day from the remains of the house where their friends had died, and they each in turn held it and prayed on it before giving it to me as a gift, a way for us to stay in solidarity with each other on my return home.

I am sitting beside the old fireplace and it triggers another memory, this time of my brother Mark when he was seven years old. It was Christmas Day, not long after we fostered him, and this was still our living room and the open fire still our main source of warmth. Our presents were piled high under a Christmas tree, and before we could open them Mum and Dad insisted that we all convince Mark that Santa Claus had come down the chimney in the night – having previously scattered some of the logs stacked beside the fire to prove it. I had been a little surprised because the rest of us had never been brought up to believe in Santa, but I greatly admired their efforts to ensure Mark was not disappointed on his first Christmas with us.

I think Mark is in heaven now. He feels like my big brother now, even though he was five years younger than me. He died at thirty-nine years old, two years ago, in Medjugorje. I had found him, after two days of searching with Milona, Charlie and other dear friends, in a beautiful little secluded field full of fragrant flowers. He had been praying prostrate when he died (probably of a heart attack), his shoes placed neatly beside him. In a carrier bag beside him was the food he was carrying back to our guest house – a little treat intended for my son, Ben. Mark had been ill and in terrible pain for most of his adult life. One day when I was driving him to a hospital appointment, he told me that he understood that prayer was the part he could play in the mission, and that he had developed a deep belief that when he offered his suffering up it had meaning and power. We made a cross of stones in the field where he had lain. It is a wonderful spot to sit when the sun is going down, just as it was when he died, and to watch the lengthening shadows cast by the trees that line the old stone wall. From there you can see the church's twin spires and Krizevac across the vineyards. Mark left this life magnificently.

As I pray now in the chapel, I feel an overwhelming sense of gratitude; to Mark, for all he shared with me and taught me, to Mum and Dad for inviting him, a stranger then, into our family and to God for taking him home the way He did. And I thank God once again for giving us this work to do for His little ones. I ask Him to teach us how to share the bread that belongs to all. I ask Him to clothe this work always in His love and to help us remember that this work is not ours, but His, and I pray that He might move many more people to take part in this mission so that all those hungry children might soon be fed.

And then I decide to leave the writing of that letter until another day, and while there is still time, I head up the river to swim with my children.

14

Love Reaches Everywhere

> Love is a fruit in season at all times,
> and within reach of every hand.
> MOTHER TERESA

The journey to the first million children ended very close to where it began. In the village of Chirimba, Malawi, less than one hour's drive from Balaka – where twelve years earlier I had met with Edward and heard the words that ignited this mission – an assorted group of people gathered to celebrate the milestone. The village primary school, nestled beneath rugged cliffs, was part of a cluster of schools in Machinga District to which we had just expanded our programme – an expansion that led us past that magic number of one million.

The amazing choir from the Jacaranda School for Orphans arrived in their battered minibus, having left Blantyre many hours before dawn. A little later some besuited politicians and dignitaries appeared, and then some press and media too. A few speeches had to be made before the fun could begin, although the crowd of volunteers and pupils eventually lost patience with a long-winded politician and simply left him speaking to himself while they headed over to where the choir were warming up. Before long we were being regaled by their (by now familiar) songs about Mary's Meals. And, as always, 'One Cup of Porridge' and 'Children of Africa' brought tears to our eyes, before the choir surprised us with an upbeat new song written specially for the occasion called 'One Million!'

Then something began to excite the crowd of children even more. Chris Watt, a photographer and friend of Mary's Meals for many years, had started to set up his drone on the school football field for a planned aerial photograph. A screaming crowd of kids surrounded him as he held his remote control, while a curious device whirred beside him. Suddenly the incredible flying machine took off and a short, stunned silence was followed by the loudest screams of excitement I have ever heard. The children stared and pointed and jumped up and down and gesticulated and screamed some more. By now I had completely given up hope of the children forming the 1,000,000 in the way that they been practising for Chris's special photograph, but then their teachers and the Mary's Meals team began to guide them towards their allotted places, even while they continued to shout and laugh. Each year-group had been organized to stand within shapes marked by sand to create one of the digits. And to my amazement, I could see the shapes forming. Then I looked at my watch and realized I should already have left to catch the only flight that would get me back to London in time for the launch of the first edition of this book, which was scheduled for the following day. As Dalitso and I sped off, I could see the little drone hanging above the perfectly disciplined groups of children. I am sure that long after they have forgotten the reason for the celebration at their school that day, those children will reminisce in later life about the time that little flying machine appeared in their school playground. And, despite my lack of faith, the picture taken from the drone turned out to be a very wonderful one.

The next few months became a bit of a blur. The reaching of the first million presented us with unprecedented opportunities to tell our story and invite people into the mission. A new march towards the two million had already begun in our minds as we celebrated in Chirimba and we were determined to take advantage of every single opening the new interest in our work was presenting.

The following evening, I attended the launch of *The Shed that Fed a Million Children* in a delightful Edwardian bookshop on Marylebone High Street. I really did not know quite what to expect, having never attended the launch of any book before, let alone my own. It was a thrill to see piles of the hardback on the counter and on the shelves, and a reassuringly healthy crowd of people gathered. Signing books for people felt very strange indeed – something I hadn't understood I would be asked to do, and something I have never lost a sense of awkwardness about in the years since. I even developed a special 'book signature', so at least it looked vaguely like my name, unlike my normal signature.

Being invited to sign things became a bit of a feature of 2015. When I got to New York a few days later, we launched the book in the Facebook offices, and to my surprise they asked me to sign their famous wall. A few months later I was invited to speak at the HarperCollins offices near Glasgow, and afterwards they gave me a tour of a brand-new exhibition they had just opened, which told the interesting story of their company, and showed me their own large white wall for signing. Except that, unlike the Facebook one, it was completely blank. It just so happened that a quirk of timing meant I was the first author they had invited to sign it. I cringed inwardly as they handed me a marker pen. They were obviously uninformed about the horrible appearance of my signature. A sense of panic heightened as I took in the virgin expanse in front of me while my enthusiastic hosts looked on.

'Are you sure? What do you want me to write?' I asked lamely, trying desperately to think of a reason to say 'no thanks'.

'Whatever – just sign your name and write "Mary's Meals" if you want,' they offered kindly.

I turned back to the board and managed to scrawl my name, uglier and even more of a mess than usual, but felt relieved that I had at least managed that. Then I wrote 'Mary's Meals'. Or at least I nearly did. I actually wrote 'Mary's Meal's' in indelible marker pen on their nice white wall. I have no idea where that extra apostrophe came from. It made no sense. It was not a mistake I had ever made before. These were words I had to write nearly every day. There was a little silence behind me, and then someone ran off for a wet rag. They scrubbed as quickly as they could at that nasty little uninvited apostrophe, which soon became an even nastier indelible dark smudge. After the trust and support HarperCollins have shown me throughout this book project, I will always feel a wave of shame when I think of that moment.

But most of the book signings were just great fun. At Glasgow Caledonian University a lovely crowd turned up, including all my own family and many old friends. When it came to the part of the evening when I had to make a little speech at the podium, I realized I had mislaid my own copy of the book with strategically placed Post-it notes marking some passages I planned to read. I began to ask some of the Mary's Meals team at the back of the room if they could try to find it for me but then I noticed Gabriel, our four-year-old, walking up from his seat, my book in hand, politely offering it to me. It was a lovely moment and I wished I could have packed him in my suitcase as I headed off for another overseas visit to North America.

I thought we had already been in top gear, but we seemed to find a higher one when we landed in New York. Not for the first time, the Laffonts kindly lent me their office, this time so that I could take part in a virtual radio tour, which involved doing seventeen consecutive radio interviews with radio hosts based in various parts of the USA; an extremely effective way to reach audiences all over the country and get very tired indeed of the sound of your own voice at the same time. I also did some real things too (as opposed to virtual), including filming something with CNN in Central Park and being interviewed and photographed at *Time* magazine. I am just thinking now that neither of those were ever broadcast or published and worrying that maybe I had something unpleasant stuck to my face or forgot to put my trousers on that day.

Then it was off to the good, sane folk of Iowa. Here we did a couple of public book launches, hoping that in our US heartland we might gather a good crowd to buy the book. And we certainly did. Much bigger crowds came and many more books were sold than we could ever have expected, thanks as ever to the irrepressible and infectious enthusiasm of Ellen Miller. The only problem encountered here was that we ran out of books – there were none left in the whole of the Midwest at one stage – and we had to ration the numbers of books individuals could buy at the final event in St Francis Parish in Des Moines.

Next was Toronto for some TV talk shows and then, on that same evening, to a book signing event in Niagara. This was another very moving occasion because it was hosted by friends of Bridgid Davidson, the lady who had founded Mary's Meals in Canada before she lost her battle with cancer. Bridgid's husband Mike, along with her mother and sister, came along to show their support and it was a very emotional evening. Afterwards, just as it got dark, the nearby world-famous Niagara Falls were lit up in Mary's Meals blue by huge floodlights, organized again by Bridgid's friends to mark the reaching of the first million. It was a spectacular sight and, like the shot of the children making the number 1,000,000 in Chirimba, it became an iconic picture of Mary's Meals and the first million. I am embarrassed to admit that I never actually saw that amazing sight in person, as exhaustion had taken hold of me and by the time they flicked the floodlight switches I was snoring in my hotel room.

Thankfully, my life has not generally been like that in the six years since the celebration of the first million. The vast majority of my time, I am glad to say, has not involved cameras or signing things and I have been blessed indeed to have spent precious time, with barely a camera in sight, in my shed – and in some of the impoverished and marginalized communities that have become part of the Mary's Meals family in recent times: a prison in Madagascar where children are incarcerated; a primary school in a leper colony in South Sudan; a remote mountain school in Haiti (although this one did involve quite a lot of cameras, given Gerard Butler was with me and we were making a new film); and isolated villages in the vast, arid wilderness of Turkana, Kenya. In each of these places I met people serving their local communities with great strength and dignity. Everywhere the local ownership on which Mary's Meals is built was evident. And often, without looking for it, I was moved by expressions of remarkable faith.

While making that film in Haiti (which in the end we called *Love Reaches Everywhere*), Gerard Butler and I talked at some length with a parent whose children were missing school because of hunger. The situation of the family was desperate. At one point Gerry asked her, 'What scares you the most?'

She looked at him, incredulously, and then with a dazzling smile answered, 'I am a child of God. I am afraid of nothing!' She put enormous emphasis on the 'nothing'. It was not an answer we expected or were looking for, but its obvious sincerity moved us deeply.

On a horribly hot day in South Sudan, Alex Keay and I were both feeling quite unwell as we arrived at another school where Mary's Meals had recently begun serving meals. We had come straight from Madagascar where we'd picked up a nasty stomach bug that was leaving us battling dehydration. Our hearts sank as we found ourselves standing in front of thousands of singing pupils who began to take turns to make speeches. Unexpectedly, as we stood swaying in front of them, two older pupils emerged from their ranks, walked up to us and calmly placed their hands on our foreheads. In the short silence that ensued we realized they were praying for us. Once again, any illusion of us being 'the givers' and them being 'the receivers' was shattered in that moment.

We were able to reach out to all sorts of new communities in the world's poorest, hungriest places, because meanwhile support for our work was growing in all sorts of new places too.

In the Czech Republic, where Karel and Lucy, inspired by reading the first edition of this book, decided to donate all the money they had saved for their new family home in order to found Mary's Meals in their own country, support for our work exploded. Never have I seen it grow so fast! Tens of thousands of people there are generously supporting our mission. And since then, something very similar and equally spectacular has happened in neighbouring Slovakia, and in Poland too.

But amazing events were not only confined to these new places. In 2019, Julie and I travelled back to Croatia for the ten-year anniversary of Mary's Meals support there. We enjoyed an amazing evening of dancing and singing in Slavonski Brod, a town we had last visited nearly thirty years previously when it was being ripped apart by war and was home to many thousands of refugees. Where people had once queued at our truck for the food parcels we were distributing, they were now fund-raising vigorously for the work of Mary's Meals.

At the main event in the capital, Zagreb, the following evening, I received a very wonderful surprise when I finished making my short speech. One of the volunteers climbed onto the stage and presented me with a parcel, which on opening turned out to be a Croatia football top. I was happy enough with that, being a big fan of their amazing national team, which had reached the World Cup final the previous year, but only when I turned it over in my hands did I realize it was much better than that. It was a signed gift from Luka Modrić, who was the holder of the Ballon d'Or (so recognized as the best footballer on the planet). He and his family support Mary's Meals partly because they were themselves refugees in the coastal town of Zadar when Julie and I used to deliver aid there. Little did we know that among the crowds of kids there was one who would grow up to be a global superstar!

When I think of the multitude of wonderful things that have happened since the first edition of this book was published – far too many to tell here – many of them are like that: the fruits of seeds planted long ago and sometimes mentioned in earlier chapters of this book. For example, I will always cherish the sublime day when Jimmy Belabre, the young musician from Cité Soleil in Haiti, sang his heart out in front of tens of thousands of people at the annual youth festival in Medjugorje. They listened, spellbound, to his Mary's Meals story and to him telling them that, 'if Mary's Meals can do impossible things, then I can do impossible things too!' And then we all danced along to his songs, with tears in our eyes. I can see it now – collared priests doing the conga under a bright Medjugorje sun.

And then suddenly, at the start of 2020, my thirty years of perpetual motion suddenly came to an end. Like millions of others around the world, I found myself unexpectedly confined to home by a pandemic. For eighteen months I did not once check in at an airport or spend a night away from my family. I have been able to do many things that were not previously possible for me – growing vegetables, keeping chickens, spending every weekend and evening with my family and getting involved in coaching shinty with the kids in our village.

While I would certainly never have wished for this pandemic, or the terrible suffering it has caused, I also feel deep gratitude for this time of stillness. These strange times have offered up many chances to rethink things, to learn new ways and to make choices about the things that matter most. It has certainly been like that, not just for me as an individual but for the Mary's Meals family too. All sorts of surprising and important lessons have been taught us during this strange season.

At the start of the pandemic, when schools all over the world began to close, we questioned briefly how an organization whose sole purpose was to serve daily meals in a place of education could move forward. But almost immediately we recognized that our work could not stop, and that while there might sometimes be good reason to suspend the formal education of children, there could never be a justification for stopping serving them food, especially when we knew that the children to whom we had promised a daily meal depended on it. And for the time being, the 'place of education' the world over had become our family homes. And so we immediately began looking at how we could find new ways to keep that promise until schools reopened. Across the thousands of communities served by Mary's Meals, we worked with local leaders and public health officials to quickly establish a new system, whereby parents collected our food from the schools' stores and took it home to cook for their children. In this way nearly all the children in our programme kept eating Mary's Meals during school closures.

Meanwhile we faced at least as much fear about how our funding could possibly hold up. Numerous fund-raising events were cancelled because of lockdowns and many regular volunteer activities had to cease. We knew too that many of our kind supporters around the world were facing new anxiety and economic hardship. Surely they would not be able to keep giving?

In March 2020 I remember driving home from our main office in Glasgow – an office that has not been open since that day, as I write – and stopping at a supermarket to do our weekly food shopping. As I struggled with my trolley through the unusually crowded aisles, Julie messaged me to say our kids' schools were closing. As I started to absorb that, I found myself staring at the shelves where the pasta was normally displayed. They were entirely empty save for some ripped-up pieces of cardboard bearing the name of an Italian brand. Between that supermarket and one nearby I managed quite easily to buy some alternative staples for our week ahead, although by now several other items were being rationed (another new experience for me). As I drove home along the banks of Loch Lomond, I was contemplating an uncomfortable set of unfamiliar feelings. For the first time in my life, for a fleeting moment, I considered what we would actually do if all our shops began to run out of food.

'To have enough food to eat and to be able to go to school one day.' Edward's dreams were of things I have taken for granted my whole life – as a child and a parent. The empty supermarket shelf and the indefinite closure of our schools were tiny inconveniences compared with the daily struggles of millions of our brothers and sisters. The impoverished subsistence farmer whose one field of maize has been decimated by drought cannot just go and replace it by buying potatoes and rice as I had just done. And for millions, disrupted schooling is not some unusual event but just the normal run of things when contending with unaffordable school fees, child malnutrition and the need for children to work to help their family survive. But even while recognizing that I still had no idea what it really feels like to live so precariously, I began to feel grateful for those unsettling moments during that strange day in March, which offered opportunities to deepen feelings of solidarity and compassion.

I do not know whether experiences like this have played any part in people being even more generous in the months since, but I do know that something very wonderful indeed has been happening within the Mary's Meals family. Our presumption that donations would decrease under COVID-19 has been spifflicated. A counter-intuitive, dramatic new growth in support for our work has coincided with this pandemic. I have watched, open-mouthed, as our armies of volunteers across all sorts of countries have adapted and found new ways to spread the word and fund-raise despite new constraints that would have justified them accepting defeat. Supporters, despite their own suffering and all sorts of new things to deal with in their lives, have been faithful and more generous than ever. As a result, our growth has, in fact, accelerated – both in terms of income and numbers of new people supporting our work. Something quite beautiful, which I do not pretend to fully understand, has been going on and it is enabling us to move forward even faster to work with many more new communities that have been waiting for Mary's Meals. And this is especially wonderful given the devasting impact the pandemic is having on the world's poorest nations and the fact it is believed that many more people will die of hunger than COVID-19.

Meanwhile, my own confinement to home provided me with other valuable new perspectives. As I was unable to go out to give talks and meet people myself, the emphasis of my leadership role shifted healthily towards supporting and enabling others. It became a time when, with some relief, the extraordinary story of Mary's Meals felt less and less like my story. Of course, it never was my story, but my part in it began to feel less important than it ever did. While I sorely missed being able to sit in the dust of a playground chatting to Mary's Meals volunteers or walking a mountain path with barefoot, laughing children, this new virtual world had its advantages. During one working day, without leaving my shed, I would find myself talking to friends on several different continents and almost feel I was really with them.

One of the greatest joys was that instead of repeatedly telling the story of Mary's Meals from my own perspective,

I had the opportunity to talk with and listen more carefully to the stories of others. Video calls were allowing me to give talks to audiences in various parts of the world without travelling there, but they also became a great way for me to invite people 'into the shed' and to get to know them over a cup of tea. One of those inspiring people was Felix, who was suffering a much more profound confinement at his home in Germany than my temporary COVID-induced one.

I had previously met Felix's parents and know his amazing aunt Marianne, who is a volunteer leader of Mary's Meals in Germany, but until these video calls I had never met him, even though he had studied at the University of St Andrews in Scotland before embarking on a brilliant international career.

In 2016, following spells of study and work as a business consultant in Tokyo, Helsinki, Paris and Chicago, Felix began his MBA in Singapore. He was twenty-eight years old and already a deeply committed supporter of Mary's Meals, making generous annual donations to our mission. Not long after arriving in Singapore, Felix joined a group making a trip to Malaysia to take part in an advanced diving course. It was a trip that ended in tragedy. On the ascent from a 30-metre dive, something went horribly wrong and Felix was lifted unconscious from the water with blood streaming from his nose. A huge and complicated emergency rescue ensued (they were diving off a remote island) and for many weeks he remained in a coma. His chances of survival were considered to be tiny and his doctors were working on the assumption that he had suffered massive brain damage.

When Felix talks to me today about those days – which of course he cannot remember – he speaks mainly about the faith of his family.

'Of course, the accident and time afterwards was a really tragic experience for me, my family and friends, but we never stopped praying and believing in Christ's power to heal and rescue us. One might imagine such a tragic accident could lead to a distrust – but I never questioned my faith. Maybe a special grace came. Of course, moments of doubt came too, but nothing serious. And then even distant people who heard my story began believing and praying for me – it became a really beautiful experience. Huge prayer groups and prayer chains were formed. My sister organized it so that every minute of the day and night someone was praying for me.'

A couple of weeks before Christmas, Felix finally woke from his coma. Incredibly, he began to speak again – in fact, he was still multilingual. But he could not move from the neck down. The international high-flyer suddenly found himself setting some very different life goals, trying to relearn basic bodily functions and finding ways to cope with his disabilities. He spent the next fifteen months in intensive rehabilitation at a specialist unit in Heidelberg.

'I have painful memories, but also good memories of that time,' he told me one day during a video call. 'I made very good friends with the nurses and other people there.'

Eventually, in 2018, he returned home to live with his parents in Frankfurt. Despite all of this, Felix never lost his desire to support the work of Mary's Meals. During 2020 he had an idea. He decided to devote his twice-weekly gait trainer (Lyra) therapy sessions to 'running' for Mary's Meals.

'Training on the Lyra is really demanding,' he explains. 'On some days it is so painful that I just have to stop. Using leg orthoses and special straps, I am pulled up into an upright position and then begin to walk. It would be more accurate to say that the machine walks me. It might sound trivial, but I can walk at 2.7 km/h, which both for me and the machine is extremely fast.'

He decided to turn this into a kind of sponsored event to raise funds for the work of Mary's Meals in Kenya. His aim was to try to raise €9,150 – enough for us to feed another 500 children. But 'Felix Runs for Mary's Meals' became a campaign that grew and grew. People began donating from all over the world. Even some celebrities, like singer Amy Macdonald, began sharing his initiative online. In the end, he raised over €142,000 – enough for us to feed 7,700 children for a year!

'It was very hard. I really exhausted myself.' Felix says now. 'But I am also a little proud!'

I find it hard when talking to Felix not to get emotional. Even to join a video call with me requires huge effort from him. When I ask him about where he finds his strength, he returns to his faith.

'I have always had faith. I have always known God exists. Deep inside me I have that knowledge. My father is Protestant and my mother Catholic. We were raised to believe that Jesus Christ is our Saviour and nothing else matters – the different confessions or denominations are less important. During my time as a student, I was a little more distant from my religious life – not so alive in faith – but I never stopped praying. Every evening I prayed by myself.'

'But what about now? What has your experience of faith been through this terrible experience?' I ask him.

'Every evening now as a family we read together a little spiritual booklet, along with two or three Bible verses. The core message of this book is to trust that God will do things. That we need to take one day at a time. I try to live that way now. My family is really impressed by this – it feels like I have a gift from God. I really worry very little now.'

At this point in our conversation, he smiles because his camera has started shaking quite violently and he can see I am distracted by it. He calls to his mum in the room next door and explains his legs have started to shake – she comes in and begins to rearrange things for him.

'Don't worry, it is no problem for me – I just didn't want you to wonder why my camera was shaking like that,' he laughs as the shaking subsides.

'Surely you have some low times?' I ask him, increasingly fascinated by his joy.

'Of course, I feel sad now and again. My life is at times a little shitty.' He flashes another grin. 'But I don't feel sad so often. Of course, I am missing out a lot when my friends travel and meet up. But I live in such a beautiful house, a lovely garden, with loving parents and my very cute dog, Paula. I am not in war-torn Syria or Yemen … or Tigray. Every day I have nutritious meals. Yes, my life could be better, but it could be a lot worse too! I try to make lists of things to be grateful for – every day I do this. It is always a long list. I enjoy listening to the birds sing. Life is good! I try to appreciate the little things. Maybe we shouldn't compare ourselves to people who look like they have more than us – maybe it's better to look at those who have less.'

When I compile my own extremely lengthy list of things to be grateful for (and I now resolve to do so on a regular basis), conversations with Felix will be near the top.

Another series of calls taking place at this time would also feature on any such list, although my regular discussions with Sister Medhin in Ethiopia were sometimes so shocking and so far removed from my own reality that they left me deeply troubled. Sometimes I almost wished for the transition time that a long-haul flight home had previously provided, or that at least that there were some way to adjust between talking to someone about the fear of starvation and sitting down to dinner with Julie and the kids.

I first met Sister Medhin, an Ethiopian nun, on a visit to Tigray in 2016. She and her small community (Daughters of Charity) welcomed me into their little house in the city of Mekelle, and from there we spent a few days travelling to villages across Tigray in which we planned to start serving Mary's Meals. This was my first visit to a country I had long been fascinated by, but there was no room in our hectic schedule for any kind of sightseeing, although on one of our car journeys Sister Medhin pointed out some of the famous ancient 'cave churches' set in the cliffs that towered above us. And one afternoon we managed to call in briefly for a coffee at the hotel where apparently Bob Geldof stayed during his Live Aid campaign. But most of the time was spent in villages set in rocky, arid landscapes, talking about and planning for the introduction of Mary's Meals. In one small primary school we crowded into the headmaster's little office and discussed the data he had available. He described a depressingly familiar tale of his school's battle with hunger – a battle they seemed to be losing based on the number of pupils dropping out each year. As we stood up to take our leave, we heard a lunch bell ring outside and the shuffling sound of children leaving their desks and classrooms. By the time we emerged from the dark room squinting into the dazzling sun, the children were sitting in a long silent row in the shade of a classroom wall. None of them were speaking, let alone playing. And there was no food this lunchtime – or any other. This was a lunch break without lunch and a playground without play. The silence of those huddled kids spoke more loudly than any word voiced in my conversation with the headmaster, and I was so happy when a few months later we began serving Mary's Meals in that school.

But as I write this, I do not know what has become of that village and its children, and there is part of me that does not even want to think about it.

At the end of 2020, with the world consumed by its epic battle with COVID-19, a very different kind of conflict erupted in Tigray. I believe – or at least hope – that in normal times the tragedy that ensued and is still unfolding as I write, leaving 5.2 million people in urgent need of humanitarian aid, would have horrified the world and moved it to act. When this same place was gripped by famine in the 1980s the world certainly did respond. Like many of my generation, Live Aid was a formative experience for me. My earliest memory of making a donation to charity was in response to that musical extravaganza which so gripped the world. Today, the comparative lack of interest in this current humanitarian disaster in Tigray troubles me deeply, as do my regular calls with Sister Medhin.

During the first few months of this war the communications blockade was almost complete. But deeply disturbing reports were leaking out of ethnic killings and allegations that rape, sexual violence and hunger were being used as weapons of war. Terrible things that should have been met by global outrage, political pressure and an outpouring of support for a desperately needed humanitarian response were instead unfolding largely unnoticed by a very distracted world.

And then, as some telephone networks became operational again, we began having regular calls with Sister Medhin. She began to describe the horror around her. Sometimes the conversation felt like a much-needed opportunity for Sister Medhin to pour out her own sadness and pain. But mainly she wanted to talk about the suffering of others and the opportunities to help them. The more personal conversations were interspersed with practical questions about how we could support an immediate emergency response. Until the conflict erupted, we had been planning some very large-scale expansions into new schools in Tigray. We were excited about reaching tens of thousands more Tigrayan children with a daily school meal and a huge amount of preparatory work had been done. But with schools closed and a huge proportion of the population forced to flee their homes, our focus had swiftly shifted to how we could provide urgently needed emergency support. And soon, through the heroism and resilience of the Daughters of Charity, we were feeding tens of thousands of displaced people who had fled the countryside and were living in Mekelle and other towns in Tigray – ironically, mainly in schools that had now become centres for internally displaced people.

As well as her daily efforts to meet the urgent material needs of destitute people pouring into the city, Sister Medhin was also doing a lot of listening to deeply traumatized people. She understood that sometimes this was what they needed more than anything else – just someone to hear their story.

'You know, these people in the centres come with so many different stories. Some young girls are raped. Even some women, even though they are with their husbands, would be also raped. Especially the women, you know, when you start to talk to them the first thing they do is start crying. And I can really, very deeply, feel their pain. You know, it pains me as though it has happened to me. That is how I feel it, it may never be the same but that is how I feel it. So you see men, when they are sharing what they went through, it is very difficult for a man to cry but they cry as well. They cry, they stop talking to you for so many minutes. You have to wait, let them cry, express their emotions. People are so traumatized, and I fully understand. Some of them told us that they had to walk on dead bodies, you know, because so many people were dead, they were practically walking on dead bodies to escape for themselves.'

On these calls we always had to presume we were being listened to by people who were determined that these crimes would not be spoken of or reported on. We had to speak cryptically and sometimes I had to try to join the dots of what she was trying to tell me. And I knew that often there was much left unsaid.

On one occasion, when we managed to reach her on the phone, Sister Medhin had just learnt that thirteen members of her own family – her brother and cousins – had been killed. They had been attacked, in several different incidents, while working in the fields. She was, of course, distraught. But in the coming days, while dealing with her own shock and raw grief, she continued with her fellow sisters to keep working for those suffering around her, whose plight she kept wanting to speak of. And her concern didn't stop with the displaced people – she was worrying for her own sisters too.

'Some of the sisters have asked me for some sort of training in how best to help and manage to cope – it is very difficult for us, we are broken from our own family side, the direct beneficiaries that we serve, the whole situation. You know even when birds fly, I'm not exaggerating, sometimes the shadow of birds can scare us. We have become so sensitive. We need support.'

On one call I asked Sister Medhin the same question I had asked Felix: 'How do you find the strength?'

'One thing for sure is the Holy Eucharist every day, the grace that comes with it, and the fact that for me especially, I meet other organizations doing the same thing, we all share the pain, we all share our stories. Some of the times we all cry, both men and women, you know, and that gives you some relief. And the way you reassure us, the donors, especially Mary's Meals, you really feel so confident, full of strength to go out, with courage to meet the needs and the demands of our people. Knowing you have backbones, you know, you have people behind you, supporting you with prayers, supporting you financially, supporting you in so many ways and I think that really makes me very strong and courageous.'

This theme of solidarity was something Sister Medhin returned to often. It was something I have been aware of right from the beginning of this work in Bosnia – how much it means to people who are suffering to know that they have not been forgotten. I think, especially when people are suffering ethnic violence and are stripped of basic rights, they are desperate for a sign that they have not been abandoned – that at least some people still recognize them as fellow human beings.

One day Sister Medhin told me a wonderful story about this. She described being in a public place in Mekelle where people were watching a news report from a local TV station. She was amazed to hear the reporter suddenly talk about the fact that Mary's Meals in Ireland had just launched an emergency appeal for the people of Tigray. She said a huge, emotional roar of approval went up from those gathered around the televisions.

It was lovely to share that story with our co-workers in Ireland the next day – especially as, yet again, the people of that small nation, with its own painful history of famine, were donating to our appeal in quite an extraordinary way.

When I was telling Julie about Sister Medhin's constant thanks for our prayers she suggested organizing a special virtual Rosary for peace in Tigray. Hundreds of people from different countries joined us, praying together in their own languages for the suffering people and for peace. To our delight, that evening the phone connection held up and Sister Medhin was able to join us, reciting Hail Marys in

Tigrayan with gunfire in the background. Many of us were moved to tears – especially at the end of the prayer when Sister Medhin spoke to us.

'Let all of those who are helping in any way possible know that we are grateful to Mary's Meals ... I keep thanking God, every single day, and especially for the last three months. It is God's special blessing, not only for the support you all give, but for me, for my own vocation also, as a Daughter of Charity. You are helping me to remain strong and faithful to my vocation and that is really very meaningful for me. It is only prayers that have kept us going. Nothing else. We do not know what tomorrow will bring so we are just thanking God for each day.'

Prayer was indeed something else that found new ways to express itself in the Mary's Meals family during this time of COVID-19. In recent years we had begun an annual Mary's Meals pilgrimage of thanksgiving to Medjugorje. In 2018 and 2019, more than 200 people from many different countries gathered with us there for three days of prayer. It was a beautiful experience and one that many of us were looking forward to repeating in 2020 until it became clear that travelling there in person would just not be possible. Once again Julie came up with an idea, but this one grew! What started off as a video call from the shed so we could give a little talk and lead some short prayers became a three-day event of video prayer, with more than 10,000 people from over 100 countries joining in. Prayer came first in the story of Mary's Meals and it seemed very clear that for many of our supporters this order of events – prayer, then action – was still their preferred way of doing things. A particular delight of the pilgrimage was our multilingual Rosary on video, with prayers being led in more than twenty different languages, including the languages of those in ethnic conflict in South Sudan.

Repeatedly we saw that barriers presented by the pandemic were being transformed into opportunities. The pilgrimage that might have been attended by 200 people in Medjugorje became one attended by 10,000. Many fund-raising initiatives experienced similar metamorphoses. Of course, not every new barrier was overcome and the Mary's Meals family is one that does not wish to remain forever in a virtual world. There are many parts of this story that could not have unfolded virtually – and frankly, this book would have been a hard read minus the pints in pubs, hugs in war zones and hot Likuni Phala being slurped from mugs. But when we happily leave these days of pandemic behind, we will have learnt a few things and we will be much stronger for it.

Perhaps, more than anything, we have learnt anew that Mary's Meals, when rooted in love, is relentless. Six years after celebrating reaching one million children we are now feeding two million children. And, without pausing for breath, we now march towards three million, and beyond that to the realization of our vision. We know we will hit bumps on the road, but they will not stop us continuing our journey together.

Today I spoke to Jerry and Dennis, two men who set off a few weeks back to cycle 1,500 miles from Claxton, Georgia, up the Atlantic coast to Bar Harbor, Maine, in order to raise $14,000 to provide 658 children with Mary's Meals in Thumba Primary School in Malawi. Their sign reads 'Cycling

4 God's Children', and people all along the route have been asking them what they are doing.

'Our philosophy is, tell it well and tell it all,' Dennis told me, holding up to his laptop camera the information cards they have been distributing on the route.

'And sometimes we tell people about Mary's Meals even when they don't ask!' laughed Jerry.

Both of these gentlemen are over eighty years old. Dennis mentioned in passing that the day before their trip began he had been diagnosed with prostate cancer and asked me to pray that his surgery in a few weeks' time went well.

'But tell Magnus your story, Jerry.' he said.

'Well, I was born a cripple. Spent half my childhood in a Shriners Hospital. I do have small legs and feet, but I learnt to walk. And who knows what I would have been like if I hadn't faced that difficulty in my life. Things like that make you bitter or better. I hope it made me better.'

A couple of weeks ago, nearly one thousand miles into their trip, the pair were travelling down a hill and went round a corner that ran into a dead end. Jerry hit a ditch at about 20 mph.

'It was the worst day of my life,' said Dennis. 'He was unconscious for about ten minutes. But there was a lovely couple there who helped me while we waited for the ambulance.'

'Anyway, we'll be back on the road soon,' Jerry interjected. He was sitting beside his wife, Julie, at home, having just returned from a lengthy stay in hospital. 'My neck's a bit stiff, but as soon as that feels better we'll be ready to go again.'

'How long do you have to go to get to Maine?' I asked, feeling almost guilty by now at what these guys – and their wives, Julie and Shirley, who had also joined our group call – were putting themselves through.

'About 500 miles, I think. But actually Maine is not the end. It is just the beginning.'

'Yeah, we were working it out,' Dennis said. 'We reckon if we can recruit a bigger group like us we could raise a million dollars for Mary's Meals.'

And so it goes on, this story. A story that moves food up faraway mountains and inspires elderly men to make epic journeys. More than ever, I stand in awe of it and feel increasingly small in the midst of it. And, yes, to me too this feels like 'it is just the beginning'. How can it be otherwise when so many millions of children are hungry this day?

New Epilogue

One windy autumn afternoon my son Gabriel, now nine years old, and I were enjoying a walk through the big woods near our house. It is a wild wood, full of all sorts of trees – pine, beech, oak, alder, holly, ash, chestnut, larch and many others too. We had been to see 'the tallest trees in the whole of Dalmally' – two enormous pines that tower above an old stone wall and look over green fields that slope up to the heathery hillside beyond.

As we walked back through layers of brown leaves, I was thinking about a little book I had just read called *The Man Who Planted Trees*. It is a masterpiece written in the 1950s by Jean Giono about his encounter with an old shepherd who he found living alone in the barren plains of the lower French Alps. It turned out that over many years this solitary shepherd had made it his daily routine to plant thousands and thousands of acorns. Over a span of forty years his efforts transformed a landscape and the lives of many people within it. I was very taken by the story, especially because in our part of Scotland there is currently much interest in reforesting the hills and glens that our ancestors cleared of trees, and which have been kept clear by sheep and deer ever since.

I was pondering Giono's tale as we strode beneath a canopy of ancient trees when Gabriel asked: 'Dad, is that an acorn?'

He bent to pick up a perfect little acorn in the leaves at his feet. And as he did so he spotted another – and another. We returned home with our pockets full of them.

The next morning, early, we headed off to the biggest oak tree we know of. It hugs the bank of the pool in the River Orchy where we swim and it has impossibly long limbs stretching along the banks and out over the water. When I was Gabriel's age I remember playing in its branches and I think it must be many hundreds of years old. At the base of its trunk, between exposed, gnarled roots there is a large hole in which otters live. Despite being acquainted with this tree for many years, I am ashamed to say that I had never before looked for acorns on it, or beneath it – but that was our quest this bright, chilly morning.

And straight away we could see that the branches, even those within Gabriel's reach, were laden with thousands of them. Those overhanging the slow-moving river were especially thick with them. And our timing was just right, with many already on the ground and others falling off at our slightest touch. We spent hours working our way around the tree and filling our bags with acorns that would otherwise have fallen into the river and been swept downstream or onto the ground to be gobbled up by sheep and deer. But even then, there were many more acorns left behind – we didn't even begin to pluck the branches above our reach, or those that would have required us to wade into water deeper than our wellies.

The next few days we spent, with the help of Gabriel's big sister Bethany, planting them in pots. Hundreds and hundreds. I have no idea where exactly we will transplant the saplings if they grow – and even now as I write I am aware quite a lot of them have already been stolen by red squirrels. But I love to think of the oak forest that the survivors may one day grow into, in which the grandchildren of those squirrels might forage – and the grandchildren of my own children too.

Acknowledgements

Dear Julie, I wouldn't have finished page one without your encouragement and I thank you with all my heart. Thank you for always believing in me despite all the evidence to the contrary. My dear children – Calum, Ben, Martha, Toby, Bethany, Anna and Gabriel – the fact that you older ones never once complained about me being even more busy and distracted than normal, and you younger ones almost never scribbled or drew pictures on my manuscript, and hardly ever ate any of my pages, makes me proud. Dear Mum and Dad, thank you. Without you there would be no Shed, no Mary's Meals – and no me either come to think of it.

Thank you, colleagues at Mary's Meals; without your tireless work all of those children would not be eating in school today and I know I do not thank you nearly enough. Katy, thank you in particular for moving me from talking about the idea of this book to actually doing something about it. Daniel, Kim and Louise, thank you for all your hard work and advice, and for being so patient with this cranky, insecure first-time author. Agnes, Jane, Siobhan, Kirsten and Susan, thank you for supporting this second edition in so many ways. Sonia, thank you for believing in this project from the first time I met you, and to all of you at HarperCollins – Andy, Minna, Morwenna, Jean Marie, Carlos and Bengono – you have all been so kind and patient.

I also want to thank every single one of you around the world who takes part in this mission. I hope those of you I write about in this book are happy with the way I have retold our stories and that those of you who have walked this road with me for many years, but who do not feature within, understand that I simply couldn't fit it all in one book!

And thank you Jesus for it all. It is all yours, the praise, the glory, the things that have happened and those still to come.

We'd love to hear your feedback on this new edition of the book. You can get in touch by emailing:

MagnusInTheShed@MarysMeals.org

For more information about Mary's Meals please visit our website:

www.MarysMeals.org